All Year Long!

All Year Long!

Funny Readers Theatre for Life's Special Times

Diana R. Jenkins

Teacher Ideas Press

An imprint of Libraries Unlimited
Westport, Connecticut • London

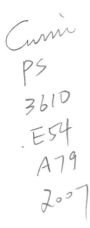

Library of Congress Cataloging-in-Publication Data

Jenkins, Diana R.
    All year long! : funny readers theatre for life's special times / Diana R. Jenkins.
        p. cm.
    ISBN 978-1-59158-436-0 (acid-free paper)
    1. Children's plays, American. 2. School children—Juvenile drama. 3. School year—Juvenile drama.
4. Schools—Juvenile drama. I. Title.
    PS3610.E54A79 2007
    812'.6—dc22   2007009446

British Library Cataloguing in Publication Data is available.

Library of Congress Catalog Card Number: 2007009446
ISBN: 978-1-59158-436-0

First published in 2007

Libraries Unlimited/Teacher Ideas Press, 88 Post Road West, Westport, CT 06881
A Member of the Greenwood Publishing Group, Inc.
www.lu.com

Printed in the United States of America

The paper used in this book complies with the
Permanent Paper Standard issued by the National
Information Standards Organization (Z39.48–1984).

10 9 8 7 6 5 4 3 2 1

Dedicated to Mike, with love and thanks

Contents

Introduction

Maybe you've already tried plays with your students. You've experienced the tortures of unending rehearsals and the stresses of live performances. You've felt the anguish of forgotten lines and prop flops, set collapses, and costume malfunctions. Perhaps you've even had the heart-dropping experience of having your star player turn up absent on the day of the big show.

It's enough to make you forget about classroom theatre altogether, isn't it? But don't give up without trying readers theatre. You'll find this method streamlines play performances, reducing complications while still giving kids the benefits of participating in theatre. And it's fun, too!

What Is Readers Theatre?

In readers theatre, actors hold onto their scripts and read their lines instead of memorizing them. This one simple change from "regular" theatre eliminates many problems! Students who have trouble memorizing can still play large roles. A play doesn't have to be rehearsed as many times since rehearsals focus on improving performance rather than getting everybody's lines down by heart. Nobody has to worry about forgetting lines – or having a scene messed up by someone else's memory lapses. And the absence of an actor isn't a devastating event.

Another advantage of readers theatre is the simple staging. Costumes, sets, props, and movement can be included in a readers theatre performance, but they are not necessary. Readers theatre scripts are designed to make sense and to be entertaining without all those extras. The actors can just sit throughout the play and simply read their scripts!

Before You Start

Before you use any readers theatre script with your students, be sure to read it yourself. Ask yourself if the content, theme, characters, and vocabulary will be appropriate and fun for your group. (You should also do this with the supplemental readings.) Note any concepts or vocabulary that need to be taught before your students read the play.

Make at least as many copies of the script as there are parts in the play. (Extras can come in handy, especially when you're using the play for a whole-class activity—or when actors lose their scripts!) Highlighting one character's lines in each script helps students follow along. Covering the scripts or putting them in binders is a good idea because they'll see a lot of use and abuse. You probably want to make a copy of the play for yourself so you can write notes about a particular performance directly on the script instead of in this book.

Making It Work

Many kids haven't had successful theatre experiences, so keep things simple and fun to start out. Since reading aloud without preparation can be stressful, give your students a chance to preview a script before you use it in your classroom. Let them do the first few readings of the script from their desks so they don't feel any pressure to "perform." You can even change casts from scene to scene so everybody gets a chance to join in the fun.

You might decide to just use a script as a one-time supplemental activity in your classroom, but multiple readings (on different days) can really benefit your students. As they become more familiar with a play, their fluency and expression get better. You can help students further improve these skills by sharing the presentation suggestions included in the introductory material of each play and by discussing each character's motivation. If a student has a problem with poor expression, model some of his lines and have him "echo" you. Most kids enjoy "copying" the teacher!

Performing Readers Theatre

Once students are comfortable with reading scripts from the safety of their desks, you can try a traditional readers theatre performance just for your class. Set up a few chairs or stools at the front of the room. If the play has a narrator, he or she can use a lectern or simply stand off to one side. The other actors just sit, holding their scripts, and read their parts. You can have the actors keep their backs to the room when they're not in a scene and turn around when they are, but you don't have to do that. A readers theatre performance can be kept as simple as you like!

After your students have performed for each other a few times, you might want to put on a "real" performance. Be sure to rehearse enough that the actors feel comfortable with their parts and read with good expression, but don't overdo it. Remember—memorization is not necessary! Performing for peers or adults is tough, so start out with a class of younger kids. They'll love seeing a play, and your students won't feel so stressed with an audience of "little kids." Later, you can work up to presenting plays to same-age students, parents and grandparents, or adult audiences outside the school.

As your students become more experienced with theatre, they may want to move away from the bare-bones readers theatre format. They'll begin to look up from their scripts, use more facial expression, turn to each other, and gesture. They might ask if they can stand, move around, and enter and exit the stage area. The plays in this book include a few directions about movement in case you want to stage a more "regular" performance. Remember—you can always stick to the traditional readers theatre format. You'll still get a great performance that audiences will love!

You may also find that students ask for costumes, sets, and props. Again, these are not essential to successful readers theatre, but suggestions are included in the introductory material for each play in case you decide to use them. It usually works best to introduce these items later in the rehearsal process because students get distracted by them and lose focus on improving their performances.

To involve more students and to make a longer program, you can work on several plays at the same time. Divide your class into casts and assign each group a different play. While you rehearse with one cast, the others can get together and read through their scripts or work on costumes, props, or sets. In readers theatre, an absence doesn't ruin a performance, but things will go even more smoothly if you have one cast understudy another by watching rehearsals or reading through another group's scripts.

The Benefits

Readers theatre can be a valuable experience for any child. Language arts skills such as reading, speaking, and listening are improved with even the simplest performances. Reading or performing these plays helps kids appreciate storytelling and literature and understand character development, dialogue, and story structure.

You can use readers theatre to build writing skills, too. For example, you might ask students to write the endings to interrupted lines. This not only improves their writing skills but also makes dialogue more natural. Instead of actors pausing before they're actually interrupted, they can go on with the line until the next actor speaks. Another good activity is having students rewrite the last scene of a play, changing the ending. With experience, students can write totally original plays.

Readers theatre has plenty of nonacademic benefits, too. Putting on a performance—even just within the classroom—takes creativity, hard work, and important social skills like cooperation and teamwork. Readers theatre can make a group of students feel closer as they accomplish something great together. And kids can take pride in their individual achievements, too. The child who's always played the third pilgrim on the left can finally feel like a real actor. Now there's a genuine boost to self-esteem!

Beginning of the School Year

The Curse of the Nerd

Summary

When they start junior high, Anya is glad to have her old friends along. Then Jen acts like a total dork and makes Anya look like one, too. Will Anya cut her loose to save herself from the curse of eternal nerd-dom?

Costumes, Sets, and Props

❖ All characters can wear contemporary clothing.

❖ A few tables, stools, or students' desks can serve as the cafeteria and the classrooms.

❖ If props are desired, schoolbooks, notebooks, and pencils can be used for the classroom scenes. Food trays could be used in the cafeteria.

Presentation

Anya, Rose, and Jen should each have a distinctive "teacher" voice.
Jen is bubbling over with enthusiasm. Steven and his group act cool, showing little emotion and speaking sarcastically.

Supplemental Reading

Anderson, Jessica Lee. *Trudy*. Minneapolis, MN: Milkweed Editions, 2005.

Birdseye, Tom. *Attack of the Mutant Underwear*. New York: Holiday House, 2003.

Gorman, Carol. *Dork in Disguise*. New York: Harper Trophy, 2000.

Muldrow, Diane. *Into the Mix*. New York: Grosset and Dunlap, 2002.

Cast of Characters

Anya	Pablo
Rose, Anya's friend	Mr. Martino, English teacher
Jen, another friend	Ms. Basu, Math teacher
Steven	Mr. Jacobs, Science teacher
Christine	Extra students (nonspeaking), if desired
Ella	

Beginning of the School Year

The Curse of the Nerd

Scene One

(Anya, Rose, and Jen enter.)

Anya: *(to audience)* All through elementary school, the teachers warned us about junior high. Like … *(changes voice)* "Just wait until you get to junior high, young lady."

Rose: Yeah! And … *(changes voice)* "You won't get away with that at the junior high."

Jen: How about … *(changes voice)* "Work hard now or you'll never make it at the junior high."

Anya: I always hated that one, but the worst one was … *(changes voice)* "You'd better get your act together or you're going to be a complete social outcast at the junior high and then you'll be cursed with eternal nerd-dom until the day you die!"

(Rose and Jen stare at her.)

Anya: Okay, okay, so none of the teachers ever said *that,* but let's be honest. We're all afraid it could happen. We worry about getting our lockers open and finding our classes and flunking out, but mostly we worry about fitting in at the junior high.

Rose: It's true.

Jen: I'm not worried. Not one little bit.

Anya: Right. Anyway, I'm glad to have my friends by my side for the first day of school.

(Steven, Christine, Ella, Pablo, and extra students enter, mill about, chat.)

Rose: Me, too. Just look at this school! It's like ten times as big as our elementary.

Anya: Let's go find our lockers.

Jen: Hey, why don't we make some friends first? Like … how about those people there?

Anya: I don't know if that's—

Jen: Hi, everybody!

Steven, Christine, Ella, Pablo: *(dully)* Hi.

Jen: I'm Jen, and this is Rose, and this is Anya, and we're new here.

Steven: Duh. We're all new here.

Jen: I know! Isn't it fantastic to start a new school? I just know junior high is going to be fantastic. And I'm going to make all kinds of fantastic new friends.

Steven, Christine, Ella, Pablo: *(stare)*

Anya: So … uh … I guess we'll look for our lockers now.

Christine: *(sarcastic)* Fantastic idea.

Jen: See you guys later! Maybe we'll have some classes together. Wouldn't that be fantastic?

Anya: Come on, Jen! The bell will ring soon.

Jen: Oh. Well, bye, everybody!

(Pablo mutters something to others, and they laugh.)

Anya: *(to Rose)* I don't believe it. We've been in the building for five minutes and Jen has already made us look like hopeless dweebs. Now we're cursed!

Rose: Cursed?

Anya: Yes! You know … like I said before. *(in "teacher" voice)* Cursed to eternal nerd-dom.

Rose: Come on, Anya. Everything will be okay once Jen calms down a little.

Jen: *(shrieks)* Here are our lockers! Aren't they fantastic?

Anya: Well, that better happen soon.

Scene Two

Anya: *(to audience)* Combination locks can be confusing at first, but let's face it. Opening a lock isn't rocket science. Left, right, left. How hard is that?

Jen: I can't get my locker open.

Anya: Try it again.

Jen: I tried it three times already. I can't do it! I can't do it! I can't—

Rose: Relax, okay? We'll help you.

Jen: What if it won't open? I'll have to carry all my books everywhere I go! I'll look like a complete idiot!

Anya: Yeah. We wouldn't want that to happen. Give me your combination and I'll open it.

Jen: Five … fourteen … twenty-one.

Anya: Okay … five … fourteen … twenty-one … and voilà! Wait a minute. That didn't work.

Jen: See?

(Bell rings.)

Jen: Oh, no! That's the warning bell. We're going to be late to our first class. You know what the teachers used to say … *(in "teacher" voice)* "Tardiness will not be tolerated at the—"

Anya: Sheesh! Calm down, Jen. It's just a simple lock, okay? It's not that difficult.

Rose: Don't worry.

Anya: *(to audience)* I tried that stupid combination over and over, and I couldn't get it to work. *(to Jen)* Are you sure you gave me the right numbers?

Jen: Yes, I'm sure. I know! Let's ask our new friends to help us.

Anya: They're not our—

Jen: Hey, you guys! Hey, over here! Yoohoo!

Anya: Jen! Everybody's looking at us.

Jen: Not everybody. *(takes a deep breath and bellows)* HEY, YOU OVER THERE! *(to Anya and Rose)* Here they come.

Steven: What do you want?

Jen: Can you help me get my locker open?

Christine: You're kidding, right?

Pablo: It's not that hard.

Anya: That's what I told her. Heh. Heh.

Jen: Well, you can't get it open either.

Ella: Are you sure you're using the right combination?

Jen: Yes. Show them, Anya.

Anya: Okay … five … fourteen …

Pablo: You're doing it backwards! It's right, left, right.

Steven: Not left, right, left. Brother!

Christine: Let's get to class.

(Steven, etc. exit.)

Jen: Thanks, you guys! Thanks so much! Thanks! See you later! Bye!

Anya: They're gone already, Jen. Quit yelling! And here! Your locker's open.

Jen: It's a good thing they came along to help me out. Friends just make life easier, don't they?

Anya: Right. Sure. *(muttering to Rose)* When they're not making you look stupid.

Rose: You *were* turning the lock backwards.

Anya: So? She's the one who's ruining everything, Rose. We're doomed.

Rose: No, we're not.

Anya: Yes, we are. Completely, totally, utterly doomed.

Rose: Whatever.

Scene Three

Anya: *(to audience as Mr. Martino and other students form class)* All morning long, Jen pulled us deeper and deeper into her dorky world. Like we were fifteen minutes into English class when she appeared at the door and …

Mr. Martino: So now let's talk about what we'll—

Jen: Is this Spanish class?

Mr. Martino: Sorry, no.

Jen: *(hysterical)* I can't find my class! I've been all over this school and I can't find it! I'm so tardy now that I'll probably get kicked out! On my first day! *(notices Anya and Rose and speaks normally)* Oh, hi, you guys. So you have this class together? *(to teacher, resuming panic)* I don't know what to do! I don't know where to go!

Mr. Martino: Let's step out in the hall, and I'll point you toward the Language Lab.

Jen: *(sobbing)* Okay. Thanks. *(cheery)* Bye, everybody! *(exits with Mr. Martino)*

Ella: What a loser!

Steven: No kidding. *(to Anya and Rose)* And she's your friend?

Rose: Yes! She's really nice.

Ella: *(rolling eyes)* Isn't that fantastic?

Anya: *(to Rose)* See? Jen is putting the whammy on us. We're cursed!

Rose: Don't be ridiculous.

Anya: *(to audience as Rose exits and Ms. Basu replaces Mr. Martino)* Jen showed up half an hour late for our math class even though it was right across the hall from the Language Lab. By then we were in the middle of doing what the teacher called …

Ms. Basu: An assessment of your current mathematical skills.

Anya: *(to audience)* Which was just like a test. A hard test. That took a lot of concentration.

Jen: *(enters)* I'm sorry I'm late! I can't find anything in this building! Please don't give me detention! Please!

Ms. Basu: Just have a seat and work on this assessment of your current mathematical skills.

Jen: What kind of math is this? I don't know how to do all this stuff!

Ms. Basu: That's okay. Do your best. It's just an assessment of your current mathematical skills.

Jen: But what does this symbol mean? And how do you do problem fourteen?

Ms. Basu: Do whatever problems you can. This is just an assessment of—

Anya: *(to audience)* Well, you get the idea. Ms. Basu had to explain things over and over. Jen looked like a fool. And I was the friend of the fool. After class, she latched onto me and flapped her big loud mouth and made sure the whole world knew that.

Jen: I'm so glad we have math together! It's fantastic to have a class with my best friend!

Christine: *(to Pablo as all exit except Anya and Jen)* I can't stand all these freaks.

Pablo: Why didn't they keep them back in grade school?

Anya: *(muttering)* We're cursed! Cursed!

Jen: What was that?

Anya: Uh … you first, Jen. Go ahead.

Jen: Okay! *(exits)*

Scene Four

Anya: *(to audience)* I had to do something quick. If I didn't change the way things were going, I might as well have "dweeb" tattooed on my forehead. I'd never escape the curse—never! *(as Rose enters)* When I met up with Rose at lunchtime, I tried to get her to face the truth. *(to Rose)* Listen … Jen is a nice person—and—

Rose: Yes, she is. Remember that time your science fair project got run over by the bus? And Jen helped you redo the whole thing?

Anya: Of course, but that's—

Rose: And how about when she gave you that cool necklace for your birthday? The one that had been in her family for years?

Anya: Yeah, that was great, but—

Rose: And wasn't it sweet when—

Anya: Look, Rose, Jen is great. But we're in junior high now. And if we're going to survive, we have to cut her loose.

Rose: How can you say that?

Anya: It's the truth, that's how. Let's face it: Jen is dead weight. She's already drowning in … in … in the Sea of Nerd! And she's going to drag us under, too, if we don't break free from her. Today!

Rose: But the three of us have been friends forever.

Anya: *(as others, except Jen, enter and take seats)* Are you with me or not?

Rose: Not! *(exits)*

Anya: *(goes up to Steven, Christine, Ella, and Pablo)* Is someone sitting here?

Ella: Yeah—the Invisible Man.

Anya: Funny. *(sits)*

Pablo: Where's your buddy?

Anya: Who?

Christine: That weird girl. *(imitating Jen)* Ooh! Ooh! Junior high is so fantastic! Ooh! ooh! will you be my new fantastic new friend? And ooh! ooh! now I'm lost! And—

Anya: Oh, her. We're not really friends.

Steven: She says she's your friend.

Anya: Yeah, she's always doing that. I feel sorry for her, but she drives me nuts, you know.

Ella: We know! *(Everyone laughs.)*

Anya: She's like a pesky fly—always buzzing around. *(Everyone laughs.)* Or a mosquito that you just can't shoo away. *(Everyone laughs.)* No, wait! She's like a leech. *(Everyone laughs.)*

Steven: Good one!

Anya: Yeah, she's a leech that sucks all the cool out of everything. *(Everyone laughs.)*

Pablo: You're pretty funny. What's your name again?

Anya: Anya.

Christine: So, Anya, when do you have art?

Anya: *(to audience)* It worked! I got rid of the curse before it became permanent. And I made a new group of friends on the very first day of junior high. I hate to sound like Jen, but I felt fantastic! Yep. Fantastic. *(losing enthusiasm)* I sure did. Just great. Really. Really great.

Ella: Want to walk to the lockers with us?

Anya: *(imitating Jen)* Ooh! Ooh! Fantastic!

(Everybody laughs and exits, except Anya.)

Scene Five

Anya: *(to audience)* I didn't see Jen for the next couple of periods. Which gave me plenty of time to get in good with my new group. But I knew I would have to face Jen some time, and when I did … well … I'd have to cut her off. Not that we couldn't still be friends. We could, of course, but only outside of school. Somehow I had to get her to understand that. *(Rose and Jen enter.)*

Jen: Hi! We both have science now. What do you have?

Anya: Science.

Jen: Fantastic! We can all walk there together.

Anya: You guys go ahead. I need to get something out of my locker.

Jen: Okay. We'll wait.

Anya: No, that's all right. It might take me a while. These locks!

Jen: I think I know how to do it now. I'll help you.

Anya: Look, Jen … I just don't want to walk with you.

Rose: Anya!

Jen: Why not?

Anya: Well … because … you know, junior high is a time for personal growth.

Jen: I know! *(in "teacher" voice)* "Remember, boys and girls, junior high is a time for—"

Anya: So I'm going to really get out of my comfort zone, okay? I'll just hang out with new friends at school, see? The three of us will do stuff together outside of school, of course, but while we're here, I think we should just act like we don't know each other. You understand.

Jen: *(hurt)* Oh. Okay. So see you later. *(exits)*

Rose: I cannot believe you! That was so mean. Wait, Jen! *(exits)*

(Mr. Jacobs, Steven, Christine, Ella, Pablo, Rose, and Jen enter and form class.)

Anya: *(to audience)* I felt sorry about hurting Jen, but I had to do it. I mean … *(in "teacher" voice)* "What happens in junior high can affect you for the rest of your life." *(back to normal)* Right? So if you get yourself labeled a geek then, your life is ruined. Right? I had to ditch Jen. *(takes seat and says softly)* I had to.

Mr. Jacobs: Not another scheduling problem! There shouldn't be so many people in this class.

Pablo: I'd be glad to leave.

Mr. Jacobs: Everybody just stay where you are and talk quietly among yourselves while I get this mess straightened out. *(exits)*

Steven: Gee, I hope we don't study insects this year.

Ella: Like flies, you mean. I just hate flies, don't you, Christine?

Christine: Well, duh. Like who … *(pauses as Ella gestures at Jen)* Yeah. I hate those pesky flies.

Pablo: They are so annoying, aren't they? Buzzing around … bzzzz … bzzz … ooh, fantazzztic!

(Jen looks their way.)

Anya: *(quickly)* You know, insects are interesting, really! Like did you know that there are more insects than any other animal? There can be millions of them on just one little acre of land! Millions! *(looks relieved when Jen looks away)*

Ella: Fascinating. But they're still annoying. Especially mosquitoes.

Steven: *Especially* the ones you can't shoo away. *(Makes a shooing motion at Jen, who turns around when they laugh.)* Right, Anya?

Anya: *(glancing at Jen)* I … I guess.

Christine: *(after Jen has turned away)* Leeches are the worst.

Anya: But they're not insects. They're actually—

Pablo: Whatever they are, leeches are disgusting. They just suck the cool out of everything, right, Anya?

Ella: Right?

Anya: Come on, you guys.

Steven: Do you know any leeches, Anya?

Anya: I … uh … I … .*(to audience)* That's when something unbelievable happened. Something that changed everything. No … not everything. Just me.

Scene Six

Jen: *(to Steven, etc.)* Leave her alone!

Ella: What?

Jen: Stop it! Stop making fun of Anya! She's not a pest. She's a fantastic person and you're lucky to even know her.

Steven, Christine, Ella, Pablo: *(crack up)*

Steven: You think we're talking about Anya?

Pablo: What an idiot!

Ella: We were talking about—

Anya: Why don't you people just … just buzz off?

Christine: You're kidding, right?

Anya: No. I'm not.

Steven: *(to friends)* Dweebs! They stick together like … like …

Rose: Like glue. Right, Anya?

Anya: Right.

Ella: Whatever.

Mr. Jacobs: *(enters)* Okay! Some of you are moving to the other science class. *(indicating Steven, etc.)* This half of the room can follow me there. *(exits)*

Christine: Good! Now we don't have to study nerdanetrics with all these nerds.

Pablo: Or dorkology.

Steven: Or dweebological … uh … dweebics. *(Steven, etc. exit.)*

Jen: You know … I'm starting to think they're not really that fantastic.

Rose: I think you're onto something there.

Anya: Thanks, Jen, for standing up for me like that.

Jen: Sure. Any time.

Anya: I couldn't believe you did that after all the stuff I said. I thought you would never have anything to do with me ever again.

Jen: Oh, you can't rid of me that easily!

Anya: Well … thanks. And I'm sorry about what I said, okay?

Jen: Okay. Thanks.

Anya: So it looks like we're stuck with each other then.

Rose: Yeah. I guess we're cursed! *(laughs)*

Anya: *(smiling)* Right. Cursed.

Jen: Can you believe it? Our first day in junior high is almost over. I don't know why the teachers made it sound so bad. It's fantastic!

Anya: Well, they did get one thing right. *(in "teacher" voice)* "The very best thing about the junior high is taking your friends along with you to share everything."

Rose: The teachers never said anything like that.

Anya: Well, they should have!

From Diana R. Jenkins, *All Year Long! Funny Readers Theatre for Life's Special Times.* Westport, CT: Teacher Ideas Press. Copyright © 2007 by Diana R. Jenkins.

My Family Tree Is Full of Nuts!

Summary

Jake hates it that he has to waste Labor Day at a family reunion. Isn't the holiday all about relaxing? Being around his crazy family isn't relaxing at all! But Jake learns there's more to his family—and the Labor Day holiday—than he thought.

Costumes, Sets, and Props

Aunt Frannie could wear a pirate hat. Cousin Albert can wear a long beard. The twin cousins could dress alike.

A few tables and chairs could be used to suggest Jake's bedroom and the picnic areas.

Presentation

❖ The Narrator stands to one side throughout play.

❖ Great Aunt Sweeney, Florence, and Annabelle can use a baby-talk tone with Jake.

❖ The twins are nauseatingly singsong when they are rhyming.

❖ The old man is crotchety and intimidating to start out.

Supplemental Reading

Bailey, Linda. *How Can a Brilliant Detective Shine in the Dark?* Toronto: Kids Can Press, 2001.

Jango-Cohen, Judith. *Ellis Island.* New York: Children's Press, 2005.

Murphy, Patricia J. *Our National Holidays.* Minneapolis: Compass Point Books, 2002.

Quattlebaum, Mary. *Family Reunion.* Grand Rapids, MI: Eerdmans Books for Young Readers, 2004. (Poetry)

Walter, Mildred Pitts. *Ray and the Best Family Reunion Ever.* New York: Amistad (HarperCollins), 2002.

Cast of Characters

Narrator	Annabelle
Jake	Edison
Dad	Fredison
Mom	Aunt Frannie
Great Aunt Sweeney	Cousin Albert
Florence	Old Man

Labor Day

My Family Tree Is Full of Nuts!

Scene One

Narrator: Jake had big plans for Labor Day.

Jake: You bet! It feels like we've already been back at school forever, and I need to relax. Taking it easy … doing absolutely nothing. ... That's what Labor Day is all about!

Narrator: Uh … not exactly. It's actually about honoring all the people who work.

Jake: Right. The important thing is that people are off on Labor Day. Including me! I'm not going to lift a finger all day. First, I'll sleep in until whenever. Then I'll have some breakfast and rest up for lunch. Then I'll—

Narrator: But what about the family reunion?

Jake: The what?

Narrator: *(to audience)* To get on with our story … Jake's relatives on his dad's side were having a huge family reunion on Labor Day.

Jake: This is the first I've heard of it!

Dad: *(entering)* Hey, Jake … big news! We're having a huge family reunion on Labor Day. Won't that be great?

Jake: Sure. You and Mom go and have a wonderful time.

Dad: But you're invited, too!

Jake: Oh, that's okay. I have a busy schedule that day.

Dad: You can't miss the reunion. The whole family hasn't gotten together like that in years! And everyone will be there. Do you remember Aunt Frannie?

Jake: Is she the one with the Chihuahuas?

Dad: You do remember!

Jake: How could I forget? She dressed them like cowboys.

Dad: And what about Cousin Albert? His beard must be down to the ground now.

Jake: Oh, boy.

Dad: Even Uncle Moogie is coming. Remember how you used to love his collection?

From Diana R. Jenkins, *All Year Long! Funny Readers Theatre for Life's Special Times.* Westport, CT: Teacher Ideas Press. Copyright © 2007 by Diana R. Jenkins.

Jake: I was a little kid then, Dad. I don't like getting that close to other people's teeth anymore.

Dad: I can't wait to see everybody. Can you?

Jake: Actually I … I mean … I was thinking … sure, Dad.

Dad: Your mother is going to be so excited. *(exits)*

Jake: Great! Now my day of rest is ruined.

Narrator: Maybe you'll have a good time.

Jake: I don't think so! My dad's family tree is full of nuts—and I get to spend a whole day with those loonies.

Scene Two

Narrator: On the morning of the big day, Jake suddenly came down with a terrible illness.

Jake: It's terrible, all right.

Narrator: Oh, come on. Do you really think you're going to get out of this thing?

Jake: I have to try, man. I mean … someone has to protect Labor Day, right? In honor of everyone who wants to do nothing.

Narrator: I told you. It's not—

Jake: Whatever.

Mom: *(enters)* Jake, we'll leave in … why aren't you ready?

Jake: *(coughs weakly)* I don't feel so hot, Mom.

Mom: Oh, really? *(feels his forehead)* You don't seem to have a fever.

Jake: Are you sure? I feel awful! My head hurts and my stomach is gurgling around and my toes are cold and my ears are buzzing and my neck itches and *(noticing her skeptical look)* I … uh … feel really weak.

Mom: Hmmm … could it be you have familyreunionitis?

Jake: I'm sick! Really!

Mom: Jake, this reunion means the world to your father. You are going with us, and you are going to act happy about it. Understand?

Jake: *(with stiff grin)* You bet, Mom.

Mom: *(exiting)* Be ready to leave in ten minutes.

Jake: *(still grinning)* Yes, ma'am.

Narrator: *(to audience)* So Jake was stuck—trapped—doomed, I guess you'd say.

Jake: *(still grinning)* Why don't you … oh! *(returns face to normal)* just be quiet? This is already the worst day in my life without you flapping your yap about it.

Narrator: You don't know that.

Jake: Of course I do. No good day involves human teeth and Chihuahuas and … and rhyming.

Narrator: Rhyming?

Jake: Just wait until you meet my twin cousins.

From Diana R. Jenkins, *All Year Long! Funny Readers Theatre for Life's Special Times.* Westport, CT: Teacher Ideas Press. Copyright © 2007 by Diana R. Jenkins.

Scene Three

(Mom, Dad, and Great Aunt Sweeney enter.)

Narrator: When Jake and his parents arrived at the reunion, the first person they talked to was Great Aunt Sweeney.

Great Aunt Sweeney: Oh, my! This isn't Little Jakie, is it?

Dad: Yes, it is, Auntie.

Great Aunt Sweeney: *(squishing Jake's face)* Isn't he just the cutest thing? Florence! Looky here! It's Little Jakie!

Florence: *(enters)* Not Little Jakie?

Mom: Hello, Florence. Yes, this is our son, Jake.

Great Aunt Sweeney: Isn't he just the cutest thing? *(squishes Jake's face then "passes" him to Florence to squish)*

Florence: He is! Just the cutest thing! Hey, Annabelle! Get over here and look at Little Jakie!

Annabelle: *(enters)* Oh, my goodness! Little Jakie! Aren't you precious? *(squishes Jake's face and "passes" him back to Great Aunt Sweeney to squish)*

Great Aunt Sweeney: Why, I remember when you were just a little bitty thing! We all had a special nickname for you.

Jake: Little Jakie?

Great Aunt Sweeney: That's right! You remember! He always was a smart little fellow. And cute! *(squishes Jake's face)*

Jake: *(still squished)* Dad?

Dad: So who else is here, Auntie?

Great Aunt Sweeney: *(releasing Jake)* Everybody! Come along and say hello. *(exits with Dad, Florence, and Annabelle)*

Mom: Remember, Jake. You're happy to be here. Right?

Jake: *(forcing grin)* Sure! Happy!

(Mom exits.)

Jake: *(releases grin and turns to Narrator)* I don't think my face can take much more of this stupid reunion.

Narrator: Oh, come on, you can handle it. *(mocking)* Little Jakie.

Jake: Don't call me that!

Scene Four

Narrator: Luckily for Jake there were some kids his own age at the reunion.

(Edison and Fredison enter.)

Jake: Oh, no! Not those guys.

Edison: Hello, I'm Edison.

Fredison: Hello, I'm Fredison.

Edison: Are you our cousin, Little Jake?

Fredison: Or have we made a big mistake?

Jake: *(muttering)* No, I made the big mistake coming to this freak show.

Edison: Speak up! Speak out! Enunciate!

Fredison: We can't understand if you don't pronunciate!

Jake: *(putting on fake grin)* Yes, I'm Jake. So … how are you guys doing?

Edison: We are fine. Hope you are, too!

Fredison: Yes, we're fine. How about you?

Jake: Yeah. Fine. Well, I guess I'd better go mingle.

Edison: Talk to Great-great-grandpa. He's a blast!

Fredison: He knows all the family's past.

Jake: Okay. Well … see you later … uh … alligator. *(exits)*

Edison: *(to Fredison)* What's that supposed to mean?

Fredison: *(to Edison)* I don't know. I mean … uh … what a scene! In between? Uh … injured spleen? Rats! Why do I always have to talk second? *(They exit.)*

Scene Five

Narrator: As the reunion went on and on, Jake got more and more stressed out.

Jake: *(enters)* Wouldn't you? These people are bizarre.

Aunt Frannie: *(enters)* Little Jakie! Oh, dear. I bet you were looking forward to seeing Yapalong Cassidy and Wyatt Arf.

Jake: Who? Oh. The Chihuahuas.

Aunt Frannie: I'm sorry, but I don't raise Chihuahuas anymore. Now I have Clydesdales. They make darling pirates!

Jake: Aren't Clydesdales like honking big horses?

Aunt Frannie: They sure are! Sorry, but I couldn't bring them today. You understand.

Jake: Sure, Aunt Frannie. Sure. Well, I'll see you later.

Aunt Frannie: Oh. Okay. Talk to you later, matey! Arrrr! *(exits)*

Jake: Yeah. Ar.

Cousin Albert: *(enters)* Who are you?

Jake: I'm Jake. I mean … Little Jakie.

Cousin Albert: You don't say! Hmph! You haven't grown much, have you? My beard is longer than you are.

Jake: I think it's longer than anyone here.

Cousin Albert: Yep! Would you believe I haven't shaved in thirty years?

Jake: Yes. Yes, I would.

Cousin Albert: Hey! There's Moogie! I can't wait to see what he's added to his collection. I hear he has the largest human molar in the world. *(exits)*

Jake: Well, I can wait. I can wait forever.

Edison: *(offstage)* Where's our cousin, Little Jake?

Fredison: *(offstage)* We need him for the potato race.

Edison: *(offstage)* Fredison, that doesn't rhyme.

Fredison: *(offstage)* Hey, you try going second sometime!

Jake: I can't take this anymore! I have to get out of here.

Narrator: So Jake ran off to the next picnic area. There he found an empty shelter. Well, he thought it was empty.

Jake: This is a good place to hide out awhile.

Old Man: Hey! What are you doing in here?

Scene Six

Narrator: The old man sitting at the picnic table looked pretty crabby.

Jake: I … uh … .

Old Man: Aren't you from the family reunion down that-a-way?

Jake: Yes, sir.

Old Man: So why are you hanging around here bothering me?

Jake: Sorry, but I had to get away for a few minutes. To tell you the truth, my family is weird. Like off-the-charts weird.

Old Man: Oh, really?

Jake: Really! I can prove it. What's the craziest thing anybody in your family ever did?

Old Man: Hmmm … I guess that would be when my parents and my sister and I came here from Ireland.

Jake: What's so crazy about that?

Old Man: Are you kidding? We left our home—the only home we'd ever known—and crossed the ocean in a ship that looked like it might sink at any moment. We didn't have cushy, high-speed jets to gallivant around in back then. You young people today are spoiled rotten, you know that?

Jake: But I've never been on a jet.

Old Man: Are you sassing me, boy?

Jake: No, sir.

Old Man: Hmph! Anyway … we traveled all the way around the world to come to a country we'd never seen before to start a whole new life. Doesn't that sound crazy to you?

Jake: It sounds scary, actually.

Old Man: Oh, it was. But my parents wanted a better life for our family, and they would do anything to get it. When we got here, they started working and they never stopped. They put in long hours at those nasty factories, and then they did odd jobs on the side. My poor mother ironed for hours every week. With a real iron iron! Not these sissy irons they have today. And my father blah blah blah … *(continues to blah on as if telling stories)*

Narrator: At first Jake was bored with the old guy's stories. But then he got kind of interested.

From Diana R. Jenkins, *All Year Long! Funny Readers Theatre for Life's Special Times.* Westport, CT: Teacher Ideas Press. Copyright © 2007 by Diana R. Jenkins.

Jake: *(to Narrator)* I guess things really were hard back in the day. I mean … those people worked all the time and they still barely survived!

Narrator: *(to Jake)* But their hard work made things better for their kids.

Jake: Yeah. And they worked hard so *their* kids would have it better than *they* did. And it went on like that all through the years. Hey! I guess parents still do that today, too, don't they?

Old Man: Of course they do! Blah blah …

Jake: *(to Narrator)* I get it now. Today is supposed to honor all those hardworking people, right?

Narrator: Right. I tried to tell you that.

Jake: So Labor Day is a day off, but it's not about goofing off.

Old Man: Of course it's not! Where did you get an idea like that, Little Jakie?

Jake: I don't know. I guess I never really thought … Little Jakie!

Scene Seven

Narrator: Little Jakie took a—

Jake: Hey!

Narrator: Okay, *Jake* took a good look at the old man sitting beside him.

Jake: Wait a minute! Are you related to me?

Old Man: I'm your great-great-grandpa. The head of your whole family. The family you said was crazy. Wanna take all that back now?

Jake: I'm sorry. I didn't know you were you. I didn't mean to … Hey! Why aren't *you* at the reunion?

Old Man: Listen, I can only handle that circus for so long. Then I need a break.

Jake: So you think they're strange, too!

Old Man: All right. Our family *is* a bit peculiar. But they're good people—the kind of hardworking people who made this country what it is today. Like Moogie. He quit school to support his family when his father died. So what if he has a strange fascination with teeth? *(shudders)* And Frannie worked two jobs and never bought herself a stitch of new clothes when her kids were growing up. If she wants to dress up elephants now, who cares?

Jake: I … I didn't know that stuff about them.

Old Man: Well, maybe it's time you got to know your family a little better. Yathink?

Jake: Yes, sir. I do.

Old Man: Then we'd better head back.

Scene Eight

Narrator: *(to audience as relatives enter)* So they returned to the reunion, and Jake tried to look past the strange behavior of his relatives and see the good in them.

Jake: *(to audience)* Which wasn't always easy! But I talked to people …

(Jake moves along the line of relatives.)

Great Aunt Sweeney: *(squishes Jake's face)*

Jake: *(talking as best he can with squished face)* School's been going pretty well so far. My teacher gives a lot of homework, but I'm keeping up.

Great Aunt Sweeney: That's wonderful! *(gives one last squish)*

Jake: *(to audience)* And I heard some interesting stories … .

Cousin Albert: So I got in trouble with the coach for not shaving! The Reds were very strict about their players being clean-shaven in those days.

Jake: I didn't even know you were a professional baseball player. That's amazing!

Cousin Albert: Oh, yes! I can tell you all kinds of stories about it.

Jake: Great! *(to audience)* And I played with my cousins …

Edison: Congratulations, Jake! You won the race.

Fredison: Wow! You set an amazing pace.

Jake: Is there a prize for first place?

Edison: No, but … hey, that rhymes!

Fredison: You're a poet.

Jake: Don't I know it? *(Fredison and Jake look expectantly at Edison.)*

Edison: I … uh … there's a boat. Want to row it?

Fredison: *(muttering to Edison as Jake moves on)* See? It's not so easy.

Jake: *(to audience)* And I just got a little closer to my family.

Old Man: It was good to see you, Jake.

Jake: You, too, Grandpa.

(Mom and Dad enter. Everyone hugs and makes good-byes. Relatives exit.)

Dad: Wasn't that wonderful? I think we should have a reunion every Labor Day, don't you?

Jake: That's a great idea, Dad.

Dad: I'll go get the car. *(exits)*

Mom: Thanks, Jake. *(hugs him and exits)*

Narrator: *(to Jake)* See, Little Jakie? You had a good day.

Jake: Call me that again, and I'll make you pay.

Narrator: *(to audience)* Lucky for me, it's the end of the play!

The Mystery of History

Summary

Lindsey is disappointed when she doesn't get assigned to the history class taught by the cool, fun teacher. Instead, she's stuck with Mrs. Morton, the oldest, meanest teacher in the school—maybe even the world! When Mrs. Morton "picks" on Lindsey, she plots revenge.

Costumes, Sets, and Props

❖ All characters can wear contemporary clothing. Ms. Jefferson can wear shaving cream on her face for the last scene.

❖ A few desks and chairs can serve as the classroom.

❖ If props are desired, students and Mrs. Morton can have books, notebooks, pens, and pencils. Mrs. Morton needs a computer printout for the last scene.

Presentation

Mrs. Morton speaks clearly, stands up straight, and accepts no nonsense. David and the other history students are afraid of her and eager to do whatever they can to please her.

Lindsey can mime typing each of her posts on the message board.

After a performance for an audience, explorer-themed refreshments, such as cookies decorated with ships or a cake decorated with Vespucci's routes of exploration, might be served.

Supplemental Reading

Klingel, Cynthia, and Noyed, Robert B. *Leif Eriksson, Norwegian Explorer.* Chanhassen, MN: The Child's World, 2005.

Matthews, Rupert. *Eyewitness Explorer.* New York: Dorling Kindersley, 2005.

Parker, Nancy Winslow. *Land Ho! Fifty Glorious Years in the Age of Exploration.* New York: HarperCollins, 2001.

White, David. *The First Voyage around the World.* Philadelphia: Mason Crest, 2003.

Willmann, Kelly. *The European Rediscovery of America.* Philadelphia: Mason Crest, 2003.

Cast of Characters

Narrator	Vito
Lindsey	Other History Students
Sienna	Mrs. Morton
Adam	Ms. Jefferson
David	

Columbus Day

The Mystery of History

Scene One

Narrator: Ms. Jefferson had only been teaching at North Middle school for three years, but she was the most popular teacher there. Everybody hoped to get assigned to her room for history.

Lindsey: I heard that she dresses up and pretends to be all the six wives of Henry the Eighth.

Sienna: And Henry the Eighth, too.

Adam: I bet that's hilarious!

David: And educational.

Vito: My brother said that Ms. Jefferson does a mean Martha Washington. Like you'd swear you were talking to the lady herself.

David: How could he tell? Nobody knows what Martha Washington sounded like.

Vito: Not exactly, I guess, but he knew Ms. Jefferson was good.

David: That's ridiculous!

Vito: You don't know everything, Mr. Smart Brain.

David: I know you're not making sense, Vito.

Lindsey: Listen, you guys, the important thing is that Ms. Jefferson makes history fun. She even brings in snacks for her students. I really hope I get put in her class.

Narrator: But when Lindsey got her schedule…

Lindsey: Mrs. Morton? I got Mrs. Morton for history? I can't believe it!

Sienna: That's too bad, Lindsey.

Lindsey: She's the oldest teacher in the school. Maybe even the world!

Vito: And the meanest.

Lindsey: Way mean.

David: Oh, she's not mean. She's just tough. I'm sure we'll learn a lot in her class, Lindsey.

Lindsey: Right. I'm really looking forward to that.

Adam: (*aside to Sienna and Vito*) I am *so* glad we got Ms. Jefferson.

Scene Two

(Sienna, Adam, and Vito exit. Mrs. Morton and other History Students enter and form class.)

Narrator: To start her first class, Mrs. Morton passed out a huge stack of paper to each student.

Mrs. Morton: This is your class syllabus. Do not lose it.

Other History Students and David: Yes, ma'am.

Lindsey: *(to David)* What does she mean … class syllable?

David: That's syllabus. It lists what we're going to learn and everything we should read and all the assignments and projects. You know … like they give out in college classes.

Lindsey: But we're not in college!

David: No, but it's still a good way to organize everything.

Lindsey: How are we going to cover all this in one year? This must be a joke.

Mrs. Morton: History is not a joking matter, young lady.

Lindsey: *(muttering)* Of course not.

Mrs. Morton: I do not allow mumbling in my class. Speak clearly! Conduct yourself like an intelligent, well educated person not some mush-mouthed sluggard.

Lindsey: Yes, ma'am.

Mrs. Morton: And sit up! *(Everyone straightens up.)* Now, everyone, look at your syllabus and follow along as I explain my expectations for you.

Other History Students and David: Yes, ma'am.

David: *(to Lindsey)* Wow! We are going to learn so much.

Lindsey: I can't wait.

Scene Three

(Mrs. Morton and other History Students exit and Lindsey's friends enter.)

Narrator: At lunch, Lindsey had to hear all about the amazing Ms. Jefferson.

Adam: I couldn't believe she dressed up on the very first day.

Lindsey: She did?

Adam: Yeah. As Isabella of Spain—the queen who sent Columbus to the New World.

Sienna: She looked so beautiful, didn't she? With that elegant gown? And the crown?

Vito: She looked just like Queen Isabella. And she talked like her, too.

David: You mean she spoke Spanish?

Vito: No, but she sounded just like Queen Isabella anyway.

David: You don't know that!

Vito: Look, you weren't there. Ms. Jefferson does one mean Queen Isabella.

From Diana R. Jenkins, *All Year Long! Funny Readers Theatre for Life's Special Times.* Westport, CT: Teacher Ideas Press. Copyright © 2007 by Diana R. Jenkins.

David:	Whatever.
Lindsey:	That sounds a lot more fun than listening to Mrs. Morton talk on and on and on and…
Sienna:	Oh! And we had cookies.
Lindsey:	*(upset)* What?
Adam:	Yeah! Ms. Jefferson decorated them with pictures of boats.
Vito:	Those were Columbus's ships. The *Niña,* the *Pinta,* and the *Santa Maria.* I had one of each.
Lindsey:	I can't believe it! You guys didn't do anything but have fun.
David:	Actually, Lindsey, it sounds like they learned quite a bit today.
Lindsey:	Well, I learned something today, too.
Adam:	What?
Lindsey:	I learned that I'm really sorry I got stuck with Mrs. Morton for history.

Scene Four

Narrator:	Lindsey might have eventually adjusted to history with Mrs. Morton if only—
Lindsey:	If only she hadn't started picking on me.
Narrator:	*(to Lindsey)* Picking on you? Really?
Lindsey:	Really!
Mrs. Morton:	Why did the Vikings give Leif Eriksson the nickname "Leif the Lucky"?
Other History Students and David:	*(waving hands eagerly)*
Mrs. Morton:	Lindsey?
Lindsey:	I didn't have my hand up.
Mrs. Morton:	I know. In this class, I call on both volunteers and non-volunteers.
Lindsey:	But if we wanted to answer, we'd raise our hands. It's a tradition in schools, you know.
Mrs. Morton:	It's also a tradition for teachers to help their students learn as much as they can. If I called only on volunteers, many of you wouldn't pay any attention and thus would learn nothing.
Lindsey:	*(muttering)* Whatever.
Mrs. Morton:	No mumbling, please. Now speak up, Lindsey, and answer my question.
Lindsey:	I … uh … don't know the answer.
Other History Students and David:	*(gasp)*
Mrs. Morton:	Did you read the homework assignment last night?
Lindsey:	Not all of it.
Other History Students and David:	*(gasp)*

From Diana R. Jenkins, *All Year Long! Funny Readers Theatre for Life's Special Times.* Westport, CT: Teacher Ideas Press. Copyright © 2007 by Diana R. Jenkins.

Lindsey: It was the first day of school! What kind of loser does homework on the very first day?

David: I read all the homework, Mrs. Morton. And I can answer the question.

Lindsey: *(muttering)* Oh. That kind of loser.

Mrs. Morton: Since you are not prepared, Lindsey, stay after school today and catch up in the detention room.

Narrator: Lindsey couldn't believe it! Detention? On the second day of school?

Lindsey: *(to audience)* I can't believe it! Detention! On the second day of school! I bet Ms. Jefferson isn't mean like that.

Narrator: *(as everyone except David and Lindsey exit)* Over the next couple of weeks, Lindsey's problems with history kept getting worse.

Lindsey: *(to David)* I never know the answer, so why does she keep asking me stuff?

David: She asks *everybody* a lot of questions, Lindsey. She's trying to help us learn.

Lindsey: Well, she's making me look stupid in front of everybody. Over and over again!

David: You could study so you'll be prepared when she—

Lindsey: It's embarrassing when I can't answer her questions.

David: After you miss a question, do you listen for the correct—

Lindsey: I'm going to get back at her for the way she's treating me.

David: How?

Lindsey: I don't know yet. But I'll think of something. *(gives an evil laugh)*

David: What was that?

Lindsey: That, my friend, was the sound of revenge! *(evil laugh)*

David: Okay.

Scene Five

Narrator: That night Lindsey came up with an idea for getting her revenge on Mrs. Morton. She was online, visiting this message board that was popular with the kids at her school, when inspiration struck.

Lindsey: I know! I'll use a fake name and post something about Mrs. Morton. Something embarrassing. Everyone at school will read it, and somebody will tell her all about it.

Narrator: Lindsey thought for a long time and finally typed…

Lindsey: "A Mystery of History.… We all know that Columbus believed the earth was round. But here's a mystery: Why don't history books ever mention the person who taught Columbus that the earth wasn't flat? North Middle School's own Mrs. Morton!" Ha! That'll do it. *(evil laugh that fades)* Wait. When she hears about this, she'll know it's one of her students. Who else would be writing about Columbus? But she teaches six classes of history a day. She'll never guess it's me.

Narrator: When Lindsey got to school the next day, everyone was buzzing about her post.

(Lindsey's friends enter.)

Vito: If Mrs. Morton taught Columbus, then she's like ten thousand years old!

David: Sheesh! Didn't Ms. Jefferson teach you about when Columbus lived?

Vito: Sure. He was born in 1451, and he died in 1506.

David: So was that ten thousand years ago?

Vito: Approximately!

David: Look, you—

Lindsey: Hey, everybody! What's going on?

Sienna: Did you see that thing about Mrs. Morton?

Adam: On the message board?

Lindsey: Oh, that.

Vito: Wasn't it hilarious? Mrs. Morton teaching Columbus! I mean…she'd have to be ten thousand years old!

David: Give me a break.

Lindsey: Maybe she really did teach Columbus. Face it. That lady is o-o-old.

(Others, except David, laugh and exit.)

David: *(to Lindsey)* Did you put that stuff about Mrs. Morton on the board?

Lindsey: Come on, David. You know how I feel about history. It is not a joking matter.

David: Right.

Scene Six

Narrator: *(as other History Students and Mrs. Morton form class)* In Lindsey's History class, everyone watched Mrs. Morton like a hawk, wondering if she knew anything.

Mrs. Morton: I'm glad to see that you all look so attentive today. Let's talk about Ponce de Léon. Why did he name the new land he discovered "La Florida"?

(Other History Students and David wave hands eagerly.)

Mrs. Morton: Lindsey?

Lindsey: I don't know. I wasn't around back then.

Others except David: *(laugh)*

Mrs. Morton: That was almost five hundred years ago so none of us were around then.

Lindsey: *(muttering)* That's not what I hear!

Others except David: *(laugh)*

Mrs. Morton: Speak up please.

Lindsey: *(loudly)* I don't know the answer. *(muttering)* And I don't care.

Others except David: *(laugh)*

Mrs. Morton: Perhaps another detention will help your attitude. Stay after today.

Lindsey: *(standing)* Look, lady, I've had it with you. And I'm not going to take it anymore!

David: *(as others look annoyed at the interruption of play)* Hey, you never said that!

Narrator: Yeah! You can't just change your lines to what you *wish* you had said.

From Diana R. Jenkins, *All Year Long! Funny Readers Theatre for Life's Special Times.* Westport, CT: Teacher Ideas Press. Copyright © 2007 by Diana R. Jenkins.

David: Especially when we're right in the middle of a performance.

Lindsey: Okay, okay. But I *could* have said that, you know. *(sits and speaks to Mrs. Morton)*

Yes, ma'am.

Mrs. Morton: Be sure to study the second chapter while you're in detention. Now who can answer my question about "La Florida"?

David: I can! I can!

Lindsey: *(coughing)* Loser!

Scene Seven:

Narrator: *(as everyone but Lindsey and David exits)* After class, everyone was talking about whether Mrs. Morton knew about "A Mystery of History."

David: I don't think she knows. What do you think?

Lindsey: She didn't act any differently so I couldn't tell. I mean … she was just as mean as ever.

David: She's not mean, Lindsey.

Lindsey: Yes, she is! She gave me detention for not knowing something.

David: Actually, I think she gave you that detention for smarting off.

Lindsey: Whatever. She has it in for me—that's for sure. Well, I have it in for her, too.

David: You did write that thing about Columbus, didn't you?

Lindsey: So what if I did? Can you blame me after the way she's treated me?

David: She's just doing her job. She's trying to teach us what we—

Lindsey: Of course you love her. You're the teacher's pet!

David: Mrs. Morton doesn't have favorites. You're just … oh, never mind! *(exits)*

Lindsey: *(calling after him)* Sure. Walk off. How childish! Teacher's pet! Teacher's pet!

Narrator: That night Lindsey posted something new about Mrs. Morton.

Lindsey: "A Mystery of History … history books tell us that Ponce de Léon discovered Florida. And, of course, we've all heard about de Léon's search for the Fountain of Youth. But why do we never hear about his more successful partner, North Middle School's own Mrs. Morton? Guess which fountain she found?" Ha! I hope somebody tells her about this one.

Scene Eight

(Lindsey's friends enter.)

Narrator: Lindsey's new post was even more popular than the last.

Adam: I fell out of my chair! "Guess which fountain she found?"

Sienna: Yeah, that was a good one.

Vito: I wonder who's writing that stuff.

David: Yeah. I wonder. *(looks at Lindsey)*

From Diana R. Jenkins, *All Year Long! Funny Readers Theatre for Life's Special Times.* Westport, CT: Teacher Ideas Press. Copyright © 2007 by Diana R. Jenkins.

Vito: Hey, does Mrs. Morton know about it?

Lindsey: We can't tell.

David: I hope she doesn't. It could really hurt her feelings.

Lindsey: Gee. Wouldn't that be terrible?

(Bell rings.)

Sienna: Let's hurry and get to History class.

Vito: Yeah! I can't wait to see Ms. Jefferson play Amerigo Vespucci.

Adam: Hey, I can't wait for the Amerigo Vespucci cake.

Lindsey: Ms. Jefferson made you another treat?

Sienna: Yeah. It's a cake with a map of Vespucci's voyages in icing. Let's go! *(They exit.)*

Lindsey: Why did we have to get stuck with Mrs. Morton?

David: She's a good teacher, Lindsey. We're learning all kinds of stuff in her class.

Lindsey: Sure we are. Sure we are.

Scene Nine

(Other History Students and Mrs. Morton enter and form class.)

Narrator: In class that day, Lindsey could tell that Mrs. Morton knew about "A Mystery of History"—and suspected Lindsey was behind it.

Mrs. Morton: When Balboa stowed away on the ship to Central America, he wasn't alone. Who stowed away with him?

David: I know! I know!

Mrs. Morton: Lindsey?

Lindsey: That was way before my time, you know.

Other History Students except David: *(laugh)*

Mrs. Morton: Despite any rumors that might be going around, I wasn't alive then either. I learned history by reading and studying about it. You might try that, Lindsey.

Other History Students and David: *(laugh)*

Lindsey: *(muttering)* Or not.

Mrs. Morton: David! Do you remember who stowed away with Balboa?

David: Yes, ma'am. It was his dog, Leoncico.

Mrs. Morton: Very good. Now let's discuss Balboa's adventures in Panama.

Narrator: After that, Lindsey didn't even try to answer Mrs. Morton's questions. And she slouched and muttered and gave Mrs. Morton a terrible attitude.

Mrs. Morton: I hate to see you wasting your intelligence, Lindsey. I'm assigning you another detention. Please use the time to study and to think about what you're doing.

(Everyone except David and Lindsey exit.)

From Diana R. Jenkins, *All Year Long! Funny Readers Theatre for Life's Special Times.* Westport, CT: Teacher Ideas Press. Copyright © 2007 by Diana R. Jenkins.

David: Well, I guess she knows about the stuff on the message board.

Lindsey: Yeah, and she's punishing me when she doesn't even know for sure I'm the guilty one.

David: But you are the guilty one.

Lindsey: She can't prove that!

David: Anyway … she's punishing you for not being prepared. And for having an attitude.

Lindsey: Hey, she can act like that's why she's picking on me, but I know the truth. Well, she can't crack me. And she can't stop me either.

David: Whatever. *(exits)*

Scene Ten

Narrator: So Lindsey posted another "Mystery of History" that night.

Lindsey: "Sure, we know about Magellan circumnavigating the world. We even know that his crew ended up eating sawdust and pieces of leather. But here's another pesky mystery: Why don't historians ever mention that the sailors couldn't stand the food their cook prepared for them? Yes, that's right! North Middle School's own Mrs. Morton drove Magellan's men to desperation with her cooking!" There! Like it would kill her to make us some cookies or something once in a while.

Narrator: Mrs. Morton called on Lindsey several times in class the next day. So that night….

Lindsey: "And why don't they tell us that Cabeza de Vaca and his men walked over two thousand miles through Mexico just to get away from Mrs. Morton's annoying questions?"

Narrator: Mrs. Morton called on Lindsey even more the following day. So that evening…

Lindsey: She's just trying to get revenge. How lame is that? Well, I'll fix her. "And shouldn't the history books tell us about how Coronado's men wanted to jump into the Grand Canyon as soon as they found it? Who can blame them with North Middle School's own Mrs. Morton on their backs all the time?"

Narrator: Finally, Lindsey saw some progress the next day.

Lindsey: Finally!

(Other History Students, David, and Mrs. Morton enter and form class.)

Mrs. Morton: Juan Rodríguez Cabrillo explored the area we now call … what?

Other History Students and David: *(wave hands eagerly)*

Mrs. Morton: Lindsey?

Lindsey: Here's a big surprise: I don't know.

Mrs. Morton: And in another surprising development, I'm assigning you detention again today.

Lindsey: *(mumbling)* Whatever. *(straightening up and speaking loudly)* I mean … whatever!

Other History Students except David: *(laugh)*

Mrs. Morton: *(upset)* Enough! History is a serious subject. It deserves your respect and so do I.

Other History Students and David: Yes, ma'am.

Mrs. Morton: *(calmer)* Let's move on. Cabrillo explored the coast of California. Then in 1543, he tripped while being chased and hit his head on a rock, causing a fatal injury. *(upset)* And, *no*, he was not running away from North Middle School's own history teacher!

Narrator: For a moment, everyone was too embarrassed to even look at Mrs. Morton. Even Lindsey felt bad that Mrs. Morton was hurt.

Lindsey: *(to Narrator)* Hey, I don't care about her feelings.

Mrs. Morton: *(subdued)* The Miwok Indians were chasing Cabrillo when the accident happened. Now let's all open our books and read about the aftermath of the Golden Age of Exploration.

Scene Eleven

Narrator: *(as everyone except David and Lindsey exits)* After class, Lindsey gloated to David.

Lindsey: Ha! I finally got to her. She was really losing it in there, wasn't she?

David: I think you should stop now. You're hurting her feelings.

Lindsey: So? She hurts my feelings all the time.

David: Oh, come on! If you just cooperated a little, she wouldn't have to be on your case. And anyway, even if she does hurt your feelings, she's not doing it on purpose. I mean … she's not *trying* to hurt you. But you *are* trying to hurt her. And you think she's mean! *(exits)*

Lindsey: *(to self)* He doesn't know what he's talking about. *(calling after him)* You don't know what you're talking about!

Narrator: When Lindsey sat down at her computer that night, she was determined to come up with the best "Mystery of History" ever.

Lindsey: I can't quit now—not when I'm finally getting under her skin. *(evil laugh)* Let's see. I've already insulted her age, her cooking, her personality…. Wow. A lot of stuff. Well, she deserved it. And she deserves whatever I throw at her tonight, right? *(laughs again but more weakly)* I'm going to get her good. *(laughs even more weakly)* I'll show her. *(coughs)* I'm going to … I'll just … Oh, man. David is right. I *am* being mean. What kind of terrible person am I?

Narrator: *(to Lindsey)* Pretty terrible, I'd say.

Lindsey: I wasn't asking you. I was asking myself.

Narrator: Oh. Sorry.

Lindsey: I've made a big mess of things. What am I going to do?

Narrator: Lindsey sat there for hours trying to think of how to make things right. Finally, she came up with an idea and started typing.

Lindsey: I hope this works!

From Diana R. Jenkins, *All Year Long! Funny Readers Theatre for Life's Special Times.* Westport, CT: Teacher Ideas Press. Copyright © 2007 by Diana R. Jenkins.   31

Scene Twelve

(Lindsey's friends except David enter. Lindsey sits in class alone.)

Adam: Did you see the message board?

Sienna: Yes! Whoever's writing that stuff has a lot of guts.

Adam: I wonder what's going to happen in Mrs. Morton's room today.

Vito: It almost makes me wish I could be in her class.

Sienna: And miss Ms. Jefferson as Hernando de Soto?

Vito: I said "almost."

(They exit as David enters and goes up to Lindsey.)

David: Hey.

Lindsey: Hey.

David: I think you did the right thing, Lindsey.

Lindsey: We'll see.

(Mrs. Morton and other History Students enter and form class.)

Mrs. Morton: Class, I read something interesting on the Internet this morning. Let me share it with you: *(reads from printout)* "Another Mystery of History. The early explorers made a lot of mistakes. Columbus never knew he had found a whole new land. Verrazano stayed on his ship instead of claiming any of North America for France. Coronado spent his life's savings trying to find imaginary cities of gold. Well, I've made a mistake, too, making fun of a teacher who was just trying to do her job. Which she did pretty well, I guess, because look at everything I've learned without even trying. So I owe a big apology to North Middle School's own Mrs. Morton." *(to class)* I appreciate the courage of our mystery historian. And I accept this apology.

Lindsey: *(muttering)* Thank goodness!

Mrs. Morton: No mumbling please.

Lindsey: Sorry!

Mrs. Morton: Now, let's get down to business. Who can tell me which European explorer discovered the Mississippi River?

Other History Students and David: *(wave hands eagerly)*

Mrs. Morton: Lindsey?

Lindsey: *(smiling)* You just never give up, do you?

Mrs. Morton: *(smiling)* No. Never.

Narrator: *(as everyone except Lindsey and David exit)* Mrs. Morton called on Lindsey a lot that day—and every day after that.

Lindsey: Man! By the time I get out of this class I'm going to know everything that ever happened to anybody ever.

David: That's impossible.

Lindsey: Okay, but I *will* know a lot of history. Thanks to Mrs. Morton.

From Diana R. Jenkins, *All Year Long! Funny Readers Theatre for Life's Special Times.* Westport, CT: Teacher Ideas Press. Copyright © 2007 by Diana R. Jenkins.

David: Yeah. She never quits. Some teachers are like that.

Lindsey: I don't know why. Hey, maybe that's the real "Mystery of History"! Like why don't—

Other students: *(run through screaming)*

Vito: *(as he passes)* Save yourselves!

David: *(looking in the direction they came from)* Is that an Aztec pyramid?

Lindsey: With legs?

David: Wait! That's Ms. Jefferson.

Lindsey: With a gigantic cake! Gee, she looks kind of unsteady carrying that thing.

David: She's going to lose it! *(runs)*

Narrator: I'm out of here! *(runs)*

Lindsey: Hey, you're the narrator! You can't just run off like that! The play's not even—*(looks offstage in terror and runs)*

(Loud noise offstage)

Ms. Jefferson: *(staggers in with face and hands covered with "icing," then wanders out again)*

Narrator: *(dragged in by Lindsey)* The end! *(They exit.)*

Yom Kippur

Starring Ephraim as Himself

Summary

Ephraim hates to go to the local deli because the owner, Mr. Lieberman, embarrasses him with his teasing. Finally, Ephraim snaps and insults Mr. Lieberman in front of everyone. Can Ephraim make things right with the deli man before Yom Kippur?

Costumes, Sets, and Props

❖ All characters can wear contemporary clothing.

❖ One table can be used as the counter. Customers can sit at other tables and chairs.

❖ If props are desired, dishes and to-go bags can be used.

Presentation

The nonspeaking customers can line up at the counter, laugh at Mr. Lieberman's jokes, and pretend to eat and drink as they sit at the deli tables.

Mr. Lieberman is loud and abrasive. After Ephraim's insult, he becomes cold and speaks in clipped tones. When Josh and Grace are being "smart," they speak in a self-consciously intellectual style.

When presented to an audience, appropriate refreshments could be provided: bagels, cream cheese, tabouleh, tuna salad, falafel, and pitas.

Supplemental Reading

Bacon, Josephine. *Cooking the Israeli Way.* Minneapolis, MN: Lerner, 2002.

Charing, Douglas. *Judaism.* New York: Dorling Kindersley, 2003.

Kaye, Marilyn. *The Atonement of Mindy Wise.* New York: Harcourt Brace Jovanovich, 1991.

Keene, Michael. *Religions of the World: Judaism.* Milwaukee, WI: World Almanac Library, 2006.

Cast of Characters

Ephraim	Mr. Lieberman
Mom	Several customers (nonspeaking)
Dad	Customer One ("Frank")
Josh	Customer Two ("Helen")
Grace	New customer (nonspeaking)

Yom Kippur

Starring Ephraim as Himself

Scene One

Ephraim: *(to audience)* Maybe I watch too much television, but sometimes my life *feels* like a TV program. My parents act like TV parents. *(Parents enter.)*

Mom: Taking care of your responsibilities is part of growing up, Ephraim.

Dad: Do the right thing, son—and you'll feel right inside.

Mom: Don't count your chickens before they hatch.

Dad: A stitch in time—

Ephraim: Thanks! Thanks, you guys! *(Parents exit.)* See what I mean? My friends are like TV friends, too. *(as friends enter)* You know how the star—that would be me—has these friends who think they're smarter than he is? My friends are like that.

Josh: We don't just think we're smart. We actually *are* smart, aren't we, Grace?

Grace: Absolutely, Josh. And the amazing thing is that we're real. Our intelligence isn't scripted for us.

Josh: Of course not! We're blessed with natural talents that far outshine those of our friend here.

Grace: And yet we're stuck with supporting roles that—

Ephraim: Okay, that'll do! *(Josh and Grace exit.)* But my life is totally TV when my family goes to Mr. Lieberman's deli. *(Mr. Lieberman and customers enter and take places.)* The same people are always sitting around – just like on TV shows. And Mr. Lieberman…He's like the obnoxious character on the show who's always driving the star nuts! He's been doing that to me all my life. It started when I was a little kid! *(gets on knees to play younger self as Mom and Dad enter.)*

Mom: Good morning, Mr. Lieberman.

Mr. Lieberman: What's so good about it?

Dad: The sun is shining! The birds are singing! The—

Mr. Lieberman: Who's the munchkin?

Mom: You remember, Mr. Lieberman. This is our boy, Ephraim.

Mr. Lieberman: It can't be. Your kid's smaller than that. And good-looking, too.

(Mom, Dad, and Customers laugh.)

Dad: Well, he's growing like a weed.

Mom: And we think he's pretty darn cute.

Mr. Lieberman: *(to Ephraim)* So, kid, who are you really?

Ephraim: *(in little kid voice)* I'm Ephraim!

Mr. Lieberman: No way. I know Ephraim, and you're not Ephraim.

Ephraim: Yes, I am! *(starts bawling)*

Mr. Lieberman: Sheesh, kid, can't you take a joke?

Dad: Calm down, Ephraim. Mr. Lieberman is just teasing you.

Ephraim: Oh. Okay.

Mr. Lieberman: You know, the real Ephraim has a much better sense of humor.

(Mom, Dad, and Customers laugh.)

Scene Two

Ephraim: *(to audience)* That was only … oh. *(stands)* That was only the beginning of my problems with Mr. Lieberman. Since then, he has bugged me every single episode! I mean … every time I'm in the deli. Like sometimes he makes stupid jokes.

Dad: Good afternoon, Mr. Lieberman.

Mr. Lieberman: What's so good about it?

Mom: Well, it's—

Mr. Lieberman: *(to Ephraim)* So, what'll you have? Soup? Bagel? Hey, you want tabouleh?

Ephraim: No, sir.

Mr. Lieberman: You sure you don't want tabouleh?

Ephraim: I don't want tabouleh!

Mr. Lieberman: Good! Nobody should bully nobody!

(Mom, Dad, and Customers laugh.)

Ephraim: Yes, sir.

Mr. Lieberman: What? You think people *should* bully other people?

(Mom, Dad, and Customers laugh.)

Ephraim: No! I didn't mean that. I was just … whatever!

Scene Three

Ephraim: *(to audience)* If Mr. Lieberman isn't torturing me with his stupid jokes, he's embarrassing me in front of everybody.

Mom: Mmm … that coffee smells good.

Ephraim: I'll save us a table. How about this one?

Dad: Okay. What do you want? You want tabouleh? *(laughs)*

Ephraim:	Funny. I'll take an onion bagel. *(sits)*
Mom:	Good afternoon, Mr. Lieberman.
Mr. Lieberman:	What's good about it?
Dad:	It is kind of rainy, but—
Mr. Lieberman:	So where's the kid?
Mom:	He's sitting over there.
Mr. Lieberman:	*(yelling across room)* Hey! You! *(Ephraim slumps and tries to hide.)*
Customer One:	Me?
Mr. Lieberman:	Like I have anything to say to you, Frank. Hey! You! Kid!
Customer Two:	What do you want?
Mr. Lieberman:	Since when are you a kid, Helen?
Customer Two:	My name isn't Helen! It's—
Mr. Lieberman:	Whatever. HEY! KID!
Ephraim:	Yes, sir?
Mr. Lieberman:	What are you doing over there? Are you too high and mighty to talk to me?
Ephraim:	No, sir.
Mr. Lieberman:	Then get over here!
Ephraim:	Yes, sir. *(slinks over)*
Mr. Lieberman:	So … you want tabouleh?
	(Mom, Dad, and Customers laugh.)
Ephraim:	Funny. Real funny.

Scene Four

Ephraim:	*(to audience as Mom and Dad exit)* If my life was really a TV show, we'd just go on like that forever—or until we were canceled. But in my reality, I got more and more annoyed with that guy. Finally, one day I just snapped. *(turns to Mr. Lieberman)* Good morning, Mr. Lieberman.
Mr. Lieberman:	What's so good about?
Ephraim:	I was just being—
Mr. Lieberman:	Hey, is there anybody behind you?
Ephraim:	No, sir.
Mr. Lieberman:	Step to the left, and let me see.
Ephraim:	I'm just here to pick up some bagels, okay? A dozen mixed, please.
Mr. Lieberman:	Come on, come on … step to the left.
Ephraim:	*(does it)* There!
Mr. Lieberman:	Hmmm … nobody back there. Where are your parents, little boy?
Ephraim:	I'm not a little boy, Mr. Lieberman. I'm old enough to come over here by myself.
Mr. Lieberman:	You can't be! It seems like only five maybe six months since you were born.

From Diana R. Jenkins, *All Year Long! Funny Readers Theatre for Life's Special Times.* Westport, CT: Teacher Ideas Press. Copyright © 2007 by Diana R. Jenkins.

Customers:	*(laugh)*
Customer Two:	Isn't that the truth?
Mr. Lieberman:	Who asked you, Helen?
Customer Two:	My name's not—
Mr. Lieberman:	Whatever. So why aren't your parents here with you?
Ephraim:	Look, you're lucky that anyone comes in this dump at all!
Customers:	*(gasp)*
Mr. Lieberman:	*(to other customers)* He's calling my establishment of business a dump? *(to Ephraim)* You're calling my establishment of business a dump?
Ephraim:	Okay, okay, it's not a dump. It's more like a circus! A circus run by a clown!
Customers:	*(gasp)*
Ephraim:	So could you just cut out all the lame jokes and annoying garbage and ridiculous … uh … ridiculousness and give me my bagels?
Mr. Lieberman:	Certainly. *(gives him the bagels)*
Ephraim:	*(pays)* Thanks.

(Customers exit, glaring at Ephraim. Mr. Lieberman exits without looking his way.)

Scene Five

Ephraim:	*(to audience as friends enter)* At first I felt pretty psyched about standing up to Mr. Lieberman. I told my friends all about it. *(to friends)* And then I said he'd better cut the clown act and hand over my bagels.
Josh:	You didn't say that!
Ephraim:	Oh, yes, I did. That guy has been pestering me my entire life! And not just me either. He annoys everybody. It was about time someone put him in his place. I'm glad I did it!
Grace:	Well, of course you are. Who wouldn't be proud to insult an elderly man, right, Josh?
Josh:	You're so right, Grace. One of the important lessons in life is you should attack harmless people before they attack you.
Ephraim:	I didn't attack him! I just gave him a dose of his own medicine.
Grace:	*(turning serious)* But it just doesn't seem like something you would do, Ephraim. It's kind of mean.
Ephraim:	Whatever.
Grace:	Well … see you later.
Josh:	Don't kick any puppies, okay? *(They exit.)*
Ephraim:	Give me a break! *(to audience)* The stuff my friends said bothered me, but I pushed the feeling away. So what if I was kind of rude? Wasn't Mr. Lieberman rude to me? And anyway … what did he care if some kid mouthed off a little bit? *(sighs)* That's what I told myself, but I had to face the truth the next time my family went to the deli.

(Mr. Lieberman, other customers, Mom, and Dad enter.)

From Diana R. Jenkins, *All Year Long! Funny Readers Theatre for Life's Special Times.* Westport, CT: Teacher Ideas Press. Copyright © 2007 by Diana R. Jenkins.

Scene Six

Dad: Good afternoon, Mr. Lieberman.

Mr. Lieberman: Good afternoon.

Dad: There's not a cloud in … It's really … I mean … We'll have two garlic bagels with cream cheese and two coffees. And what do you want, Ephraim?

Ephraim: Tuna salad on an onion bagel, please. And tea.

Mr. Lieberman: Very well.

Mom: So … how are you today, Mr. Lieberman?

Mr. Lieberman: Fine.

Dad: Are you feeling okay?

Mr. Lieberman: I'm fine.

Mom: And how's business?

Mr. Lieberman: Fine. Here's your order.

Dad: Thanks. *(family sits)*

Mom: I wonder what's wrong with Mr. Lieberman.

Ephraim: He said he was fine.

Dad: But he didn't make a single joke.

Ephraim: Which was great if you ask me! He ruins the show!

Dad: What show?

Ephraim: I meant to say that he ruins the place. People get tired of his annoying jokes.

Mom: Everyone loves Mr. Lieberman!

Ephraim: *(muttering)* Not everybody.

Dad: Okay, then. *Lots* of people love him. Like Mrs. James. *(points to Customer Two)*

Ephraim: You mean Helen?

Mom: I thought her name was Myrtle.

Dad: I don't know what her first name is. I just know she's had a hard time since her husband passed away. And Mr. Lieberman usually won't let her pay for anything.

Ephraim: Really? But that's so nice. And he's always yelling at her!

Mom: Mr. Lieberman doesn't yell, Ephraim.

Mr. Lieberman: *(as new customer enters)* Hey! Don't just stand there! Get over here and order!

Mom: Okay. He has a big voice. But he also has a big heart.

Dad: He donated a lot of money so you kids could have basketball goals at the park.

Ephraim: He did?

Mom: Yes, he did. He donates to every good cause around town.

Dad: And he gives jobs to people that no one else wants to hire.

Mom: And he—

Ephraim: Okay, okay! He's great! I get it! *(to audience as others exit)* You might think I was feeling really terrible about that time, but I mostly felt mad. Like I had accidentally missed the most important episode of the season! How was I supposed to know someone so obnoxious was really a good guy?

Scene Seven

Ephraim: *(as friends enter)* I unloaded on my friends, of course, expecting some support. Ha! *(to friends)* I didn't know he did all those nice things! I wouldn't have said that stuff to him if I'd known!

Grace: So if he was some kind of cold-hearted miser guy, then it'd be okay to disrespect him?

Ephraim: I didn't mean that!

Josh: You shouldn't have insulted him at all! I mean…you shot him down in front of everybody!

Grace: I bet you really hurt his feelings.

Ephraim: So?

Grace: Come on, Ephraim. Stop pretending you don't care. I know you feel bad.

Ephraim: *(to audience)* Why did she have to say something like that? Something so … true!

Grace: *(to Ephraim)* I'm smart, remember?

Ephraim: Right. *(to audience)* Anyway … the anger drained right out of me, and I felt awful! *(to friends)* Okay, okay, I shouldn't have done it. And I'm sorry I did. But there's nothing I can do about it now.

Josh: Nothing?

Grace: Nothing at all?

Ephraim: Nothing!

Grace: Gee, Josh, isn't it about time for a special day?

Josh: Gosh, Grace, I think you're right. In just a few days it will be…hmmm…what's it called?

Grace: Yom Kippur. *(turns to Ephraim)* Maybe you've heard of it?

Ephraim: You guys are so funny.

Josh: I believe that's the Day of Atonement, isn't it, Grace? A day to ask God's forgiveness?

Grace: That's right, Josh! But before one can make things right with God, one must first make things right with all those whom one has wronged.

Josh: Must one?

Grace: One must!

Ephraim: Okay, okay! This is like the worst episode of my life.

Josh: And yet it isn't a TV program at all, is it, Grace?

Grace: No, Josh. This is Ephraim's life, uncut and uncensored!

Ephraim: Time for you guys to go.

Josh: *(laughing)* See you later! *(exits)*

Grace: *(serious)* You can do it, Ephraim. *(exits)*

Scene Eight

Ephraim: I knew I should apologize to Mr. Lieberman. It was the right thing to do, of course. And also my friends were right about Yom Kippur. I *should* straighten things out before the holy day. But in real life, apologizing is not as easy as it looks on television. It's hard to admit you did something wrong! And facing somebody and asking their forgiveness for being a low-life worm? That's really rough. So I stayed away from the deli. I even pretended that I wanted to study when my parents went there.

(Parents enter.)

Mom: You *want* to study?

Ephraim: Sure. Calvin Coolidge was a really, really, really interesting president.

Dad: Really?

Ephraim: Just bring me back something.

Dad: Well…okay.

Mom: *(as they exit)* Should we see if he has a fever?

Ephraim: *(to audience as customers, Mr. Lieberman, Grace, and Josh enter)* But I couldn't keep away from the deli forever. I knew that. And when Mom sent me to pick up our break-the-fast food order just before Yom Kippur started, I finally had to face Mr. Lieberman. *(to Grace and Josh)* What are you guys doing here?

Josh: I'm helping Grace.

Grace: And I'm picking up my family's order. What about you?

Ephraim: Yeah. Me, too.

Grace: Is that all?

Ephraim: Yes, that's all!

Josh: You know, Grace, sometimes I wonder why we even bother to share our wisdom with Ephraim.

Grace: I have the same feeling, Josh. Our entire explanation of Yom Kippur seems to have fallen on deaf ears.

Ephraim: I just can't do it, okay? Apologizing is so embarrassing. I mean…it makes you look like a complete wuss. And I already feel like a such a loser. Saying I'm sorry isn't going to change that!

Grace: But apologizing isn't about how *you* feel, Ephraim. It's about the other person.

Ephraim: Yeah … well … I can't do it. Let's get in line. *(They stand behind Customer Two.)*

Mr. Lieberman: *(to Customer Two)* Put your money away. I'm not taking it. Not one penny!

Customer Two: You're too kind.

Mr. Lieberman: Yeah, yeah. Now how about moving out of the way, Helen?

Customer Two: Sure … Mr. *Liebowitz. (moves away and sits)*

Mr. Lieberman: *(to Ephraim, Grace, and Josh)* I think her memory's going. But mine isn't. Here's your family's order. *(hands two bags to Grace)* And here's yours. *(hands bag to Ephraim)*

From Diana R. Jenkins, *All Year Long! Funny Readers Theatre for Life's Special Times.* Westport, CT: Teacher Ideas Press. Copyright © 2007 by Diana R. Jenkins.

(Grace and Ephraim look in bags then switch and pay.)

Grace: *(handing one bag to Josh)* Thanks, Mr. Lieberman.

Ephraim: Yeah … uh … thanks. *(turns to go)*

Mr. Lieberman: Wait a minute, kid. I got something to say to you.

Ephraim: Yes, sir?

Mr. Lieberman: I just … look, kid … I know I can get a little loud sometimes….

Customer One: *(to Customer Two)* A little?

Mr. Lieberman: And I joke around a lot … too much maybe…. What I'm trying to say is … well … I didn't mean to give you such a hard time. And I'm sorry, okay?

Ephraim: Sure. No problem. It's forgotten.

Mr. Lieberman: Good. Now stop holding up the line, will you?

(Ephraim, Grace, and Josh move away and stop to talk.)

Josh: *(to Ephraim)* He apologized to you!

Ephraim: I know.

Josh: *He* apologized to *you!*

Ephraim: I know! Let's go.

(They start to walk out, but Ephraim stops.)

Grace: What's the matter?

Ephraim: I…I need a minute to think. *(Everybody freezes and Ephraim moves closer to the audience.)* I wanted to walk on out the door. I mean … it felt like the end of the episode. Why not go on with my life and let the credits roll? But the most important moment in a TV show is when the main character does the right thing. And wasn't that what mattered in reality, too? I had to ask myself: was I going to be the star in my own life? *(looks at Mr. Lieberman then back at the audience)* The answer was … yes.

Scene Nine

(Everyone unfreezes as Ephraim returns to Mr. Lieberman.)

Ephraim: Could I talk to you, Mr. Lieberman?

Mr. Lieberman: Sure, kid. It's not like I have a business to run or anything.

Ephraim: I just wanted to say … well … that stuff I said the other day … it wasn't … I mean … *(brightening)* I falafel!

Mr. Lieberman: You want falafel? Why didn't you say so before?

Ephraim: No! I falafel! You know … it's a joke … like when you ask me if I want tabouleh.

Mr. Lieberman: You want tabouleh, too? You know, your mother didn't say anything about tabouleh when she called in the order.

Ephraim: That's not what I mean. *(sighs)* I'm trying to say I *feel awful* about the stuff I said to you. I falafel, okay?

Mr. Lieberman: That is one terrible pun, kid.

Ephraim: I know. I just wanted to let you know how sorry I am. Really sorry. I hope you can forgive me.

Mr. Lieberman: *(with great kindness)* Of course, I can. You're a good kid, Ephraim. A good kid. *(back to normal)* Now get out of here! Scram! I got customers!

Ephraim: Yes, sir! *(walks over to Grace and Josh)*

Grace: You did it!

Ephraim: Yeah. And it felt pretty good. Now I'm really ready for Yom Kippur.

Josh: See? You should listen to us.

Ephraim: Okay, okay!

Grace: This bag is getting heavy. Let's go, Josh. See you later, Ephraim!

Josh: Later!

Ephraim: *(as they exit)* Thanks, you guys. *(to audience)* And so…we've reached the end of a very special program. Stay tuned for our next episode…starring Ephraim as himself! *(realizes rest of cast is staring at him)* Uh … I… *(backs out, looking embarrassed)*

Mr. Lieberman: *(to customers)* So he's a bit strange. Who cares? You can't falafel about a good kid like that!

Fall Break

Win/Lose/Win

Summary

Darrell and his football team, the Bears, are bad winners. They're so psyched about defeating their rivals, Sheena and the Tigers, in an away game that they trash the school. The home team is a bunch of bad losers and they run amok, too. Now mortal enemies must spend their fall break together cleaning things up. Can they make peace?

Costumes, Sets, and Props

❖ The coaches and players can wear sports clothing if desired and carry sports equipment such as whistles, towels, water bottles, or footballs. Mrs. Brandt, the principal, should dress appropriately.

❖ A few chairs could be used as benches in the locker rooms.

❖ Props can be mimed, but if props are desired, buckets, sponges, and other cleaning materials can be used.

Presentation

The narrators stand on opposite sides of the stage. Each team stands near the narrator who supports them: Narrator One and the Bears, Narrator Two and the Tigers.
The Tigers always speak in unison.

During the vandalism, the teams can mime doing damage. If space allows, they could tear through the room, ending up back on stage.

In the last scene, when Darrell and Sheena are trying to convince Patrick they have changed, the Bears and Tigers should nod agreement and act friendly to each other. Darrell can try to involve the audience in chanting for Patrick.

Supplemental Reading

Bruchac, Joseph, et al. *Sports Shorts.* Plain City, OH: Darby Creek, 2005.

Buckley, James Jr. *Great Moments in Football.* Milwaukee, WI: World Almanac Library, 2002.

Kauchak, Therese. *Good Sports: Winning, Losing, and Everything In-between.* Middleton, WI: Pleasant Company, 1999.

Messler, Mireille. *Competition: Deal with It from Start to Finish.* Toronto: Lorimer, 2004.

Cast of Characters

Narrator One, who favors the Bears   Coach Sartini

Narrator Two, who favors the Tigers   Sheena

Darrell   Tigers (two or more)

Patrick   Coach Lloyd

Bears (two or more)   Mrs. (Mr.) Brandt, principal

Fall Break

Win/Lose/Win

Scene One

(Darrell, Patrick, and Bears enter and freeze. Narrators enter and stand on opposite sides of stage.)

Narrator One: Everyone hates a bad loser.

Narrator Two: But a bad *winner* is worse.

Narrator One: I don't think so!

Narrator Two: Well, you're wrong. There's nothing worse than a bad winner.

Narrator One: That's ridiculous!

Darrell: *(moving just his mouth)* Psst! We're trying to put on a play here.

Narrator One: Oh. Sorry. We'll get right to it, Darrell.

Darrell: It's about time!

Patrick: Really!

Narrator Two: So! Everybody hates a bad *winner*. And Darrell was one of the worst winners ever. So was the rest of his football team. When they won their first game of the season, they reacted like this:

Darrell, Patrick, and Bears: *(unfreeze and perform victory dance)* We wo-on! We wo-on! Uh-hu-uh! We wo-on! *(etc.)*

Narrator Two: Disgusting, huh?

Narrator One: So they're proud of their accomplishment. What's wrong with that?

Coach Sartini: *(enters)* Hey, hey, hey! Let's show some good sportsmanship, Bears.

Narrator Two: *(to Narrator One)* See? Sportsmanship!

Narrator One: Whatever.

Coach Sartini: Now everybody go shake hands with the other team and congratulate them on a good game.

Bears: Yes, sir (ma'am). Okay. *(etc.) (They exit, followed by coach.)*

Patrick: *(to Darrell)* That was stupid. We shouldn't have acted like that.

Darrell: We're the winners, Patrick. We can act however we want to act. That's what winners do, right?

Patrick: *(as they exit)* I don't know….

Scene Two

Narrator Two: When the Bears won their next game, they were even more obnoxious. Thanks to Darrell!

Darrell: *(runs in, points to one side, and shouts)* We are the winners! You are the losers! We are the winners! You are the losers! *(etc.)*

Patrick: *(enters)* Come on, man. Don't do that.

Darrell: Why not? We're the winners.

Patrick: What kind of winner rubs it in?

Darrell: The winning winner who won the game, that's who! *(turns to side)* We are the winners! You are the losers! *(etc.)*

Bears: *(enter and join Darrell)* We are the winners! You are the losers! *(etc.)*

Patrick: You guys!

Narrator Two: What terrible behavior!

Narrator One: *(raising voice to be heard)* Well, it's true. They *are* the winners. And the other team did lose.

Narrator Two: *(raising voice)* But it doesn't show good *(coach enters and team suddenly becomes quiet)* sportsmanship! *(in normal voice)* I mean … sportsmanship.

Coach Sartini: Come on, Bears! This is not the kind of conduct I expect out of you.

Patrick: Sorry, Coach.

Coach Sartini: I want you all to be good sports. Understand?

Darrell, Patrick, and Bears: Yes, sir (ma'am).

Coach Sartini: Now let's go congratulate the other team. *(exits)*

Darrell: *(looks at rest of team)* We won, right? And that means we can do what we want, right?

Bears: Yeah! Right! *(etc.)*

Patrick: Sheesh! Didn't you guys listen to what Coach Sartini said?

Darrell: His (her) ideas are so out-of-date. But we respect him (her), so we'll just celebrate when he's (she's) not around. Right, team?

Bears: Right!

Darrell: *(chanting quietly as he exits)* We are the winners! We are the winners!

Bears: *(join in quietly and exit)* We are the winners! We are the winners!

Patrick: Brother! *(exits)*

From Diana R. Jenkins, *All Year Long! Funny Readers Theatre for Life's Special Times.* Westport, CT: Teacher Ideas Press. Copyright © 2007 by Diana R. Jenkins.

Scene Three

Narrator Two: After that, the Bears hid their sorry attitudes from their coach.

Narrator One: Look! We're just supposed to narrate! So how about a little objectivity?

Narrator Two: I call it like I see it. *(to audience)* Coach Sartini thought the team was displaying good sportsmanship since they saved their gloating for when (s)he wasn't around. But the truth was: the Bears had a serious problem.

Patrick: *(sticking head back in)* Hey, not all the Bears!

Narrator Two: *(to Patrick)* You're on the team so it's a problem for you, too.

Patrick: Yeah. I guess you're right about that. *(exits)*

Narrator Two: *(to audience)* The truth about the Bears finally came to light the last game before fall break.

(Tigers enter and freeze.)

Narrator One: Yes, let's talk about that game.

Narrator Two: Let's! The Bears won again, and—

Narrator One: Even though they weren't on their home turf.

Narrator Two: And after the game, they—

Narrator One: And the losing team, the Tigers, were terrible losers—like I was talking about before.

(Tigers unfreeze.)

Sheena: What a bunch of cheaters!

Tigers: Yeah! Cheaters!

Sheena: They're such wusses they can't win without cheating!

Tigers: Yeah! Wusses!

Sheena: They tackle like old ladies!

Tigers: Yeah! Old ladies!

Coach Lloyd: *(enters)* What's with the attitude? Where's your sense of sportsmanship?

Sheena: I think we lost it when their stupid kicker won the stupid game in the last few stupid seconds.

Tigers: Yeah! Stupid!

Coach Lloyd: Hey, their kicker is very talented—not stupid. The Bears played a good game, and so did you guys.

Sheena: *(muttering)* They cheated.

Tigers: *(muttering)* Yeah! Cheated!

Coach Lloyd: That's enough of that. Now let's congratulate the winners.

Sheena and Tigers: Yes, sir. (ma'am)

Narrator Two: *(as Bears and Coach Sartini enter)* And the Tigers did what the coach said. They shook hands with the Bears.

Narrator One: But they weren't good sports about it.

(Two teams mingle, shaking hands unwillingly, except for Patrick who has a good attitude.)

Patrick: *(shaking Sheena's hand)* You have a fantastic team. Great job!

Sheena: *(shaking Patrick's hand)* Uh … well…. Good job with the kicking.

Patrick: Thanks.

Darrell: *(shaking hands with Sheena)* Good game.

Sheena: *(tightening grip)* Congratulations.

Darrell: *(wrestling a bit)* Thanks.

Sheena: *(getting rougher)* Sure.

Patrick: Come on, you guys!

Narrator One: *(as Patrick and Sheena arm wrestle)* But Sheena started trouble with Darrell.

Narrator Two: No, Darrell started trouble with Sheena.

Coach Sartini: Hey, break it up!

Coach Lloyd: Stop it!

Coach Sartini: Everybody off the field!

Coach Lloyd: Now!

(Teams move to opposite sides and freeze as coaches exit.)

Narrator One: See? Those bad losers caused a big problem.

Narrator Two: That was Darrell's fault!

Narrator One: No, it was Sheena's fault!

Sheena: *(moving only mouth)* Gee. I hope our play isn't disturbing you two.

Narrator Two: Shut up, will you? We're trying … oh! Right. On with the play!

Scene Four

Narrator One: *(as Sheena and Tigers unfreeze and act out the following)* The Tigers headed off to their locker room. On the way there, Sheena kicked over a trash can and ripped down a poster. The other bad losers soon joined her in damaging anything they could get their hands on. And when they got to the locker room, they continued their rampage. They broke a bench! They poured shampoo everywhere!

Narrator Two: Hey, those bad winners, the Bears, were even worse!

(Bears unfreeze and act out the following, with Patrick looking disgusted.)

Narrator Two: As they headed for their locker room, Darrell led his team into a classroom. The Bears turned over all the furniture and tore up every piece of paper they could find. Then they ran on down the hall and trashed the coach's office.

Coaches: *(enter and yell in unison at own teams)* Stop! Right now! What's the matter with you people? You're in big trouble now! *(Kids stop, but look sullen.)*

Mrs. Brandt: *(enters)* I cannot believe this! Whatever happened to good, old-fashioned sportsmanship?

Coach Lloyd: I'm really sorry, Mrs. Brandt. Believe me, the Tigers *will* clean up their mess!

Mrs. Brandt: I'm the principal here. I'll decide their punishment. *(turns to Tigers)* You *will* clean up your mess. Starting tomorrow morning.

Sheena: But it's fall break!

Coach Lloyd: Too darn bad, Sheena!

Mrs. Brandt: Coach! Please! I'll handle this. *(turns to Sheena)* Too darn bad, Sheena!

Sheena: *(muttering)* Whatever.

Mrs. Brandt: And what do you have to say, Coach Sartini?

Coach Sartini: I deeply apologize, Mrs. Brandt. And my team will be here tomorrow, too, to help with the cleanup.

Mrs. Brandt: I run this school, Coach. I make the decisions around here. *(turns to Bears)* You will all come here tomorrow and help with the cleanup.

Darrell: And give up our fall break?

Mrs. Brandt: Of course! Be here at seven sharp. *(exits)*

Coaches: *(in unison to own teams)* Yeah! Seven sharp! Now, everybody go home! *(They exit along with Bears and Tigers, leaving Patrick, Darrell and Sheena behind.)*

Patrick: Thanks a lot, you guys. *(exits)*

Darrell: *(to Sheena)* Whoever heard of trashing your own school? What a bunch of idiots!

Sheena: Oh, yeah? Well, what kind of dopes trash stuff when they win?

Darrell: Sheesh! Don't you ever watch TV? Everybody knows that winners are on a big high, and they get to go wild.

Sheena: I never heard anything so stupid.

Darrell: Look! You're the one —

Mrs. Brandt: *(returning)* Go home! Now! *(They all exit.)*

Narrator One: There's going to be trouble tomorrow.

Narrator Two: Yathink?

Scene Five

(Darrell, Patrick, Sheena, Bears, Tigers, and coaches enter and start cleanup.)

Narrator One: The next morning, the coaches made everybody start by cleaning up the visitors' locker room.

Sheena: We didn't make any of the mess in here.

Narrator One: Typical bad loser attitude!

Darrell: We won so we shouldn't have to clean up anything.

Narrator Two: Typical bad winner attitude!

Patrick: Well, I didn't make any mess at all.

Narrator One: Typical … uh….

Narrator Two: Innocent bystander?

Narrator One: I guess. *(to audience)* The coaches supervised things pretty closely to start out, but then they decided to work on the damage in the coach's office. *(Coaches exit.)* That's when Sheena started causing problems.

Narrator Two: She *accidentally* kicked over Darrell's bucket.

Narrator One: Right.

From Diana R. Jenkins, *All Year Long! Funny Readers Theatre for Life's Special Times.* Westport, CT: Teacher Ideas Press. Copyright © 2007 by Diana R. Jenkins.

Sheena: Oops!

Darrell: Hey, what do you think you're doing?

Sheena: Oh. Gee. Sorry. I guess you'll have to mop that floor again.

Darrell: How about *you* mop it up, loser?

Sheena: How about you make me?

Patrick: Oh, come on! Can't you get along for five minutes?

Darrell: She started it.

Sheena: It was an accident!

Coach Sartini: *(enters)* What's going on in here?

Darrell: Nothing, Coach.

Sheena: We'll be finished real soon.

Coach Sartini: Good! *(exits)*

Darrell: *(to Sheena)* Oh, you'll be finished, all right. When we get out of here, the Bears are going to finish the Tigers for good.

Bears: You bet! Yeah! *(etc.)*

Sheena: You just try it!

Tigers: Yeah, try it!

Patrick: Stop it already! Let's just get things cleaned up so we can go home and enjoy a few minutes of vacation. Okay? *Okay?*

Darrell: Okay, okay.

Bears: Okay. Yeah. *(etc.)*

Sheena: Whatever.

Tigers: Yeah, whatever.

Patrick: Good! I'll get some more water in the bucket. Let's get back to work!

Narrator One: Everyone did what Patrick said.

Narrator Two: But not for long! Pretty soon the Bears stirred up more trouble.

Narrator One: No, it was the Tigers.

Narrator Two: Oh, yeah? Well, let's just see what happened.

Scene Six

Narrator One: After the visitors' locker room was cleaned up, the coaches moved everyone to the home locker room.

Darrell: This is ridiculous! The winners should be celebrating, not cleaning up the losers' mess.

Patrick: Both teams trashed the school—both teams should clean up.

Darrell: Hey, whose side are you on?

Patrick: I'm not on the side of anybody who does stuff like this. I mean … it's so lame.

Darrell: Are you calling me lame?

Patrick: Never mind, Darrell. Let's just get finished.

Sheena: Well, I want you to know I agree with you, Patrick.

Patrick: You do?

Sheena: Sure. I think Darrell is lame, too.

Tigers: Yeah! Lame!

Darrell: You take that back right now!

Sheena: Make me!

Darrell: *(drawing back fist)* Don't think I won't!

Sheena: *(drawing back fist)* Go ahead and try it, loser!

(The cast moves in slow motion throughout following:)

Narrator One: That's when it happened. Patrick was determined to prevent any fighting….

Narrator Two: And he ran forward….

Narrator One: And pushed between Darrell and Sheena….

Narrator Two: And got clobbered by both of them!

Narrator One: And fell to the floor like a sack of potatoes!

Sheena: Patrick! Patrick!

Darrell: Are you okay?

Sheena: Speak to us!

Tigers: Yeah, speak to us!

Patrick: I'm okay. Just help me up.

Darrell: Hey, sorry about that, dude.

Sheena: Me, too.

Darrell: If this stupid loser hadn't caused so much trouble—

Sheena: You're the loser, you loser!

Tigers: Yeah, loser!

Darrell: Hey, my team hasn't lost a game all year. That makes us winners, you loser!

Bears: Yeah! You tell him! *(etc.)*

Patrick: That's it! I've had it! I have had it!

Tigers: Yeah, had it!

Sheena: *(to Tigers)* Hello? He's not on our team.

Tigers: *(mutter and look embarrassed)*

Patrick: As soon as we get out of here, I'm not on any team. I quit!

Everybody else: What?

Darrell: But we said we were sorry for hitting you.

Sheena: And we won't do it again.

Patrick: Sheesh! You don't get it, do you? I'm not quitting just because you accidentally hit me. That's only one part of a huge problem. You *(pointing to Bears)* are the worst winners I have ever seen! And you *(pointing to Tigers)* are the worst losers! You people are ruining football for me. So I quit!

Sheena: But you're a really good player.

From Diana R. Jenkins, *All Year Long! Funny Readers Theatre for Life's Special Times.* Westport, CT: Teacher Ideas Press. Copyright © 2007 by Diana R. Jenkins.

Darrell: And we can't win without you. Don't you care about the team?

Sheena: And the sport?

Patrick: Of course I do! I love football. I love playing against tough competitors and giving it my personal best. That's what it's all about. But you all act like winning is everything—on the field and off! You don't know what good sportsmanship means—or any other kind of respect either—and you don't care. I don't want to be around losers like you.

Darrell: But, Patrick—

Patrick: Let's get this job finished.

Sheena: But, Patrick—

Patrick: *(with quiet forcefulness)* Now.

Scene Seven

Narrator One: It was dead quiet as everyone got back to work.

Narrator Two: They all knew that Patrick was right.

Narrator One: They had acted like jerks!

Narrator Two: And they were really sorry.

Narrator One: But they didn't know how to fix things.

Narrator Two: Until Darrell and Sheena reached for the same broom at the same time.

Darrell: Hey, I was going to use that!

Sheena: I had it first!

Darrell: Look! I…. *(looking toward Patrick)* I mean … you go ahead and use it, Sheena.

Sheena: Oh, yeah? Well…. *(looking toward Patrick)* Oh. Thanks, Darrell.

Darrell: Sure. No problem. We're all in this together, you know.

Narrator One: From that moment on, things began to change.

Narrator Two: Not that everything was perfect, but the Bears and the Tigers treated each other with some respect.

Narrator One: And got along pretty well for the rest of the day.

(Coaches and Mrs. Brandt enter.)

Coach Lloyd: Everything looks great!

Coach Sartini: Good job!

Mrs. Brandt: I'll be the judge of that. *(looks around)* Everything looks great! Good job!

Patrick: Can we go home now?

Mrs. Brandt: Yes, you may. And I hope you've all learned your lesson.

All the kids: Yes, ma'am.

(Coaches and Mrs. Brandt exit. Patrick starts to exit.)

Darrell: Wait, Patrick! We really *have* learned our lesson.

Sheena: Yeah. Can't you tell?

Darrell: We're going to try harder to be good sports.

Sheena: And treat other people the right way.

Darrell: So don't quit, okay?

Sheena: Yeah, don't quit, Patrick.

Patrick: I don't know….

Darrell: *(looking at others as he chants)* Patrick! Patrick! Patrick! *(etc.)*

Sheena, Tigers, and Bears: Patrick! Patrick! Patrick! *(etc.)*

Patrick: Okay, okay already!

Darrell: So you're staying on the team?

Patrick: Yes, I'm staying. Sheesh! Now let's go home. *(exits)*

Darrell, Sheena, Bears, Tigers: *(exiting)* Patrick! Patrick! Patrick!

Narrator One: *(moving next to Narrator Two)* So Darrell and the Bears became *real* winners.

Narrator Two: Sheena and the Tigers are winners, too, you know.

Narrator One: Well, sure! Just not in a winning-football-games kind of way.

Narrator Two: So? They're winners in real life. And anyway, I bet the Tigers beat the Bears the next time they play.

Narrator One: What? I don't think so.

Narrator Two: *(getting into Narrator One's face)* Oh, yeah? Well, I do!

Narrator One: *(pushing a bit)* No way! The Bears are going to—

Patrick: *(enters and clears throat)*

Narrator One: *(stepping back)* I … uh … That's going to be a good game, huh?

Narrator Two: Yeah! So … see you there?

Narrator One: Sure!

(Narrators exit, acting friendly.)

Patrick: *(as he exits)* Patrick! Patrick! Patrick!

Election Day

If You Say So

Summary

John knows he could never win an election because people find him obnoxious. He decides to run the presidential campaign of a friend. Herschel doesn't have a mind of his own, so John figures he can control everything from behind the scenes once Herschel is in office. But what if Herschel doesn't want to be his puppet?

Costumes, Sets, and Props

❖ The lady in the audience should have a strange hairdo. The man in the audience should wear mismatched clothing. Other characters can wear normal, contemporary clothing.

❖ A few desks and chairs can represent various locations throughout the play.

❖ If props are desired, the following can be used: sign-up sheet, pen, booklet, mirror for Mrs. Galvin to use at the end of Scene Three, and Candidate's Statement.

Presentation

John is obnoxious and unpleasant except when he is trying to manipulate someone.

Herschel starts out as an amiable and gullible person, but he is sharper and wiser by the end of the play. In Scene Four, his actions and expressions are exaggerated as John instructs him.

Supplemental Reading

De Capua, Sarah. *Running for Public Office.* New York: Children's Press, 2002.

Donovan, Sandy. *Running for Office: A Look at Political Campaigns.* Minneapolis, MN: Lerner, 2002.

Edwards, Nancy. *Mom for Mayor.* Chicago: Cricket Books, 2006.

Rallison, Janette. *All's Fair in Love, War, and High School.* New York: Walker, 2003.

Cast of Characters

John	Mrs. (Mr.) Galvin
Lady in audience	Angela, Susan, and Franco—potential voters
Malcolm and Lee, John's friends	Audience member
Herschel, presidential candidate	Carla and Dave, Herschel's opponents
Two people talking in audience	Man in audience

Election Day

If You Say So

Scene One

John: People don't like me much. I don't know why. *(to lady in audience)* Whoa! Bad hair day?

Lady: Well, I never! *(exits)*

John: What's her problem? Anyway, I always get this negative response for some reason, and I've accepted it. But when I got to the middle school, the whole thing became a big problem. It happened like this….

(Malcolm, Lee, and Herschel enter.)

Malcolm: *(to John)* Are you going to run?

John: Why would I run? Did you have beans for supper again last night?

Malcolm: No!

Lee: He's asking if you're running for class president.

John: President? What are you talking about?

Malcolm: Didn't your homeroom teacher talk about the election?

John: Maybe. She sent me out in the hall—again!—so I didn't hear the announcements. I could really help her run things more efficiently if she'd just listen to me. So what about this election?

Lee: In two weeks, we're electing our class president.

Herschel: We're going to do it on the real election day so it will be a true lesson in democracy.

John: Man, you are totally brainwashed.

Herschel: I am?

John: You believe everything you're told. That's brainwashed!

Herschel: Okay … if you say so.

John: So … class president … I always wanted to be the president of something.

Malcolm: I know. That's why I thought maybe you'd run.

Lee: Not that you'll get elected.

John: Thanks for your support, Lee.

From Diana R. Jenkins, *All Year Long! Funny Readers Theatre for Life's Special Times.* Westport, CT: Teacher Ideas Press. Copyright © 2007 by Diana R. Jenkins.

Lee: You know what I mean. You're not the kind of person who gets elected to anything.

John: Yeah. If only people knew the real me.... *(notices two people whispering in audience)* That is very rude! If you're going to run your mouths, you can just get out of here! *(after they exit, turns back to friends)* I'm really a caring person with some good ideas. Nobody ever gets that.

Malcolm: Yeah. Go figure.

John: If only my brains could be inside someone else's body. Then I'd be elected in a landslide! Yeah … it'd have to be somebody really likable. Somebody who can get along with anyone. And somebody without a mind of … I know! It should be somebody like you, Herschel.

Herschel: Me? I-I-I'm sorry, John, but I can't let you experiment on me.

John: Sheesh! You've been watching too many old movies. We can't really put my brain in your body, you dope!

Herschel: Oh. Of course not.

Lee: So what are you talking about, John?

John: I'm talking about putting my brain behind Herschel's campaign.

Herschel: My campaign?

John: Yep! You're going to be our class president!

Scene Two

John: *(to audience as others freeze)* Herschel wasn't exactly the *perfect* candidate. People liked him, but they didn't think of him as presidential. I would have to groom Herschel into what *looked* like leadership material. Not that he had to actually lead. Once he was elected, I'd run things behind the scenes. Herschel would do whatever I told him to do.

Herschel: *(as everyone unfreezes)* You want *me* to run for class president?

John: Sure! You'd be great!

Herschel: I don't know, John. I don't think anyone will vote for me.

John: You're popular with the kids who came here from our elementary school. Isn't he, guys?

Lee: He's right. People do like you.

Malcolm: I'd vote for you.

Herschel: Thanks.

John: A *lot* of people from our old school will vote for you, but that's not enough to win you the election. You need other kids to vote for you, too. Luckily, I have plenty of ideas about how to make that happen. So I'll be your campaign manager, okay? With me running things, you can't lose, Herschel! It'll be easy to win.

Herschel: Really?

John: Sure! Just listen to me, and I'll get you the position you're dreaming of.

Herschel: I'm not exactly dreaming of being president.

From Diana R. Jenkins, *All Year Long! Funny Readers Theatre for Life's Special Times.* Westport, CT: Teacher Ideas Press. Copyright © 2007 by Diana R. Jenkins.

John: You're not? But don't you want to help your fellow citizens here at Central Middle School? Don't you want to make life better for us as we struggle through the trials and tribulations of life here at Central Middle School where we're struggling to get our educations?

Herschel: I guess.

John: Then you were meant to be our leader, Herschel. It's your destiny!

Herschel: Oh. Well, if you say so.

John: Good. Let's go to the principal's office and sign you up as a candidate.

Scene Three

(Lee and Malcolm exit, and Mrs. Galvin enters.)

John: Hi, Mrs. Galvin. We're here to sign up for the election.

Mrs. Galvin: *(aghast)* Oh, my! You're running for office, John?

John: No, not me. Herschel's going to run for class president.

Mrs. Galvin: Well, that's a re— I mean … how nice! Sign this list, Herschel. *(holding out booklet)* And here's a booklet about the election and—

John: *(snatching booklet away)* I'll take that!

Mrs. Galvin: *(irritated)* The booklet is for the candidate, John.

John: Don't worry yourself into any more gray hairs, Mrs. Galvin. I'm his campaign manager so I need to see the booklet, too.

Mrs. Galvin: Oh. Well, all right, I guess. Good luck, Herschel!

Herschel: Thanks!

Mrs. Galvin: *(sneaking look in mirror as she exits)* Gray hairs! I don't have any gray hairs.

John: Okay, let's see what the booklet says about the president. *(flips pages)* Here it is. "Creative thinking and good communication are important for the class president, but it is most essential that he/she be willing to serve others." What a bunch of baloney! The most important thing about being class president is the ability to handle power.

Herschel: Power?

John: Yeah … uh … you know … you use the power of the office to help people. We have to get you elected so you can do that. I'll read this booklet during study hall, and then we'll meet at my house after school and start planning our strategy, okay?

Herschel: Sounds good to me. *(exits)*

John: *(to audience)* Doesn't everything?

Scene Four

John: I found out some important information from the booklet like how big our campaign posters could be—not very!—and how much we could pay people to vote for us—nothing! *(shakes head in disbelief)* I also found out that Herschel needed to write a Candidate's Statement about where he stood on the issues. And

From Diana R. Jenkins, *All Year Long! Funny Readers Theatre for Life's Special Times.* Westport, CT: Teacher Ideas Press. Copyright © 2007 by Diana R. Jenkins.

he would have to debate his opponents the day before the election. I had my work cut out for me, but I knew I could mold Herschel into a winner!

(Herschel, Lee, and Malcolm enter.)

John: *(to Lee and Malcolm)* What are you two doing here?

Lee: We want to be on Herschel's campaign team.

John: I guess that's okay. But don't do anything stupid that will make him lose the election.

Malcolm: Hold on! You mean the campaign team is supposed to help the candidate win?

Lee: Gee. Who knew?

John: Funny. Okay, Herschel, we have to make you look presidential. So stand up straight.

Herschel: Okay.

John: Now look serious.

Herschel: Okay.

John: Not that serious!

Herschel: Okay.

John: Well, more serious than that!

Herschel: Okay.

John: Just act like you're somebody responsible who can handle being president.

Herschel: Okay.

John: Perfect! Now say, "I'm really concerned about that, and I'm going to look into the problem."

Herschel: I'm really concerned about that, and I'm going to look into the problem.

Lee: Wow, Herschel! That was impressive.

Herschel: *(dropping serious pose)* It was?

Malcolm: Yeah. You looked like a real president—not like yourself at all!

Herschel: Oh. That doesn't seem right.

John: What are you talking about?

Herschel: Isn't it dishonest to act like somebody I'm not?

John: That's what politics is all about, Herschel! Candidates put forth their best image so people will vote for them. Then they can do wonderful things for everybody once they're in office.

Herschel: But if people won't vote for the real me, then maybe I shouldn't be president at all.

Malcolm: That makes sense.

John: Only to a dope like you, Malcolm! Look, Herschel, do you know anything about politics?

Herschel: Not really.

John: Then leave everything to the person who does—your campaign manager! I promise you we're going to run a clean and honest campaign, okay? I just want to polish your image so people get to know the real you behind the person they think you are but they don't really know.

Lee: Huh?

John: So what do you say, Herschel? Will you trust me?

Herschel: Sure, John.

John: Say that like a president!

Herschel: *(acting presidential)* Sure, John.

John: Okay, now let's work on your Candidate's Statement. It's supposed to show where you stand on all the issues.

Herschel: But I'm not sure what I think about the issues.

John: That's okay. I already wrote the statement for you. You just have to memorize it.

Herschel: Oh. Okay. I guess I can do that.

(Herschel looks at statement and freezes along with Malcolm and Lee.)

Scene Five

John: I worked with Herschel for hours that afternoon, teaching him how to act presidential so he could impress anybody. Then, the next day at school, I sent him out to meet the voters.

(Herschel, Malcolm, and Lee unfreeze.)

Herschel: *(putting statement in pocket)* I'm not comfortable going up to people I don't know.

John: Well, duh. They won't vote for you if they don't know you who you are.

Herschel: My name is on all those posters Malcolm and Lee made.

John: There's so much more to running for office than campaign posters, Herschel. You have to get yourself out there … let the voters take a good look at you and see what kind of man you are … You know, no one ever said this was going to be easy.

Lee: Wait, John … Didn't you say that yourself?

Malcolm: That's right! He said if he was Herschel's campaign manager—

John: Nobody asked for your opinions. Okay, Herschel. Go meet those voters over there.

(Angela, Susan, and Franco enter.)

Herschel: Hi, you guys! I'm Herschel.

Angela: Hi. I'm Angela. And this is Susan. And Franco.

Herschel: Hi! Listen … I'm running for class president and I'm hoping you'll vote for me.

Susan: How do you feel about the school's homework policy?

Herschel: *(presidential)* I'm really concerned about that, and I'm going to look into the problem.

Franco: Homework is a problem all right! You have my vote.

Angela: Mine, too.

From Diana R. Jenkins, *All Year Long! Funny Readers Theatre for Life's Special Times.* Westport, CT: Teacher Ideas Press. Copyright © 2007 by Diana R. Jenkins.

Susan: And mine!

Herschel: *(sincerely)* Thanks! Thanks a lot!

(Angela, Susan, and Franco exit.)

Lee: Good job, Herschel!

Malcolm: Yeah. You were smooth.

John: But that's only three votes. And there must be a hundred kids here who don't know you. You have to try and meet them all, Herschel.

Herschel: Okay.

John: But don't forget to be nice to the people you already know.

Herschel: Okay.

John: And stand up straight.

Malcolm: If you keep talking, the bell will ring and he won't have time to campaign.

John: I'm just helping him, Malcolm. I don't see you doing anything to get him elected.

Malcolm: But I made twenty posters last—

John: So get on out there, Herschel, and schmooze your heart out!

Herschel: Uh … okay. *(as he exits along with Lee and Malcolm)* Schmooze?

Scene Six

John: Herschel actually did a good job campaigning. He went out and met a ton of new people. And thanks to my training, he made a good impression on them. Whenever some issue like homework or cafeteria food came up, Herschel handled things the way I'd taught him.

Herschel: *(entering)* I'm really concerned about that, and I'm going to look into the problem.

John: People fell for it every time! All we had to do was get through the debates, and Herschel would have the election wrapped up. But then he had to go and ruin everything.

Herschel: You know, I've been thinking …

John: Oh, don't do that! You might burn out brain cells you'll need when you're the president.

Herschel: That's funny, John. But, seriously … I've been thinking about how everyone hates homework and they don't want to have any.

John: Yeah?

Herschel: I just don't agree. I think we need some homework to help us learn.

John: Whatever you do, Herschel, do *not* say that to anybody else.

Herschel: Why not?

John: Because you'll never get elected if you go around saying you're in favor of homework!

Herschel: But when people ask me about my stand on that issue, shouldn't I be honest?

From Diana R. Jenkins, *All Year Long! Funny Readers Theatre for Life's Special Times.* Westport, CT: Teacher Ideas Press. Copyright © 2007 by Diana R. Jenkins.

John: No! I mean … you shouldn't lie, of course, but you don't have to blab the whole truth either. Just say what I told you to say. That makes everybody happy.

Herschel: It just seems so … I don't know … fake!

John: It's how politics works, okay? If you don't play the game, you don't get elected. And if you don't get elected, you can't do anything good for the voters. And if you can't do *that*, then what use are you to the people of these United States, home of the brave, land of the free?

Herschel: Well … I …

John: Come on, Herschel. You were meant to be a patriot—and an instrument of democracy.

Herschel: If you say so …

John: I do! And I'm right! Now let's talk about the debate.

Scene Seven

John: I practiced and practiced with Herschel! He just didn't understand what a debate was all about. *(to Herschel)* What's your opinion of Central's no-cell-phones policy?

Herschel: *(presidential)* I'm really concerned about that, and I'm going … *(back to normal)* But shouldn't I actually answer the question?

John: You *are* answering it! You're saying you're concerned. *Really* concerned.

Herschel: But I don't think—

John: There you go again! Remember … I'm the brains behind your campaign. Leave all the thinking to me.

Herschel: But won't I have to think when I'm arguing the issues? I mean … it *is* a debate!

John: And the point of a debate is to say nothing that could lose you any votes.

Herschel: It is?

John: Of course!

Herschel: But what if one of the other candidates challenges something I've said?

John: Then you say, "My opponent makes a good point. I will consider all sides of this important issue when I am in office."

Herschel: But that doesn't really say anything.

John: Right! And if you handle the whole debate like that, you'll be the hands-down winner!

Herschel: If you say so. It just seems like voters should know where I stand. And so should I!

John: Your Candidate's Statement tells where you stand. You'll say that at the beginning of the debate and all your opinions will be clear. Do you have it memorized?

Herschel: Yes, but—

John: Let's hear it.

From Diana R. Jenkins, *All Year Long! Funny Readers Theatre for Life's Special Times.* Westport, CT: Teacher Ideas Press. Copyright © 2007 by Diana R. Jenkins.

Herschel: (*quickly recites*) I would be honored to be your president and lead you through the trials and tribulations of life here at Central Middle School. A good education is the backbone of a successful life, but there's more to life than—

John: That's terrible! You're going to have to act sincere, Herschel.

Herschel: How can I be sincere when I'm not expressing any real ideas about anything?

John: Hey, I spent a long time writing that statement!

Herschel: Sorry, John, but I—

John: I've worked hard on this whole campaign. Just so you could have your dream come true.

Herschel: I know! And I appreciate that.

John: Do you? Do you really?

Herschel: Yes, I really do. Now just let me try the statement again.

John: Well … okay. Let's hear it.

Herschel: (*presidential*) I would be honored to be your president and lead you through the trials and tribulations of life here at Central Middle School. A good education is the backbone of a successful life, but there's more to life than just a good education. Friends bring—

John: Much better! Man, I can taste victory, can't you?

Herschel: (*sadly*) Yeah. Sure. If you say so. (*exits*)

Scene Eight

John: I was feeling confident about winning the debate—and the election! Soon I would be running everything! I had lots of changes I wanted to make at our school. First, I was planning to organize a strike to force teachers to stop assigning homework altogether. Then I was—

Audience Member: But that's not what Herschel wants!

John: Herschel doesn't know what he wants until I tell him what he wants.

Audience Member: You're unbelievable!

John: And you're disturbing our performance. Out you go!

Audience Member: Hey, you can't—

John: Security! Security!

Audience Member: All right! I'm going. (*exits*)

(*Herschel and other candidates enter and take places for debate. Other students enter and sit to one side to watch debate. All freeze.*)

John: Anyway … For once I would have the power to *make* people listen and do what I wanted. Not that I would be some kind of dictator. I'm not like that, you know. (*to Herschel who unfreezes*) Just do what I told you. Don't think any stupid thoughts of your own and go ruining my plan! I am your brain … remember that!

Mrs. Galvin: (*enters*) Let's get started, people.

(*Everyone else unfreezes, and John sits.*)

Mrs. Galvin: First, let's hear our candidates' statements about the issues. Carla?

Carla: I really want to be president because I really want to do something nice for people because I'm really a people person and I really hope you'll vote for me. Thank you. Really.

(Everyone, except John and Herschel, raises hands to applaud then freezes.)

Herschel: *(to self)* She didn't say anything about the issues!

John: *(to self)* Man, she's good.

(Everyone unfreezes and applauds.)

Mrs. Galvin: That was very nice, Carla. Okay, let's hear your statement, Dave.

Dave: I can sum up my position with one word—lunch in the cafeteria! You know what I mean.

(Everyone, except John and Herschel, raises hands to applaud then freezes.)

Herschel: *(to self)* He didn't really explain what he thinks … or what he's planning!

John: *(to self)* Wow! He won't lose any votes with that statement.

(Everyone unfreezes and applauds.)

Mrs. Galvin: Thank you, Dave. Now we'll hear from Herschel.

Herschel: *(takes out statement, looks at it, and refolds it)* I want to talk to you about some important issues and what I think about them.

John: *(jumping up)* WHAT? Wait! Wait a minute!

Mrs. Galvin: Behave yourself, John.

John: But I need to talk to Herschel! Right now! It's an emergency!

Mrs. Galvin: Sit down and listen.

John: But … but … but … .

Mrs. Galvin: NOW!

John: *(collapses into seat as everyone freezes)* I'm doomed!

Scene Nine

John: *(to audience)* I couldn't believe the things Herschel said.

Herschel: *(unfreezes)* Sure, homework is a pain, but it helps us, too. *(freezes)*

John: He had an opinion about everything.

Herschel: *(unfreezes)* The cafeteria ladies work hard, but we need healthier lunches. *(freezes)*

John: And he shared every one of those opinions.

Herschel: *(unfreezes)* And if your work isn't complete, then I don't think you *should* get to go on a field trip. *(freezes)*

John: He went on like that, ignoring everything I taught him! He didn't even sound presidential!

Herschel: *(unfreezes)* I'm not the smartest person in school. Or the coolest either. And I've never been the president of anything. But if you vote for me, I'll do my best. Thanks. *(freezes)*

From Diana R. Jenkins, *All Year Long! Funny Readers Theatre for Life's Special Times.* Westport, CT: Teacher Ideas Press. Copyright © 2007 by Diana R. Jenkins.

John: I figured Herschel had upset a lot of people with those … *ideas*. There was no way we were winning the election now. My dream was crushed! Why couldn't he just follow orders?

(Everyone unfreezes and heartily applauds Herschel.)

John: What is … but I thought … Hey, they like him!

Malcolm: Of course they do! He's the only one with any real ideas.

Lee: Yeah. And you can tell he cares about making a difference.

Mrs. Galvin: Good job. Now let's move on to the question-and-answer part of our program.

John: *(as everyone freezes)* Herschel did a great job with that, too. You couldn't really call it a debate because Carla and Dave weren't much of a challenge.

Carla: *(unfreezes)* Sure I believe in a quality education because … um … I'm really, *really* a people person. *(freezes)*

Dave: *(unfreezes)* There are two things that make a quality education: a good cafeteria, good food, and good vending machines. *(freezes)*

Herschel: *(unfreezes)* A good education is important, and I have some ideas about how we can get the best education possible. Like how about a tutoring program to help kids with homework? And maybe we could have a special reward for kids who improve their grades. *(freezes)*

John: Everybody was impressed with Herschel. And you know what? So was I. He had put a lot of thought into the issues. The idea of getting elected by being real seemed pretty crazy to me …

(Everyone unfreezes and applauds Herschel.)

John: But obviously it was working.

Scene Ten

Mrs. Galvin: That's the end of our pre-election debate. Please go to lunch now.

(Everyone, except John and Herschel, exits.)

Herschel: Are you mad at me?

John: Nah! It was a revolutionary plan, I'll say that, but a good one. I know you're going to win.

Herschel: We'll see tomorrow. But win or lose, I want to say thanks for all your hard work.

John: No problem. So … maybe we should be talking about what we'll do after you win.

Herschel: You mean … to celebrate?

John: Well, of course, we'll celebrate! But I'm thinking about what we can accomplish with the power of the presidency.

Herschel: *(annoyed)* "We"?

John: Heh-heh. I meant "you," of course. But I'd be glad to keep helping you … you know … give you ideas … shape your policy … .

Herschel: *(getting mad)* Pull my strings like I'm your puppet?

John: What? Where'd you get an idea like that?

From Diana R. Jenkins, *All Year Long! Funny Readers Theatre for Life's Special Times.* Westport, CT: Teacher Ideas Press. Copyright © 2007 by Diana R. Jenkins.

Herschel: From my brain. I do have one, you know.

John: Sure you do! I'm just saying—

Herschel: Hey, you're not in charge of the world, okay? You can't force your opinions on everybody and boss them around and manipulate them. Nobody likes it when you act like that.

John: So?

Herschel: So if you quit doing that stuff, you'll get along with people a lot better.

John: Really?

Herschel: *(kindly)* Sure. And you'll make some more friends, too.

John: I don't know …

Herschel: Just give it a try.

John: Well … okay. Change is tough, you know.

Herschel: Believe me, I know! But you can do it, John.

John: If you say so …

Herschel: Later! *(exits)*

John: Herschel did win the election—by a landslide! I think I *helped* Herschel, but, in the end, he's the one who really made that happen. Of course, I'm kind of disappointed I can't run my agenda through him, but it's great that he's finally developed some backbone. And what he said about me … well … it's not something I liked hearing, but it actually helped. I'm trying to be a better … *(looking at man in audience)* Dude! What are you wearing?

Man in audience: Excuse me?

John: Well, look at yourself! You look like a … I mean … I … Sharp, man! Sharp!

Man in audience: Thanks. You know … you're not really such a bad guy.

John: *(smiling)* If you say so! *(exits)*

Give Me a Break!

Summary

Callie is proud of herself for starting a Thanksgiving food drive at school. It's hard work, but she doesn't mind since she's such a generous person. Then the drive attracts the attention of Mabel, an annoying person who doesn't have any friends. She thinks Callie is so nice *she'll* be friends with her! But Callie wouldn't be caught dead hanging around with someone like Mabel!

Costumes, Sets, and Props

- ❖ All characters dress in normal, contemporary clothing except Mabel who dresses strangely.

- ❖ A few shelves, desks, and chairs can serve for the locations in the play.

- ❖ If props are desired, the following can be used: canned food, decorated cardboard box, art supplies, and grocery sack of food.

Presentation

Callie is self-righteous in general and testy with Mabel in particular.
Mabel is odd and annoying but enthusiastic and grateful. She often speaks too loudly.

Supplemental Reading

Clark, Sandra. *You Can Change Your World! Creative Ways to Volunteer and Make a Difference.* Grand Rapids, MI: Fleming H. Revell, 2003.

Grace, Catherine O'Neill, and Margaret Bruchac. *1621—A New Look at Thanksgiving.* Washington, DC: National Geographic Society, 2001.

Gray, Kathlyn. *Volunteering: The Ultimate Teen Guide.* Lanham, MD: Scarecrow Press, 2004.

Perry, Susan K. *Catch the Spirit: Teen Volunteers Tell How They Made a Difference.* New York: Franklin Watts, 2000.

Cast of Characters

Callie	Extra students, if desired (nonspeaking)
Mom	Mabel
Mr. (Mrs.) Emerson	Scott
Mrs. (Mr.) Perez	Amber, Pat, and Keiko—Callie's friends
Mrs. (Mr.) Hefferman	Mabel's mother

Thanksgiving

Give Me a Break!

Scene One

Callie: I guess you could say I was shocked. See, I always thought of a food bank as a huge building, stacked to the ceiling with cans and boxes. But the first time my mom took me with her to volunteer at our local food bank, things weren't like that at all. The building was pretty small. And the shelves were almost empty!

Mom: *(entering with Mr. Emerson)* This won't feed many families, will it, Mr. Emerson?

Mr. Emerson: No, it won't. We haven't received a lot of donations lately.

Callie: Give me a break! Would it kill people to come through with a few cans of green beans?

Mom: I guess most people get busy with their own lives and don't think about the food bank.

Mr. Emerson: We're hoping to get more donations this month since so many groups have food drives in November.

Mom: I hate to think of any families going without a Thanksgiving dinner.

Callie: Me, too. Hey, maybe my school could have a food drive!

Mr. Emerson: That's a wonderful idea, Callie!

Callie: I'll talk to our principal about it on Monday.

Mom: How nice! I'm proud of you.

Callie: I guess I'm just a caring person—unlike some people. *(as Mom and Mr. Emerson exit)* I was feeling pretty proud of myself. Here I was, giving up my Saturday to work at the food bank. And I was going to lead a food drive, too. I asked myself: how many people are that giving? And I answered myself back: almost nobody! Our principal, Mrs. Perez, agreed with me about that.

Scene Two

Mrs. Perez: *(enters)* You have a good idea, Callie. How are you planning to organize things?

Callie: I think I should take a donation box to each classroom and give an inspirational talk about the food drive. You know … a lot of people just aren't naturally

Mrs. Perez: generous. They might need a little push. We can run the drive for two weeks, ending the Friday before Thanksgiving. I'm sure my mom will help me take the donations to the food bank.

Mrs. Perez: Sounds good! I'll let the teachers know you'll be visiting their rooms.

Callie: Thanks, Mrs. Perez.

Mrs. Perez: No, thank *you*. There aren't many people who have your kind spirit, Callie.

Callie: I know! *(to audience as Mrs. Perez exits)* So the next day I went to all the classrooms and explained the food drive. I had this good speech prepared. *(clears throat)* "It's time to stop thinking about yourself and start thinking about the less fortunate. That's what I've been doing. You know, some families won't have a nice Thanksgiving dinner without your help. For the next two weeks we're having a school food drive, which was my idea. Bring in non-perishable food items and put them in this box I decorated for you. All your donations will go to the food bank. Please, everybody … give generously." Pretty good, huh? Anyway … I went to my own room last.

(Mrs. Hefferman, Scott, Amber, Pat, Keiko, Mabel and students enter.)

Mrs. Hefferman: This is a wonderful thing you're doing, Callie.

Callie: I just can't help giving to others, Mrs. Hefferman. *(to audience)* So I recited my speech, and, at the end, something weird happened. *(to class)* Please, everybody … give generously.

Mabel: *(stands and applauds)* Wow, Callie! That is so nice! Fantastic idea! *(notices everyone else is staring)* I mean … uh … *(clapping slows, then stops)* So … great, Callie, great. *(sits)*

Amber: *(muttering)* Unbelievable!

Callie: *(to audience)* That's Mabel Ryan. She's always doing strange stuff like that.

Scott: Which might explain why no one wants to be her friend. No one!

Callie: No kidding. *(to class)* So start bringing in donations tomorrow. Thanks!

Mrs. Hefferman: Thank you, Callie. This is such a thoughtful idea.

Mabel: *(standing and applauding)* Yay, Callie! Way to go! *(notices everyone staring, clapping slows to a stop)* Yeah. Uh. Go. Callie. *(sits)*

Scott: Brother!

Callie: *(as others exit)* Mabel was really annoying, but I never dreamed how much of a pest she could really be! I found that out all too soon.

Scene Three

Callie: My class didn't bring in much food the next day. While everyone went to lunch, I counted the food containers in our box. I couldn't believe how few there were!

Mabel: *(enters)* Hey! Need any help?

Callie: *(jumps)* You startled me.

Mabel: Sorry! So do you want me to help you?

Callie: I think I can handle counting to … let's see … nine, ten, eleven. That's terrible!

Mabel: It's just the first day. You'll get more donations tomorrow.

Callie: I'd better!

Mabel: Hey, I know! Let's stack up the food so there's plenty of room for all the stuff people will be bringing in later.

Callie: Okay, I guess. *(to audience)* So we started stacking. And Mabel started driving me nuts!

Mabel: The food drive is a great idea, Callie.

Callie: Yeah.

Mabel: Nobody should have to go hungry.

Callie: I know.

Mabel: But lots of people do.

Callie: I know.

Mabel: Lots and lots of people actually.

Callie: I know!

Mabel: People would be surprised –

Callie: Give me a break, Mabel! I know all that! I'm the person running the food drive, remember?

Mabel: And that is so nice of you.

Callie: *(with gritted teeth)* Thanks.

Mabel: Really, really nice.

Callie: Listen, Mabel. Now that the food is stacked, I have something else to do, something that takes … uh … thought, see, so I can't talk to you. Okay?

Mabel: Oh, sure. I understand.

Callie: *(waits a moment)* So … why are you still standing here?

Mabel: I'm waiting for you. So we can go to lunch together.

Callie: Together? *(to audience)* Give me a break! I wouldn't be caught dead eating lunch with Mabel Ryan. I mean … my friends expect me to sit with them and I … uh … can't stand them up, you know. *(to Mabel)* Why don't you go ahead without me?

Mabel: Okay. I'll save you a seat.

Callie: Whatever.

Mabel: See you soon! *(exits)*

Callie: Oh, goody.

Scene Four

Callie: *(as Mabel, Amber, Pat, and Keiko enter)* I waited a bit then went to the cafeteria. Of course, Mabel was sitting all by herself—like usual! I pretended I didn't see her and went right over and sat down with my friends.

Amber: What took you so long?

Callie: I was busy with food drive stuff.

Pat: How's it going?

Callie: Not too great. There's hardly anything in our box. People can be so self-centered.

Keiko: I know what you mean. One time I—

Callie: It's really not that hard to be a little generous.

Mabel: Hey, Callie!

Callie: Oh. Hi. *(turning to others)* This world would be a better place if everyone just thought about other people and gave a little of themselves. That was my philosophy when I came up with the idea of the food drive.

Mabel: So I guess you guys are busy talking, huh?

Callie: You could tell that, could you?

Mabel: Oh, yes, I could tell. I'll just talk to you later. Bye! *(exits)*

Amber: What a dweeb!

Callie: No kidding! She actually wanted me to eat lunch with her.

Amber, Pat, and Keiko: *(laugh)*

Pat: You're kidding.

Callie: Nope. And I don't get it. I have *never* eaten lunch with her before.

Keiko: Nobody has.

Callie: Right. And why would I start now?

Amber: Really! What is she thinking?

Callie: Who knows? But she can keep her stupid ideas to herself!

(Amber, Pat, and Keiko laugh and exit.)

Scene Five

Callie: The next morning my classmates brought more donations, but not as much as I'd hoped.

Scott: *(enters)* Here's something for your food drive, Callie.

Callie: One can of creamed corn? Gee, that's so generous of you, Scott.

Scott: Well … not really.

Callie: No kidding! I was being sarcastic. One can isn't much of a donation.

Scott: Yeah, I know. Especially since I hate creamed corn.

Callie: Sheesh! You just brought it in to get rid of it?

Scott: Well … uh … kind of … .

Callie: That is so selfish! What if everybody had that attitude? What if *I* had that attitude? There wouldn't be a food drive at all if I were as selfish as you are, Scott!

Scott: Okay, okay! I'll bring more tomorrow.

Callie: And bring something good!

Scott: Okay! *(muttering as he exits)* Saint Callie!

Callie: Luckily, some people were kinder than Scott and brought in bigger donations. But guess who didn't bring in anything at all? Mabel! After all that stuff she said about how wonderful the food drive was, she didn't come through with one little can of anything! Even creamed corn! Give me a break!

Mabel: *(enters and looks in box)* Wow! You got more stuff! I'll stack up the new donations.

Callie: A lot of kids brought food today, but not everybody did. I guess some people don't really care about the needy.

Mabel: You're right about that. Not everyone is as giving as you are, Callie.

Callie: Well, I really believe in helping those less fortunate than myself. I mean … I *do* something about the problem. I don't just *talk* about it.

Mabel: That's great. Hey, this box is almost full. I can bring another box from home tomorrow. Just think! Our class might fill up *two* boxes. Wouldn't that be wonderful, Callie?

Callie: Sure. Wonderful.

Mrs. Hefferman: *(enters)* Time for Art!

Callie: *(to audience as Mrs. Hefferman exits and Scott, Amber, Pat, Keiko, Mabel, and other kids enter and sit at tables)* A chance to escape! I hurried away from Mabel and walked down to the art room with my friends. But when we got there, Mabel leeched onto me again.

Scene Six

Mabel: Hi, Callie!

Callie: Hi.

Mabel: Guess who I'm going to draw for our portrait assignment.

Callie: I don't know. *(muttering)* And I don't care.

Amber, Pat, and Keiko: *(snicker)*

Mabel: You! And I'm going to show you working on the food drive. A portrait is supposed to show a person's true personality, right? So I'm going to show your kindness.

Amber: Isn't that nice?

Pat: Isn't it though?

Keiko: Callie is just such a sweet, sweet person.

Scott: *(snorts)* Right! Saint Callie!

Callie: Who asked you, Scott?

Amber: And Callie *is* a nice person!

Mabel: Yeah. She's someone who cares about other people and—

Callie: Look, Mabel, I really need to concentrate on the assignment, okay? So how about you give me some breathing room?

Mabel: Oh. Sure. *(moves one step away)*

Amber, Pat, and Keiko: *(laugh)*

From Diana R. Jenkins, *All Year Long! Funny Readers Theatre for Life's Special Times.* Westport, CT: Teacher Ideas Press. Copyright © 2007 by Diana R. Jenkins.

Callie: More than that!

Mabel: Oh. Okay. *(moves one more step)*

Amber, Pat, and Keiko: *(laugh)*

Callie: It's not funny, you guys. *(to Mabel)* I meant that you should … like … go someplace else.

Mabel: Oh. Okay! See you later! *(moves to another area)*

Pat: She is so strange.

Callie: Tell me about it! Why does she suddenly think I'm going to be friends with her?

Scott: Don't you get it? With this food drive, you've fooled her into thinking you're some kind of saint. And a saint has to be nice to her, right?

Callie: Is *that* what's going on?

Amber: I hate to say this, but I think Scott's right.

Keiko: Me, too! She keeps saying how nice you are. I guess she thinks you're nice enough to be her friend.

Callie: Rats! Why did I have to be so generous and open-hearted?

Amber, Pat, Keiko, and Scott: *(laugh)*

Callie: What's funny about that?

Pat: Oh. You're serious. I mean … we're just laughing about Mabel. What a loser!

Amber, Pat, and Keiko: *(laugh nervously)*

Scott: Brother! Leave me out of this conversation!

Callie: You were never in it, Scott!

Scott: Whatever.

Callie: *(to friends)* Well, I am not going to be her best buddy. I guess she'll eventually get that idea. I just hope it doesn't take too long!

Scene Seven

Callie: *(as others exit)* But Mabel just couldn't take a hint. Over the next week, she kept appearing at my elbow and asking me about the food drive and telling me how nice I was and stacking up the food donations even though I didn't want her to and counting them for me even though I could count just fine, thank you, and butting into my conversations and following me around and driving me totally INSANE! And she never got the idea I wasn't interested in her friendship! I finally had to get mean with her even though that was so opposite to the real me.

Mabel: *(enters)* Hi, Callie! What are you doing?

Callie: *(jumps)* Sheesh, Mabel! Do you have to keep sneaking up on me like that?

Mabel: Oh. Sorry. So what are you doing?

Callie: I'm going around to collect the food boxes from the other rooms.

Mabel: Do you want some help?

Callie: *(muttering)* Not from you I don't!

Mabel: What?

Callie: Give me a break, Mabel! Why do you keep trying to help me all the time? Have I asked you to help me? Even once?

Mabel: No, but the food drive is such a good idea that I'd like to help.

Callie: You must be joking.

Mabel: No, I really want to help.

Callie: If you're so big on helping, why didn't you bring something to donate?

Mabel: Well … I …

Callie: I mean … look at all the food the other kids in our class have donated! Sure, I had to push them a little. Well … okay, I had to push them a lot! But I cared enough about the needy people to do whatever it took to make people give generously. It was tough, but I did it. And we now have tons of food—two whole boxes just from our room!

Mabel: Yes, the drive is a big success.

Callie: No thanks to you!

Mabel: I … I'm sorry, Callie.

Callie: *(to audience)* That's when I realized how I could get rid of Mabel for good. *(to Mabel)* I'm sorry, too, Mabel. You know, I could never be friends with someone so self-centered. Never!

Mabel: I … I … .*(runs off as Scott enters)*

Scott: What's the matter with Mabel? She looked upset.

Callie: *(shortly)* I don't know.

Scott: And you don't care either, do you?

Callie: Of course I do!

Scott: Oh, yeah … that's right. You're Saint Callie.

Callie: Look, Scott, don't talk about me. You've never even spoken two words to Mabel. And you said that no one wanted to be her friend. Including you!

Scott: I know, but maybe I've changed my mind about Mabel. *(starts to exit but turns back)* And about you, too. *(exits)*

Scene Eight

Callie: I guess I was supposed to be bothered by what Scott said, but I wasn't. Not at all. Not one bit. What did I care what he thought? Or what he meant about changing his mind about me? I did feel bad about hurting Mabel's feelings. But I had to do that. Being subtle just didn't work with that girl. It was better to be blunt and make a clean break. In the long run, that was going to hurt her less. And anyway, I couldn't keep wasting so much time and energy on her.

Mom: *(enters)* Wow! You've really collected up a lot of food. I'm impressed with the generosity of the kids here.

Callie: I think they could have given more. Some people didn't donate anything! *(to audience)* Like you-know-who!

Mom: Well, some people just don't have much to give, I guess.

Callie: It's a good thing some of us do have generous hearts!

Mom: Right. Well, let's get the boxes loaded up into the van. *(exits)*

Callie: We took the food to the food bank then stayed awhile to help the other volunteers sort things out. On Saturday, we all got together again to bag up the food. Then on Sunday, Mom and I took some of the bags and drove around delivering the food to needy families. Talk about rewarding! People were so grateful, and I felt like I was really doing something good. Finally, we came to the last stop on Mom's list. *(sits)*

Mom: *(enters and sits next to Callie as if in car)* I'm tired, but this has been a great experience.

Callie: Really! I'm glad I … uh … .

Mabel: *(enters, looks out "window," and calls over shoulder)* Hey, Mom! Somebody just pulled up in the driveway! Mom! *(exits)*

Callie: *(slumps in seat)* You know what, Mom? I am really, really tired. I think I'll just stay in the car this time. Okay?

Mom: Okay, Callie. I'll be back in a few minutes. *(exits)*

Callie: *(sitting back up)* Okay, so maybe you already figured out why Mabel was excited about the food drive. And why she didn't bring anything in. But it's easy to see things clearly when you're watching a play. It's a lot harder when things are happening in your real life. *(sighs)* But maybe I would've figured things out, too, if I hadn't been so busy feeling proud of myself and my "generosity!" Poor Mabel! I made her feel terrible, but she didn't want me to know her situation so she couldn't say anything. It's a good thing she doesn't know … uh-oh! *(slumps)*

Mom: *(entering with Mabel and her mother)* Have a wonderful Thanksgiving!

Mabel's mother: We will—thanks to you and the food bank!

Mabel: Thanks! Thanks so much! That was so nice of you! Thanks!

Mom: You're welcome, dear.

(Mabel and her mother exit, and Mom returns to "car.")

Mom: Goodness, Callie! Are you really that tired? Sit up.

Callie: *(straightening)* Yes, ma'am.

Mom: Let's head home. Now we can start planning our own Thanksgiving dinner!

Callie: Yeah. Great. Thanksgiving.

Scene Nine

(Mom exits.)

Callie: *(pacing)* That night I spent a lot of time thinking about how I had treated Mabel. And I felt terrible about it! *(pauses)* I had to ask myself: how generous was I really? Sure, I gave of myself for the food drive, but I was so selfish when it came to Mabel. *(paces a bit, then stops)* I couldn't be bothered to be friendly to her – or even just kind! *(paces a bit, then stops)* And it sure wasn't very giving to refuse her friendship when she'd been so nice to me! *(collapses in chair)* I had really

From Diana R. Jenkins, *All Year Long! Funny Readers Theatre for Life's Special Times.* Westport, CT: Teacher Ideas Press. Copyright © 2007 by Diana R. Jenkins.

messed up! And I wasn't going to feel better until I made things right with Mabel. Which I was planning when I got to school Monday morning.

Mabel: *(enters and speaks coldly)* Oh. Hi, Callie.

Callie: *(hurrying over)* Hi, Mabel! I've been waiting for you.

Mabel: Why?

Callie: To say I'm sorry for how I acted. I was the one who was selfish! I … I made the food drive all about me, and I thought I was so superior or something, and I shouldn't have been so mean to you, and … and I'm sorry, okay? I hope we can still be friends.

Mabel: *(softly)* I'm sorry, Callie. But I don't think so. *(exits)*

Callie: I couldn't blame Mabel for not wanting to be my friend. But I really wished that she would at least accept my apology. How could I get her to forgive me? I thought about that all morning long instead of concentrating on my lessons.

(Mrs. Hefferman and students enter and take seats.)

Mrs. Hefferman: Callie? Callie? Callie?

Scott: *(nudges Callie)* Yo! Wake up!

Callie: What? Oh! I'm sorry.

Mrs. Hefferman: That's all right, dear. I bet you're tired. I understand you worked on the food drive all weekend.

Callie: Yes … along with a lot of other volunteers. We took food to over fifty families on Sunday.

Mrs. Hefferman: How wonderful! Thank you for running the drive for our school.

Callie: You don't have to thank me. I should thank everybody here. You guys really came through, and your generosity made the food drive a big success. Thanks a lot! And I … uh … I'm sorry if I gave you a little too much attitude, okay?

Scott: A little!

Mrs. Hefferman: *(warning)* Scott … .

Scott: She yelled at me about corn. Corn!

Mabel: Well, I think Callie did a really nice thing, thinking up the food drive and doing all that work. She helped save a lot of people from going hungry, and that's great.

Mrs. Hefferman: I agree with you, Mabel. Now let's get out our Science books, everybody.

Callie: *(to audience as students get out books)* I couldn't believe Mabel said that after the way I had hurt her. Now *that* was generous. Why did I ever think she wasn't worth my time?

Mrs. Hefferman: Page 77, please.

Callie: I was sitting there, really wanting to make things up to Mabel, when I got a great idea. Mrs. Hefferman! Mrs. Hefferman!

Mrs. Hefferman: Yes, Callie?

Callie: Can I say one more thing about the food drive?

Mrs. Hefferman: Very well.

Callie: *(stands)* I want to thank someone else – someone who helped keep things organized and who supported me through the whole thing. *(turns to Mabel)*

Thanks, Mabel. Good job! *(starts applauding)* Way to go! You're the best! *(signals to others to join her)* Come on, you guys.

Amber: You're kidding, right?

Callie: No, I'm not. *(goes on applauding and cheering Mabel)* Yay, Mabel! Great job! *(etc.)*

Scott: *(joins in)*

(Others look puzzled, but join in, too.)

Mabel: *(smiling)* I didn't do that much.

Callie: You were really helpful. And nice, too. And … and giving. I'm sorry I didn't appreciate that at the time.

Mabel: It's okay.

Callie: Thanks.

Mrs. Hefferman: Now! Let's get on with Science, shall we?

Callie: *(to audience as others exit)* So Mabel and I became the very best of friends and we lived happily ever after! Okay … not exactly. Mabel and I *are* pretty friendly now … which isn't always easy. I mean … she still annoys me sometimes. But I'm trying to be more giving with my time – and my friendship. I mean … *truly* giving! It's hard, but I'm giving it my all. *(starts to exit but turns back and smiles)* And I'm not giving up! *(exits)*

From Diana R. Jenkins, *All Year Long! Funny Readers Theatre for Life's Special Times.* Westport, CT: Teacher Ideas Press. Copyright © 2007 by Diana R. Jenkins.

Christmas

Who Cares about Christmas?

Summary

Tamara is tired of getting Christmas gifts she doesn't like. People choose her presents as if they don't even know her! Determined to get only "good stuff," she starts a campaign of dropping hints. When no one catches on, Tamara takes more drastic measures. Sure, people get upset, but aren't they forgetting that Christmas is all about giving?

Costumes, Sets, and Props

❖ All characters wear contemporary clothing except the Narrator, who is dressed as an angel.

❖ A real Christmas tree or a Christmas tree backdrop could be used.

❖ Props can be mimed, but if props are desired, the following are needed: crocheted "computer cozy," fishing rod, a sweater with pink pigs on it, a CD, a baseball cap, a long shopping list, catalogs, and various wrapped packages or gift bags.

Presentation

Tamara is subtly sarcastic about the gifts she doesn't like. When she is trying to manipulate others, she is overly "sincere."

The angel Narrator starts out too sweet and gushy but gradually gets more and more annoyed with Tamara, becoming tense and impatient.

Supplemental Reading

Beneduce, Ann Keay. *Joy to the World, A Family Christmas Treasury.* New York: Atheneum Books for Young Readers, 2000.

Canfield, Jack, et al., editors. *Chicken Soup for the Soul Christmas Treasury for Kids.* Deerfield Beach, FL: Health Communications, 2002.

Davis, Jane. *Crochet Fantastic Jewelry, Hats, Purses, Pillows & More.* New York: Lark Books, 2005.

Dyer, Heather. *The Girl with the Broken Wing.* New York: Scholastic, 2005.

Erlbach, Arlene. *Christmas—Celebrating Life, Giving, and Kindness.* Berkeley Heights, NJ: Enslow, 2001.

Ross, Kathy. *Christmas Presents Kids Can Make.* Brookfield, CT: Millbrook Press, 2001.

Cast of Characters

Narrator (angel)	Ellen
Tamara	Roy
Grandma	Mom
Dad	Grandpa
Spring	

Christmas

Who Cares about Christmas?

Scene One

Narrator: Christmas is just wonderful, isn't it? Isn't it? Such a special time of year. Most people can't wait for the Christmas season. I know I can't!

Tamara: *(glumly)* Well, sure, you're looking forward to Christmas. You're an angel! Your life is perfect up there in heaven, with the … the wings and the … the halo.

Narrator: And God.

Tamara: Right. Well, I can wait just fine. Who cares about Christmas?

Narrator: Poor Tamara. She's always had a bit of a problem with Christmas.

Tamara: A bit of a problem? I have a big problem with Christmas. It's so disappointing! My family and friends just don't understand the true meaning of Christmas.

Narrator: Tamara felt that Christmas was about giving. But no one she knew really got that. Which was why things like this were always happening:

Grandma: *(enters)* Merry Christmas, Tamara.

Tamara: Merry Christmas, Grandma.

Grandma: Oh, I do hope you like my gift for you.

Tamara: I'm sure I will.

Grandma: Open it, dear.

Tamara: Okay … just let me get this tape off and … oh. Wow.

Grandma: Do you like it?

Tamara: Well … I'm not sure I know what it is, Grandma.

Grandma: I'll give you a hint. I crocheted it myself.

Tamara: Yeah, I can see that.

Grandma: It's a computer cozy! You drape it over your computer.

Tamara: Okay.

Grandma: It's my own idea. You know, some people put a cozy on their teapot or their blender.

Tamara: They do?

From Diana R. Jenkins, *All Year Long! Funny Readers Theatre for Life's Special Times.* Westport, CT: Teacher Ideas Press. Copyright © 2007 by Diana R. Jenkins.

Grandma: Oh, yes! And some people put a cozy over their extra rolls of toilet paper.

Tamara: Really.

Grandma: So I figured: why not a computer?

Tamara: Sure. Why not. Wow. Thanks, Grandma.

Grandma: You're welcome, dear. *(exits)*

Tamara: *(staring at gift)* Are you kidding me? A person who understands Christmas doesn't make completely useless—and bizarre! — objects for presents. You're supposed to give stuff that people might actually want. *(tosses gift aside)*

Narrator: I'm sure your grandmother crocheted that gift with love.

Tamara: I know, but it's still a big disappointment.

Scene Two

Narrator: Tamara tried to not get her hopes up too much when it came to Christmas. But sometimes she couldn't help herself.

Dad: *(enters)* You'll never guess what I got you for Christmas. Here's a hint: it's a lot of fun.

Tamara: *(skeptical)* Uh-huh. Sure, Dad.

Dad: And it's kind of sporty, I guess you could say.

Tamara: Uh-huh. Sure, Dad.

Dad: And it's out in the garage.

Tamara: Uh-huh, sure … Wait! In the garage? You don't mean? Ohmigosh! I don't believe it! Ohmigosh! Ohmigosh!

Dad: Do you want to see it now?

Tamara: Yes! Yes! Ohmigosh! Yes!

Dad: Okay then. *(mimes opening door)* Voilà!

Tamara: Ohmi. … Hey, where's the car?

Dad: Your mother went to the grocery, remember?

Tamara: No, not that car! I meant my … oh.

Dad: So how do you like your present?

Tamara: Where *is* my present?

Dad: Right there! With the big bow.

Tamara: You mean … that fishing pole?

Dad: It's not just any fishing rod. That's the No-Escape Nab-o-lator 5000. Isn't she a beauty?

Tamara: You got me a fishing pole?

Dad: Not just any fishing—

Tamara: Yeah, I got that, Dad.

Dad: Just think how much fun we'll have this spring, out on the lake together. That'll be some real quality father-daughter time. And maybe you'll let me use the Nab-o-lator now and then.

Tamara: Yeah, Dad. Sure. Who cares? I mean … use it all you want.

Dad: Thanks, honey.

Tamara: No, thank *you*, Dad. I've never received a present quite like this before.

Dad: It was my pleasure. *(exits)*

Tamara: *(pretending to call after him)* Yeah. Thanks a million, Dad. And, by the way, the spirit of giving isn't about choosing gifts that *you* like. You're supposed to think about the person who's getting the gift.

Narrator: Maybe he *was* thinking of you and all the time you two could spend together fishing.

Tamara: Maybe. Or maybe he was thinking about the Trash-o-lator 5000. *(tosses gift aside)*

Narrator: Maybe you're wrong.

Tamara: And maybe you should get down to Planet Earth more often and experience reality.

Narrator: *(annoyed)* Oh, yeah? Well, maybe you should … I mean … *(sweetly)* It's so nice of you to share your thoughts with me.

Tamara: *(sweetly)* Isn't it though?

Scene Three

Narrator: Sometimes Tamara wondered what people were thinking when they shopped for her Christmas gift. It was like they didn't know her at all.

Spring, Ellen, and Roy: *(enter)* Hi!

Tamara: Hi, you guys.

Spring: Merry Christmas, Tamara. *(hands Tamara her gift)*

Tamara: *(opening gift)* Thanks, Spring. Oh … it's a sweater. And look. It has little pink flowers all over it.

Spring: Those are pigs.

Tamara: Pigs? On a sweater?

Spring: Isn't it just precious?

Tamara: And so completely different from anything I ever wear. But who cares about that?

Spring: Right! I mean … those little piggies are just so cute.

Ellen: Here, Tamara. Open my gift. *(handing Tamara her gift)*

Tamara: Do I have to? I mean … okay. Here goes! *(opens gift)* Songs of the Lonesome Pickup Truck. Gee, thanks, Ellen. This is the first country music CD I've ever owned. The very first. Yep, this will be the only country CD in my whole collection. You know … the collection of CDs we always listen to when you come over? Well, this is the one and only country CD.

Ellen: I'm glad I found something really different.

Tamara: Oh, you sure did that.

Roy: *(hands Tamara a baseball cap)* Merry Christmas!

From Diana R. Jenkins, *All Year Long! Funny Readers Theatre for Life's Special Times.* Westport, CT: Teacher Ideas Press. Copyright © 2007 by Diana R. Jenkins.

Tamara: *(losing patience)* Roy, have you ever seen me wear a baseball cap?

Roy: Sure.

Tamara: No, you haven't! I have never had a baseball cap on my head in all my life.

Roy: You haven't?

Tamara: No! Yet somehow you decided to get me a baseball cap.

Roy: Yeah! Pretty thoughtful, huh?

Tamara: Well … uh … I … Sure. Thanks, you guys.

Spring, Ellen, and Roy: *(exit)*

Narrator: Yes, Christmas was always a big disappointment to Tamara. Then last year she decided things were going to be different.

Tamara: I'm tired of waiting for the true spirit of giving to hit everybody. I'm going to make sure I get good stuff this year—and only good stuff. This is going to be the best Christmas ever!

Scene Four

Narrator: The first step in Tamara's plan was to make a list of what she wanted for Christmas.

Tamara: *(pulls paper from pocket and unrolls long list)* I hope I didn't leave anything out.

Narrator: Are you kidding? That's the longest wish list I've ever … I mean … *(sweetly)* So Tamara made a list and memorized it.

Tamara: *(studying list)* Mutter … mutter … new computer … mutter … mutter … solid-colored sweaters … mutter … mutter … CDs by people who can actually sing … mutter … mutter … tasteful jewelry … mutter … mutter … Okay, then! *(rolls up list and returns to pocket)* Now I just have to drop a few well-placed hints, and I'll be on my way to a really merry Christmas. For once!

Mom: *(enters)* Is your homework all finished, Tamara?

Tamara: Almost. Of course I could work a lot faster if I had a better computer. You know, Mom, computers today are much more efficient than they were back in the day.

Mom: Back in the day?

Tamara: Yeah, you know … like last year when I got my old computer? Computer technology can change a lot in just one year.

Mom: It's amazing how things like that keep improving.

Tamara: Isn't it? And studies show that the advances in computers really help with learning.

Mom: Really?

Tamara: Really! I read it online. Of course, I couldn't take time to read the entire article because it was taking too darn long to download on my old computer. But I'm sure the rest of it was really interesting and educational.

Mom: Hmmmm … you've given me something to think about.

Tamara: I have?

Mom: Definitely! Well … come and set the table when you're finished. *(exits)*

Tamara: Ha! I see a new computer under the tree Christmas morning.

Narrator: So Tamara's plan seemed to be off to a good start.

Tamara: Rats! I forgot to mention how kids with flat-screen monitors score higher on standardized tests.

Narrator: Maybe I should say Tamara's *scheme* was off to a good start.

Tamara: Call it a scheme if you want. Who cares as long as it works?

Scene Five

Narrator: Over the next few days, Tamara worked on the rest of her family and her friends.

Grandpa: *(enters)* I can't believe it's December already.

Tamara: I know what you mean, Grandpa. Time flies.

Grandpa: Why, it seems like just yesterday we were celebrating Christmas.

Tamara: It is so hard to keep track of the time. Especially when you're busy.

Grandpa: I'm retired, you know. So I'm not all that busy really.

Tamara: But I am. It's hard for me to get everything finished on time and get to places on time and make time for my family and friends. I could use something to make my life easier.

Grandpa: *(looking puzzled)* Oh?

Tamara: Sure! Maybe something pretty?

Grandpa: *(still confused)* Pretty, huh?

Tamara: Gold is always pretty, don't you think?

Grandpa: *(brightening)* I sure do. You know, your grandmother is crocheting like wild fire—what with the holidays coming up.

Tamara: *(sighs)* I know, Grandpa. Could you do something about that?

Grandpa: You bet, pumpkin! Now that I know what kind of gift you're looking for. *(exits)*

Tamara: Computer … Watch … That's two things off my list. Now who else needs a hint?

Narrator: Maybe you could use one! I think —

Tamara: Who cares what you think? Oh, there's Roy. I'll talk to him next.

Scene Six

Roy: *(enters)* Hi, Tamara!

Tamara: Hi, Roy. So have you started your Christmas shopping yet?

Roy: No, I'm just thinking right now. You know … it's the thought that counts.

Tamara: Yeah. I've heard that. So, Roy, do you ever think about your gifts *after* you give them?

Roy: What do you mean?

Tamara: Well … like do you notice if the person you give a gift to ever uses that gift?

From Diana R. Jenkins, *All Year Long! Funny Readers Theatre for Life's Special Times.* Westport, CT: Teacher Ideas Press. Copyright © 2007 by Diana R. Jenkins.

Roy: No. I guess I never thought about that. Wait a minute … does this have something to do with the baseball cap I gave you last year? I never see you wear it.

Tamara: And did you ever wonder why I never wear it?

Roy: No, but I'm wondering about it now. *(stands there and thinks awhile)* He-e-ey … I get it! Gee, I'm sorry, Tamara.

Tamara: It's okay, Roy. I know you'll do better this year. Right?

Roy: You bet! Don't you worry about that. You're going to flip over this year's gift.

Tamara: Great! You know … most girls like diamonds.

Roy: Right. Diamonds.

Tamara: And things that come in pairs. *(touches ears)*

Narrator: *(muttering)* Unbelievable!

Roy: Gotcha! Well, see you later.

Tamara: Later! *(exits)*

Scene Seven

Narrator: *(obviously annoyed)* So things were moving along smoothly for Tamara. She figured it would only take a little more manipulation, and her perfect Christmas would be all set.

Dad: *(enters)* I'm sorry about your show, Tamara, but I can't miss the big game.

Tamara: I understand. If only there were some way we could both watch the programs we want.

Dad: Hmmm ... yeah … .*(exits)*

Tamara: Finally I'll get my own TV.

Ellen: *(enters)* Hi!

Tamara: Hey, have you been watching *American Pop Idol Rock Star* on Wednesday nights?

Ellen: No, I haven't seen that program.

Tamara: The singers on that show are so good. I wish I could listen to their music all the time.

Ellen: Oh, really? *(exits)*

Tamara: There! That ought to get me some decent CDs.

Spring: *(enters)* Hi!

Tamara: Oh, hi, Spring. I saved some catalogs for you. Here. *(hands her catalogs)*

Spring: Thanks! I love looking at catalogs.

Tamara: You can keep them. I was going to order some stuff, but then I decided I wouldn't. I'll probably be getting some clothes for Christmas.

Spring: Yeah, probably. Well, thanks!

Tamara: I'm sorry about all those things that I circled already. You know … the clothes that I liked and thought about ordering but then I didn't after all.

Spring: No problem! *(exits)*

Tamara: *(thinks a moment, then looks at audience)* You know … I hear it's going to be a bitter cold winter. Like the kind of cold that freezes your nose and ears and fingers into little popsicles. A person could really use some good protection for a winter like that. Like maybe a cozy new coat with some fashionable accessories like gloves and hats. *(looks at Narrator)*

Narrator: Don't look at me!

Tamara: *(looking at audience again)* And maybe some fur-lined leather boots. In size eight. *(gets out list and checks it over)* Okay then. I think that's everything. *(rolls up list and puts in pocket)* Let the giving begin!

Narrator: You … but … you … I can't … this is … aaaaargh!

Tamara: Whatever.

Scene Eight

Narrator: Tamara was really looking forward to Christmas. Of course! She was getting everything she wanted, wasn't she?

Mom: *(enters with stack of gifts)* Could you put these under the tree, Tamara? And no peeking!

Tamara: *(taking gifts)* Why peek? I can tell none of these are for me.

Mom: What makes you say that?

Tamara: They're all too small.

Mom: Big surprises come in small packages, you know. *(exits)*

Tamara: But computers and televisions don't!

Narrator: She looked through the packages and found several tagged for her. Several *small* packages.

Tamara: This can't be all that I'm getting!

Mom: *(enters with more packages)* Here are the rest of the presents.

Tamara: *(takes packages)* Mom, remember the other day when we talked about computers?

Mom: Sure! I'm so glad you mentioned how important they are for learning. I'm going to start taking some college courses next semester. I thought I'd drop a few hints and see if your father will get me one for Christmas. *(exits)*

Tamara: I hope she's better at giving hints than she is at taking them.

Grandma: *(enters)* I'm almost finished crocheting your gift, Tamara.

Tamara: Crocheting? But I thought you and Grandpa were giving me something gold this year.

Grandma: It's gold, all right. A beautiful, fire hydrant gold! *(exits)*

Tamara: Man! Can't anybody take a hint?

Roy: *(enters, pretends to swing a bat and hit a ball, grins at Tamara, exits)*

Tamara: I don't know what that's supposed to mean, but I don't think it has anything to do with diamond earrings. Sheesh! I guess my hints were too subtle for this bunch.

Narrator: *(sarcastic)* Yeah. Some people have so much trouble understanding the true meaning of Christmas.

Tamara: No kidding! I'm going to have to really hit everybody over the head with the spirit of giving. And I'm going to have to do it soon or this Christmas will be another disaster.

Scene Nine

Narrator: So Tamara came up with a whole new scheme for manipulating her loved ones into fulfilling her selfish desires.

Tamara: I just want to get some decent presents. What's so bad about that? I mean … the people who care about me *want* to give me gifts that I'll like. Because they love me. And I love them. I want them to fulfill *their* desires.

Narrator: Which would be to give you everything you want.

Tamara: Right. Anyway … it's not a scheme. I'm just going to *tell* people what to get me.

Narrator: *(exasperated)* You can't order your loved ones to –

Tamara: I'll start with my friends.

(Spring, Ellen, and Roy enter.)

Tamara: Hi, you guys. Listen … I've decided honesty is the best policy so I'm going to be perfectly honest and tell you that you give lousy Christmas presents but don't worry because we can fix that if you just listen to me.

Spring: We give lousy presents?

Ellen: I thought you liked *Songs of the Lonesome Pickup Truck.*

Tamara: I hate country music, Ellen. Which you would have known if you paid any attention at all when I played my CDs.

Ellen: Sorry. I just thought you'd like something different.

Roy: Does this mean you didn't like the baseball cap either?

Tamara: Sorry, but yes. That was a stupid idea, Roy. *(to Spring)* And the piggies on the sweater? Come on, Spring!

Spring: I'm sorry. I thought it was cute.

Tamara: Well, it wasn't.

Spring: Yeah. I get that.

Tamara: So anyway … I'll make it easy for you. You *(pointing to Spring)* can get me a sweater in a solid color. You *(pointing to Ellen)* can buy me the CD with all the stars from *American Pop Idol Rock Star.* You *(pointing to Roy)* can get me some earrings. Fake diamonds will do.

Roy: But I already got you a fantastic gift!

Tamara: I doubt that, Roy. I really doubt that.

Roy: Yeah. Me, too. *(exits with Spring and Ellen, all looking depressed)*

Tamara: Bye! See you later! Hey, you guys! I said … .well … bye.

Narrator: I think you really hurt their feelings.

From Diana R. Jenkins, *All Year Long! Funny Readers Theatre for Life's Special Times.* Westport, CT: Teacher Ideas Press. Copyright © 2007 by Diana R. Jenkins.

Tamara: Oh, they're okay. They just had to go somewhere in a hurry. I know! They're probably heading for the mall right now.

Narrator: Or maybe they're going home to cross you off their Christmas lists.

Tamara: Of course not! They're my friends, you know.

Narrator: Yeah. Friends.

Scene Ten

Narrator: Next, Tamara tried to straighten out her parents.

Dad: *(enters)* I can't wait for Christmas.

Tamara: Yeah. Right. Could we talk about my Christmas gifts, Dad?

Dad: I'm not telling you anything. My lips are —

Tamara: I want a new computer, Dad.

Dad: But you just got a new computer last year!

Tamara: And it's already out-of-date. I need a new one.

Dad: I was planning to get your mother a computer. She's starting college and –

Tamara: Hey, I know! She can use my old one. It's not like she really knows that much about computers anyway. I'm the person who can really appreciate a new computer. And my own TV? I'd really, really, really appreciate that.

Dad: Oh, really? It doesn't seem to me that you appreciate very much at all!

Tamara: But, Dad —

Dad: We'll talk about this later, young lady. *(exits)*

Tamara: Sheesh! What's he so mad about?

Narrator: I don't know. Maybe he's upset that he has an ungrateful wretch for a daughter?

Tamara: What kind of angel are you? You're not supposed to insult people like that.

Narrator: I … I can do whatever it takes to set you straight. It's … it's my job! And I have to tell you, Tamara … your whole attitude about Christmas is so wrong.

Tamara: Whatever. I have to talk to Grandma before it's too late!

Scene Eleven

Grandma: *(enters)* Could you help me wrap some gifts, Tamara?

Tamara: Sure, Grandma, but first I need to talk to you.

Grandma: Okay, dear.

Tamara: I know you're crocheting something for me, but—

Grandma: Fire hydrant gold—just like you said you wanted.

Tamara: Actually, that was a mistake, Grandma. What I really wanted was a gold watch.

Grandma: Oh. Oh, my.

Tamara: So couldn't you and Grandpa get me a watch for Christmas instead of whatever crocheted thingy you're making?

From Diana R. Jenkins, *All Year Long! Funny Readers Theatre for Life's Special Times.* Westport, CT: Teacher Ideas Press. Copyright © 2007 by Diana R. Jenkins.

Grandma: *(sadly)* I would love to do that. But we're on a fixed income. I just don't think we can afford any gifts that aren't made from yarn. I get it on sale, you know.

Tamara: Oh. That's okay. Really, Grandma.

Grandma: I'm sorry to let you down, sweetie. *(exits)*

Tamara: But … but … .man!

Narrator: What's wrong?

Tamara: I think I've really messed up.

Narrator: Gee. What makes you think that? I mean … all you did was try to manipulate everyone for your own selfish purposes then hurt their feelings and show them that you only care about what you can get out of them all in a vain attempt to teach them about the true meaning of Christmas which would be giving you whatever you want. What's wrong with that?

Tamara: You know, you're really sarcastic for an angel.

Narrator: *(sighs)* I'm sorry, Tamara.

Tamara: I just wanted to get good presents. How did I end up wrecking everything?

Narrator: Well … I think you lost track of what Christmas is really about.

Tamara: It's about giving, isn't it? I didn't get that wrong!

Narrator: It *is* about giving. God gave the world the ultimate gift—His Son. In honor of that gift, people give presents to their family and friends—to show that they care about them. But you stopped thinking about the *giving* and got all wrapped up in the *getting.*

Tamara: Yeah, I guess I did. Everybody must think I've been incredibly selfish.

Narrator: And self-centered.

Tamara: Yeah.

Narrator: And unappreciative.

Tamara: I know.

Narrator: And –

Tamara: Okay, okay! The question is: how do I make things right with everybody?

Narrator: Come on. Do you really need an angel to tell you that?

Tamara: No, I guess not. I … I just hope they can all forgive me. *(exits)*

Scene Twelve

Narrator: So Tamara went and found every single person she'd treated so badly and apologized and told them they didn't need to give her any gifts at all and, if they did, she would appreciate their kindness and … yadda yadda yadda. To her surprise, everyone accepted her apologies.

Tamara: *(entering)* Which I didn't really deserve.

Narrator: Not really.

Tamara: Hey!

Narrator: I mean … wasn't it great that the … uh … blessed rain of forgiveness … uh … rained down upon her?

Tamara: Right.

Narrator: Then Tamara spent the last few days before Christmas thinking about *giving*. The gifts of God—and the gifts she wanted to give to her friends and family. By Christmas Day, she had made or bought something really thoughtful for everyone.

Tamara: I hope they like their gifts. I want them to see how much I care.

Friends and Family: *(enter with gifts and look inside all at once)* Thanks, Tamara. I love it!

Tamara: And I love your gifts, too. *(to Grandma)* You really outdid yourself with that crocheted carpet, Grandma. It's really gold!

Grandma: Thank you, dear.

Tamara: No, thank you. *(to Roy)* And getting me a pair of baseball tickets so I'd have a reason to wear my cap somewhere?

Roy: To the baseball *diamond!*

Tamara: Great idea! *(to everyone)* Thanks, everybody, for thinking of me. I'm so lucky to have you guys in my life.

Friends and Family: *(in unison)* Thanks, Tamara. And Merry Christmas!

Tamara: *(as they exit)* Merry Christmas! *(to Narrator)* This has been the best Christmas ever.

Narrator: That's because you get it now.

Tamara: Yeah. The true spirit of giving!

Narrator: Right. Well, I guess my work here is finished.

Tamara: Thanks … uh … angel … uh … chick. (dude)

Narrator: Just doing my job!

Tamara: *(handing over a gift)* And here! Merry Christmas! *(exits)*

Narrator: A gift for me? Thanks! I wonder what it is … *(opens gift and pulls out a CD) Songs of the Lonesome Yodeler?* Cool! I love yodeling. *(exits yodeling)*

The Babysitter Has Spoken!

Summary

Mick's winter break is ruined because he has to babysit his younger siblings. It's bad enough that he can't do anything with his friends, but his brothers and sisters make things worse by behaving terribly. They act like they hate him! But didn't he hate them first?

Costumes, Sets, and Props

❖ For humor, Mick's siblings can dress like little kids: oversized T-shirts, baseball caps, blacked-out teeth, and so on. Other characters can dress normally. Mick's friends should be dressed for winter activity when they come to visit.

❖ A few chairs and a table can serve as furnishings for Mick's house.

❖ If props are desired, the following can be used: television set, dishes, glasses, silverware, and telephones.

Presentation

Mick's siblings talk and behave like little children.

Mick's parents speak in clipped tones.

Mick becomes more and more frustrated with his siblings as the play goes on, speaking more harshly and coming down harder on them.

Supplemental Reading

Murkoff, Heidi, with Sharon Mazel. *The What to Expect Baby-sitter's Handbook.* New York: Workman, 2003.

Williams-Justesen, Kim. *My Brother the Dog.* Terre Haute, IN: Tanglewood Press, 2006.

Cast of Characters

Narrator	Dad
Mick	Janell
Brandt	Ranger
Shiloh	Martin
Mom	Erica

Winter Break

The Babysitter Has Spoken!

Scene One

Narrator: Mick had all kinds of plans for winter break.

Mick: We can go skating!

Brandt: Yeah!

Shiloh: And you guys can come along when my family goes skiing.

Mick: Great!

Brandt: Oh, and how about a hike on the trails at Shady Cliffs?

Mick: Good idea!

Narrator: *(as friends exit and parents enter)* Yes, Mick had lots of plans for his vacation. *Until* his parents gave him the bad news.

Mom: New job!

Dad: Starting next week!

Mom: No babysitter yet!

Dad: Except you!

Mick: WHAT?

Mom: *(sighs)* We *said* ... New job!

Dad: Starting next—

Mick: I got that part! Are you saying I have to babysit the brats during my winter break?

Mom: Not brats!

Dad: Your siblings!

Mom: Your flesh and blood!

Mick: But I have stuff to do!

Dad: Sorry about that!

Mom: In a bind, you know!

Dad: Counting on you!

Mick: But … but … . *(They exit.)* This stinks! I'm supposed to be on vacation. It isn't fair for me to have to give that up to watch my brothers and sisters. Why did Mom have to get a new job now?

Narrator: Gee. That *is* kind of selfish of her.

Mick: No kidding!

Scene Two

Narrator: *(as Mick's brothers and sisters enter)* Mick's enthusiasm for babysitting was truly underwhelming, but his brothers and sisters were thrilled with the idea.

Janell: You're going to be our babysitter during vacation?

Mick: *(unenthused)* Yes, Janell.

Ranger: Oh, boy!

Martin: For the whole week?

Mick: Yes, Martin.

Ranger: Oh, boy!

Erica: You'll be in charge of us all day long?

Mick: Yes, Erica.

Ranger: Oh, boy!

Mick: Why do you keep saying that, Ranger?

Ranger: Because it's going to be fun!

Mick: Sure. Right. Loads of fun.

Ranger: Oh, boy!

Mick: Stop saying that already!

Scene Three

Narrator: *(as brothers and sisters exit and parents enter)* Mick had babysat for his brothers and sisters before but only for short periods of time. Since this was a long-term job, his parents went over all the rules, made him memorize phone numbers, and lectured him about safety.

Mom: Don't open the door!

Dad: Don't play with matches!

Mom: Don't climb any ladders!

Mick: Come on! I'm not going to … I mean … what was that thing about the matches again? I don't think I get that.

Dad: Funny!

Mick: And I'm supposed to leave the doors open, right?

Mom: Such a joker!

Mick: What makes you think I'm joking? Maybe I'm not responsible enough to babysit during winter break.

From Diana R. Jenkins, *All Year Long! Funny Readers Theatre for Life's Special Times.* Westport, CT: Teacher Ideas Press. Copyright © 2007 by Diana R. Jenkins.

Dad: (scolding) Mick …

Mick: (muttering) It's not right … giving up my break …

Mom: (scolding) Mick …

Mick: (muttering more quietly) I work hard … deserve a vacation …

Dad: Counting on you!

Mom: See you later! (They exit.)

Mick: (muttering) This is so lame … (looks to see if they're gone, then speaks loudly) Yeah! Really lame! And unjust, too! And undemocratic! Yeah. Totally un-American!

Scene Four

Narrator: Mick's first day of babysitting started out with a problem. He had just plopped down in front of the television when his brothers and sisters came in to interrupt.

(Brothers and sisters enter.)

Martin: So what are we going to do, Mick?

Mick: Who cares what you do?

Erica: Hey, should we play a game?

Janell: That's a good idea. We can all play something together.

Ranger: Oh, boy!

Martin: So what game should we play, Mick?

Mick: I don't care. Play whatever you want. Just get out of here so I can watch my show.

Ranger: Aren't you going to play with us?

Mick: No. Why would I do that?

Erica: Because you're the babysitter. And babysitters play games with the kids they babysit.

Janell: Yeah.

Mick: Some babysitters do that—the sorry ones who don't have anything better to do. I have something way better to do. I'm watching television.

Ranger: We'll watch with you.

Mick: No, you won't! You guys go play your game.

Erica: You can't stop us from watching television, you know.

Mick: Oh, really? Don't babysitters tell kids when they can and cannot watch TV?

Erica: Uh … yeah, I guess they do.

Mick: Well, then. I'm saying you guys can't watch TV right now. Go find something else to do. The babysitter has spoken!

Ranger: (as brothers and sisters exit) He'll play with us later.

Mick: (calling after them) Don't count on it!

Scene Five

Narrator: Mick watched television until it was almost time to make lunch.

Mick: This is going to be the most boring vacation ever!

Narrator: Just as he clicked off the television, the doorbell rang and his brothers and sisters came running like a herd of wild animals.

Brothers and sisters: *(entering)* I'll get it! No, I'll get it! Who is it? *(etc.)*

Mick: Stop! Nobody open that door!

Martin: But what if it's the mailman?

Erica: Or Santa Claus?

Ranger: Santa Claus? Oh, boy! I'll get it!

Mick: No, you won't! What if it's a burglar? Or … or a rampaging gorilla escaped from the zoo? Or an evil alien from another planet?

(Knock on door makes them all jump.)

Janell: At least it's not one of those blobby aliens without real body parts. I hate those things.

Ranger: Me, too!

Mick: Brother! Let me look through the peephole and see who it is.

Erica: Is it something alien?

Mick: Kind of. Let me open the door.

Brothers and sisters: *(running offstage)* AAAAAAAAAAAA!

Scene Six

Narrator: Of course, Mick knew better than to open the door to alien invaders or anybody else for that matter. But he was allowed to let his friends in.

Brandt: *(entering)* What took you so long?

Shiloh: *(entering)* And what was all that screaming about?

Mick: My stupid brothers and sisters think you're from another planet. So what are you doing?

Brandt: We're going sledding in the park.

Shiloh: Too bad you can't come.

Mick: Tell me about it. Being a big brother is a big pain! I mean … it hasn't just ruined my vacation, you know. It's ruined my life!

Shiloh: I wish I had some brothers and sisters. It's boring being the only child.

Mick: Are you kidding? I would *love* to be the only child again! Then for once—

Brandt: *(looking offstage)* Oh, hi, Ranger!

Ranger: *(enters)* Hi.

Mick: What do you want?

Ranger: *(softly)* Nothing. *(exits)*

Shiloh: I think he heard you, Mick.

Brandt: Yeah, he acted kind of strange.

Mick: How could you tell? *(laughs)*

Shiloh: Well, we'd better get going. See you later.

Brandt: Yeah. Later. *(They exit.)*

Mick: Now I have to make lunch. Working during vacation! What a lousy deal! *(exits)*

Scene Seven

Narrator: So Mick worked his fingers to the bone making peanut butter sandwiches and soup for his brothers and sisters.

Mick: *(yelling)* Everybody get in here and eat your lunch!

(Brothers and sisters enter, looking downcast, and sit.)

Mick: Go ahead and eat. *(waits)* I said: eat! *(waits)* Why aren't you eating?

Erica: I want my sandwich cut in half.

Mick: Just eat it, Erica.

Erica: But I'm hungry! One piece of food isn't enough.

Mick: Give me a break! It's the same amount of food whether it's cut or not. Just eat it like that!

Martin: I'm really hungry. Cut my sandwich in four pieces, Mick.

Mick: I'm not cutting your sandwiches! Eat them like they are!

Erika: Okay, but I'm still going to be hungry.

Mick: Whatever.

Ranger: I don't like peanut butter.

Mick: What are you talking about? It's your favorite food!

Ranger: No, it's not.

Mick: Since when?

Ranger: Since right now.

Mick: Well, I'm not making you something else. So eat that or go hungry.

Janell: This soup is cold.

Mick: That's because you guys keep talking. Just eat!

Janell: You can't make us eat.

Mick: Yes, I can. I'm the babysitter and what I say goes and I say EAT!

Narrator: The kids nibbled at their sandwiches and sipped a little of their soup.

Martin: This sandwich tastes funny.

Erica: There's something in my soup. I think it's a worm.

Mick: It's chicken noodle soup, Erica. That's a noodle.

Ranger: I don't like—

Mick: Everybody shut up and eat! I don't want to hear another word! Just eat and go play when you're finished!

From Diana R. Jenkins, *All Year Long! Funny Readers Theatre for Life's Special Times.* Westport, CT: Teacher Ideas Press. Copyright © 2007 by Diana R. Jenkins.

Narrator: Mick's brothers and sisters ate only a little of their lunch, then left the table.

Mick: After all my hard work? Sheesh! I give up my vacation and this is the appreciation I get.

Narrator: *(muttering)* What a sorry attitude!

Mick: Really! And if their attitudes don't improve, I'm going to have to take action!

Scene Eight

Narrator: *(as Mom enters and dials phone)* After lunch, Mick's mom called to check on things.

Mom: Brrring! Brrring!

Mick: *(answering phone)* Hello?

Mom: Hi, Mick!

Mick: Oh, hi, Mom.

Mom: How's it going?

Mick: Terrible! All they do is pester me.

Mom: *(scolding)* Mick …

Mick: It's true!

Mom: Teeth brushed?

Mick: I don't know.

Mom: Hair combed?

Mick: I don't know.

Mom: Chores done?

Mick: I don't know!

Mom: Books read?

Mick: I don't know if they did their reading or not! I don't know if they did anything! See? I told you I shouldn't babysit.

Mom: Mick …

Mick: Okay, okay! I'll get on it.

Mom: Good! Bye! *(exits)*

Mick: Bye. *(hangs up)* Rats! I hope they did all the stuff they're supposed to do.

Narrator: But Mick soon found out that his brothers and sisters had done none of those things—and they didn't *want* to do any of them!

Scene Nine

Mick: Everybody come here! *(waits)* Hey! Everybody get in here! *(waits)* I SAID EVERYBODY COME HERE RIGHT NOW! *(waits)* GET IN HERE RIGHT THIS MINUTE OR YOU'RE IN BIG TROUBLE!

(Brothers and sisters stroll in.)

Mick: It's about time. Now! Have you brushed your teeth today?

Janell: Maybe.

Martin: Could be.

Erica: It's possible.

Ranger: I'm not telling.

Mick: Did you brush your teeth or not?

Janell: Maybe.

Martin: Could be.

Erica: It's possible.

Ranger: I'm not telling.

Mick: Quit goofing around! Go brush your teeth right now. And comb your hair, too.

Janell: You can't make us brush our teeth.

Mick: Yes, I can! I'm the boss here.

Martin: You're not the boss of us.

Mick: I am, too! I'm the babysitter, and you have to do what I say.

Erica: We don't have to do everything you say.

Mick: Yes, you do.

Erica: No, we don't. What if you told us to jump off a bridge? We wouldn't have to do that.

Mick: *(yelling)* I'm not telling you to jump off a stupid bridge! I'm telling you to brush your stupid teeth so they don't rot in your stupid heads and fall out of your stupid mouths!

Ranger: You don't have to yell at us.

Mick: *(yelling)* I'm not yelling!

Janell: *(to others)* Sounds like yelling to me.

Others: Yeah. Really! I'm with you.

Mick: *(yelling)* Just go do what I told you! *(takes a deep breath and speaks more quietly)* I mean … go do what I said. NOW!

Brothers and Sisters: *(exit muttering)*

Mick: Man! Why can't they just cooperate?

Scene Ten

Narrator: Things didn't get any better as the day went on. To get his brothers and sisters to make their beds, Mick had to stand over each one and yell.

Mick: *(looking offstage)* Smooth out that sheet! No, not like that! Do it right! Now pull up the spread! Not that far! Now take the pillow and put it in the middle! The middle! You know where the middle is!

Narrator: He went through that four times. Then he tried to make everyone do the twenty minutes of daily reading his parents required.

Mick: (looking offstage) Open your book. Open it! NOW! And read. You can't read if you're not looking at the page! You're not really reading! I can tell you're faking! READ!

Narrator: Mick had never had so much trouble with his brothers and sisters.

Mick: (looking offstage) Pick up your toys! Hang up your clothes! Pick up your toys! Hang up your clothes! Pick up your toys! Hang up your clothes! Pick up your toys! Hang up your clothes! What's the matter with you people? PICK UP YOUR TOYS! HANG UP YOUR CLOTHES! (collapses in a chair) I hate this! Hate, hate, hate it! I cannot take a whole week of this torture!

Scene Eleven

Narrator: By the time his parents got home, Mick was frustrated out of his mind.

Mick: They can't make me do this anymore. They can't! Those little brats are driving me crazy!

Mom: (entering) Hello!

Dad: (entering) Hello!

Mick: Listen, you guys—

Brothers and Sisters: (running past Mick to parents) Mom! Dad! We love you! Help! (etc.)

Mom: One at a time!

Janell: Mick gave us cold soup.

Erica: With worms in it.

Martin: He told us we could starve.

Janell: And he yelled at us all the time.

Erica: All the time!

Martin: He wants our teeth to rot out.

Janell: He said we should jump off a bridge.

Mick: That's a bunch of lies!

Dad: I should hope so.

Martin: He was a terrible babysitter. Terrible!

Mick: They're the ones who were terrible. They wouldn't do anything I told them to do.

Mom: Teeth brushed?

Brothers and Sisters: Yes!

Mick: Yeah, but—

Dad: Chores done?

Brother and Sisters: Yes!

Mick: But I had to—

Mom: Books read?

Brothers and Sisters: Yes!

Mick: But they fought me the whole way! All day long! They were the biggest brats in the whole world!

From Diana R. Jenkins, *All Year Long! Funny Readers Theatre for Life's Special Times.* Westport, CT: Teacher Ideas Press. Copyright © 2007 by Diana R. Jenkins.

Janell: See? That's how he yelled at us all day.

Mick: I had to yell! You guys wouldn't listen if I didn't yell.

Martin: Oh, yeah? Well—

Mom: Wait a minute. Do you have anything to say, Ranger?

Ranger: Yes. *(to Mick)* Please don't hate us anymore. Please.

Scene Twelve

Narrator: For a moment, there was a terrible silence. Then everyone looked at Mick.

Mick: I … I don't hate you.

Janell: Yes, you do.

Erica: You said we ruined your vacation.

Martin: And your life.

Mom: Mick!

Janell: You said you wanted to be an only child.

Ranger: I heard you tell your friends.

Dad: Mick!

Janell: And since you hate us, we decided to hate you.

Martin: Yeah!

Erica: But it's hard to do.

Janell: Really! I'm tired of hating you.

Martin: Me, too. This has been the worst day ever!

Ranger: So can you stop hating us now?

Erica: Please!

Narrator: Mick had never felt so low in all of his life. He was a terrible brother! And a lousy babysitter! And a scumball worm who didn't deserve the love and admiration of his family! And a—

Mick: All right already! *(turning to family)* I'm sorry, you guys. I was mad because I couldn't do anything with my friends and I said a lot of stuff I shouldn't have said. I didn't mean it. I don't hate you, okay?

Ranger: Really?

Mick: Really. And the rest of this week we're going to have a good time, okay?

Brothers and Sisters: Yay! Great! *(etc.)*

Narrator: *(as everyone except Mick exits)* Did you really meant that?

Mick: Yes!

Narrator: I don't know if I believe you. You were pretty mean to them.

Mick: *(embarrassed)* I know. I shouldn't have acted like that. But things are going to change now.

Narrator: Oh, really?

Mick: Really! *(starts to exit and turns back)* The babysitter has spoken! *(exits, followed by Narrator)*

From Diana R. Jenkins, *All Year Long! Funny Readers Theatre for Life's Special Times.* Westport, CT: Teacher Ideas Press. Copyright © 2007 by Diana R. Jenkins.

It. Was. January.

Summary

Aimee has a bad case of the January blahs. When her service club decides to make New Year's resolutions, Aimee reluctantly resolves to be helpful. After all, she's in a service club—she has to help somebody sometime anyway. Then she discovers being helpful does something for her. Too bad the people she's helping don't like what her assistance does for them!

Costumes, Sets, and Props

❖ All characters can wear contemporary clothing.

❖ A few tables and chairs can serve as the meeting room, art room, and cafeteria.

❖ Mr. Stiller needs a candy bar and a bag of chips. Other props can be mimed. If desired, the following props can be used: school supplies and books, paper and pencil for the fundraising list, and trays and food for the cafeteria scene.

Presentation

When Aimee is overcome with the blahs, she speaks in a slow, dreary voice.

Shanika is angry and crabby in the first scene. In Scene Two, she is annoyingly cheerful. She gradually loses her cheerful attitude until she is downright hostile at the end of the play.

Supplemental Reading

Rau, Dana Meachen. *New Year's Day.* New York: Children's Press, 2000.

Wandberg, Robert. *Making Tough Decisions.* Mankato, MN: Capstone Press, 2001.

Youngs, Bettie B., and Jennifer Leigh Youngs. *A Taste-Berry Teen's Guide to Setting and Achieving Goals.* Deerfield Beach, FL: Health Communications, 2002.

Cast of Characters

Aimee	Lynn
Shanika	Randall
Burke	Extra students
Mr. Stiller	Mrs. Moreau
Georgia	

New Year's Day

It. Was. January.

Scene One

Aimee: *(in dreary voice)* January … It was January … The most boring month of the year. You know what I mean. You drag yourself back to school after vacation, feeling blah. You think about the long, long, *long* stretch of time between now and the end of the year. You ask yourself, "Will it never end?" You—

Shanika: *(enters)* I think they get the idea, Aimee. Tell them what happened. You know … explain how you went crazy last January and ruined all our lives.

Aimee: *(in normal voice)* It wasn't that bad!

Burke: *(enters)* Get real! You made everybody miserable over those stupid resolutions.

Aimee: Look, it was all Shanika's idea.

Shanika: But you're the one who turned it into a freak show.

Aimee: How about we let the audience judge that?

Shanika: Fine by me.

Burke: Get on with it already.

Aimee: *(to audience)* So anyway … it was January. I mean … *(resuming dreary voice)* It. Was. January. And this is what happened:

Scene Two

(Mr. Stiller, Georgia, Lynn, Randall, and extra students enter.)

Shanika: *(now very cheery)* Hi, Mr. Stiller!

Mr. Stiller: Hi, Shanika. And everybody else, too. This is a great turnout. I'm glad to see so many new faces here. You're going to enjoy Helping Hearts and Hands. It's such a great service club—and a good place to make friends. And, hey, welcome back to those of you who are returning. I think that … Are you okay, Aimee?

Aimee: It's. January.

Mr. Stiller: *(puzzled)* Uh-huh … Well, it's a whole new year, kids—a time for new ideas and fresh beginnings. Any ideas about what we should do for our first project of the new year?

Georgia: We could visit the nursing home.

Lynn: We could collect food for the food bank.

Aimee: We could take a nap until February.

Randall: Man! What is your problem?

Shanika: She just has the after-vacation, wintertime blahs. *(to Aimee)* Look on the bright side, Aimee. In just a few months, winter will be over and it will be spring again!

Aimee: Really? Hey, does that happen every year?

Georgia: Funny.

Burke: I guess everybody feels kind of blah at this time of year.

Shanika: I don't! I like it when the New Year starts. It's like Mr. Stiller said. You can get a fresh start on everything. He-e-ey, I know what our first project should be!

Lynn: What?

Shanika: Let's all make New Year's resolutions! You know … to improve ourselves. We could make resolutions to live healthier. Or to be kind. Or whatever. We'll become better people—and that will help *us* help *others*.

Burke: That's not a bad idea, Shanika.

Mr. Stiller: I agree.

Lynn: Let's do it!

Everyone (except Aimee): Yeah! Good idea! *(etc.)*

Aimee: *(after everyone gets quiet)* Yippee.

Randall: Come on, Aimee.

Shanika: Give it a try.

Aimee: Oh, all right. I guess it can't make things any worse than they are. *(to audience)* Unfortunately, I was so wrong about that!

Scene Three

Aimee: *(to audience as others exit)* So after a long and boring discussion, everybody decided we should all go home and think hard. Like that was going to happen. It. Was. January. Anyway, we were supposed to come up with one resolution and share it at the next meeting. It all sounded like way too much work to me.

Shanika: *(enters with Burke and Randall)* I can't decide whether to make a resolution to be kind or a resolution to be friendly or a resolution to be generous or a resolution to be something else.

Burke: I need to study more. And get more exercise.

Randall: Me, too. I … oh, hi, Aimee!

Aimee: Hi.

Shanika: What's your resolution going to be?

Aimee: Don't know.

Randall: Have you been thinking about it?

Aimee: Sure. Every waking moment.

Shanika: It's hard to decide, isn't it? I can't decide whether to make a resolution to be kind or a resolution to be friendly or a resolution to—

Aimee: Yeah, yeah. I heard you before. Maybe you should make a resolution to talk less.

Burke: Aimee!

Aimee: Sorry, Shanika. Maybe my resolution should be to have a better attitude.

Randall: That's a really good idea.

Shanika: *(through gritted teeth)* Isn't it though? I mean … *(now cheerful)* Isn't that a good idea?

Aimee: Yeah, but it sounds kind of hard. Maybe I'll do something else.

Shanika: Like what?

Aimee: I don't know.

Randall: You said you'd do this, Aimee. Quit moping around and … and think of something!

Aimee: *(excited)* Give me some time! You know, thinking takes energy! Energy I don't have!

Burke: You seem pretty energetic right now.

Aimee: Well … I … it's just … *(back to dreary)* I am so tired. Just exhausted.

Randall: Brother!

Shanika: Aimee … .

Aimee: Don't worry. I'll have a resolution by our next meeting.

Shanika: Great! *(exits with Randall)*

Burke: *(snorts)* Sure you will. *(exits)*

Aimee: *(calling after him)* Hey, I resent your lack of faith in me, Burke! *(dreary)* Or at least I would resent it if I only had the strength. *(to audience)* So I tried with everything I had to think of a good New Year's resolution. But when meeting day came, I still didn't have an idea.

Scene Four

(Mr. Stiller, Shanika, Randall, Georgia, Burke, Lynn, and other club members enter.)

Mr. Stiller: Okay, everybody! Let's talk New Year's resolutions! I'll start. My resolution is to cut the fat out of my diet.

Georgia: That's a good one, Mr. Stiller.

Mr. Stiller: My wife thinks so, too. Now, who's next?

Shanika: *(waving hand)* I have one! I've resolved to be more cheerful.

Aimee: Oh, no! Please no!

Lynn: What's the matter, Aimee?

Aimee: I … uh … have a headache. A bad headache. And I think it's going to be getting worse.

Shanika: That's too bad. But just think! You'll feel so good when the headache goes away.

Aimee: Right. *(muttering)* Like on graduation day.

Burke: My resolution is to be a more thoughtful person.

Aimee: That's going to be hard to do.

Burke: *(angry)* What's that supposed to mean?

Shanika: Don't get upset, Burke. Aimee might have meant that you're already so thoughtful it will be hard for you to improve.

Burke: *(to Aimee)* Is that true?

Aimee: Sure. *(to audience)* It's true that I might have meant that. Anyway … everybody went on and on about their resolutions. Finally, I was the only person left.

Mr. Stiller: Aimee? What about you?

Burke: She doesn't have one!

Aimee: I do, too!

Lynn: So out with it!

Georgia: Come on.

Extra students: Yeah! Come on! *(etc.)*

Aimee: Okay, okay! I was … um … thinking … and … I got it! I mean … since this is the *Helping* Hearts and Hands Club, I've resolved to be helpful!

Shanika: Wow! That's a great resolution, Aimee.

Aimee: Thanks.

Burke: Hope it didn't wear you out, thinking of that one!

Everyone: *(laughs)*

Aimee: Real funny, Burke. *(to audience)* Actually it was a simple idea. I mean … it was a service club! I'd have to help somebody sometime. And once I did, I figured I could say I'd kept my resolution. And it wouldn't take any extra effort on my part.

Mr. Stiller: Okay then. Good job, everybody. Now we need to start thinking seriously about fundraising. Our bank account is really low and we need money for our service projects.

Aimee: I have an idea, Mr. Stiller.

Mr. Stiller: Yes?

Aimee: Since Burke's resolution is to be *thoughtful*, maybe he could *think* of some fundraising ideas and make a list and present it at our next meeting.

Burke: That's not what being thoughtful means!

Aimee: Oh. Sorry. I'm just trying to be helpful. That's my resolution, you know.

Mr. Stiller: Aimee has a good idea there, Burke. You've been in a lot of organizations. I bet you could come up with some good fundraising ideas.

Burke: I'm kind of busy right now, but I guess I could do it.

Mr. Stiller: Thanks!

Burke: Hey, maybe Aimee should *help* me since she's resolved to be so *helpful*.

Mr. Stiller: What do you say, Aimee?

Aimee: *(glaring at Burke)* I say somebody's a big … um … Gee, Burke really is thinking, isn't he?

Burke: So you'll help? Great!

Shanika: Wow! This resolution thing is really working out. See, Aimee?

Aimee: *(moans)* Is it spring yet?

Scene Five

Aimee: *(as others, except Burke, exit)* The next day, Burke wanted us to meet during study hall to make the list of fundraising projects. *(to Burke)* But I have to study.

Burke: Really? You were planning to skip your usual nap?

Aimee: Look, it's January. We should all be hibernating.

Burke: I thought you wanted to be helpful.

Aimee: Well, I thought you wanted to be thoughtful. A thoughtful person wouldn't set somebody up to do work they don't want to do when they … uh … oh, never mind! Do you have anything written down yet?

Burke: Yep! Here's what I have so far: "Fundraising Ideas."

Aimee: *(after a pause)* Sounds good to me!

Burke: Look, Aimee … .

Aimee: Okay, okay! *(to audience)* So we made a list—a pretty good list. And when we finished, I realized something. *(to Burke)* He-e-ey … I don't feel so blah anymore.

Burke: Maybe that's because you forgot about yourself for one little moment and left your self-centered attitude behind.

Aimee: No-o-o, that's not it. I think it's because I was busy helping somebody. Yeah … that's it! I hate to say it, but maybe Shanika had a good idea.

Burke: See?

Aimee: Helping people really gives you a lift, doesn't it? I mean … *(blahs returning)* it just … I feel … January … It's January … .

Burke: There's the bell. Later! *(exits)*

Aimee: I. Hate. January.

Scene Six

Aimee: *(to audience)* As I dragged myself to art class, I thought about what had just happened. For one brief shining moment, I had left January behind. For a while there, I felt so … so … April! If I helped someone else, could I get that feeling back again?

(Mrs. Moreau, Georgia, Randall, Lynn, and extra students enter.)

Mrs. Moreau: All right, everyone! We'll be working on our sculptures this period. Please gather your supplies and get right to work.

(Everyone mimes working on art projects.)

Aimee: *(sitting next to Georgia and Lynn and extra students)* Hi.

Georgia and others: Hi.

Lynn: Hi, Aimee. Georgia was just about to tell us something juicy about Randall.

Georgia: Yeah. This is so good! See, Jenna told Franco who told Sammy that—

Aimee: Wait a minute. Didn't you make a resolution to stop gossiping?

Georgia: Well … yeah …

Aimee: Then you shouldn't be telling this story.

Georgia: Hey, who put you in charge?

Aimee: I'm just trying to be helpful.

Georgia: But this is something really, really good.

Aimee: It's gossip—and you said you weren't going to gossip anymore.

Lynn: Couldn't she start that after she tells us the juicy stuff about Randall?

Aimee: No. It would still be gossiping. She can't do that.

Georgia: But … but … *(sighs)* She's right, you guys.

Extra Students: *(moving away)* Man! Rats! *(etc.)*

Lynn: *(moving away)* Gee, thanks, Aimee.

Georgia: Yeah, thanks a lot! *(moving away)*

Aimee: Oh, you're welcome. I'm glad to help. *(to audience)* I really was glad! Helping somebody had worked again. My blahs were gone!

Scene Seven

Randall: *(as he approaches Aimee)* Hey, what were you guys talking about?

Aimee: Well, we were almost talking about you.

Randall: Huh?

Aimee: Georgia was going to tell everybody some gossip about you, but I reminded her about her resolution to stop gossiping so she didn't do it.

Randall: Man! That is unbelievable!

Aimee: Oh, you don't have to thank me or anything, Randall. I made that resolution to be helpful, and I'm going to stick to it. I've realized that—

Randall: I'm so sick of that stupid Georgia! She's always running her mouth about stuff that isn't her business! I'm going to give her a piece of my mind!

Aimee: *(to audience)* Here was somebody else who obviously needed my help. *(to Randall)* Don't forget your resolution, Randall. You said you were going to control your temper.

Randall: So?

Aimee: Telling Georgia off is not controlling your temper.

Randall: Yeah, but—

Aimee: You did mean it when you made that resolution, didn't you?

Randall: Of course! But I … oh, just leave me alone, Aimee!

Aimee: I'm trying to help you, Randall. See, my resolution really means something to me.

Randall: Since when?

Aimee: Since I recognized the real power of helpfulness. I have the feeling my resolution could completely turn my life around.

Randall: Give me a break! And get away from me!

Aimee: Uh, uh, uh … temper, temper.

Randall: *(sputtering)* Rfml … sezzum … gimee … frizzick … Oh, whatever! *(moving away)*

Mrs. Moreau: *(looking toward others)* My! Everyone seems to be in a bad mood today.

Aimee: I'm not! I'm feeling really great.

Mrs. Moreau: Really? But it's … it's … *(mocking Aimee's usual dreary tone)* It's. January.

Aimee: I know, but … I mean … *(dreariness returning)* Just because … You're right. It's. January.

Mrs. Moreau: There! That's the Aimee I know and love. *(exits along with others)*

Aimee: *(to audience)* The blahs were back. They fell over me like a really heavy … something … that was weighing down on me like … really hard. I felt even worse than before. I had to help somebody and get my April feeling back … If only I could summon up the energy …

Scene Eight

(Aimee's friends and extra students enter and mime eating lunch.)

Aimee: I went to the cafeteria, got my tray, and planted myself next to my friends. Luckily, my help was soon required.

Lynn: *(to Burke)* Hey, you have two slices of pizza!

Burke: So? I'm starving to death!

Lynn: But you took the last slice! I was right behind you and I got stuck with Tuna Fluff.

Randall: I hate to say this, but that can't be tuna. And the fluff? Who knows?

Lynn: Whatever. I'm not going to eat it. The point is that Burke hogged too much pizza.

Burke: I didn't know that was all they had!

Aimee: I bet you didn't even think about that, did you?

Burke: Of course not!

Aimee: That was not thoughtful. Not thoughtful at all. And you made this big resolution to be more thoughtful! But you did something so not thoughtful. Not thoughtful at all. Now I'm just trying to be helpful, you know, and I think—

Burke: Okay! Okay! I'll give her some of my pizza. Just leave me alone!

Lynn: Thanks, Aimee!

Aimee: Don't eat that, Lynn!

Lynn: Why not?

From Diana R. Jenkins, *All Year Long! Funny Readers Theatre for Life's Special Times.* Westport, CT: Teacher Ideas Press. Copyright © 2007 by Diana R. Jenkins.

Aimee: I know you love pizza, but didn't you resolve to eat vegetarian?

Lynn: Yeah, but –

Aimee: Because you didn't want any animals to die to feed you?

Lynn: Yeah but –

Aimee: Then you can't eat that pizza.

Lynn: I'll just pick the pepperoni off!

Aimee: *(shaking head sadly)* You know that's not going to make things right. Those little pepperonis gave up their lives for this pizza. Picking them off won't bring them back, will it?

Lynn: Pepperoni aren't like … They're meat, but I … You don't slaughter them … I don't think … Oh, keep your stupid pizza, Burke. I've lost my appetite!

Burke: Gee, I wonder why.

Aimee: I have a great appetite! In fact, I feel fantastic! I can't wait to help somebody else!

Others except Shanika: *(exiting)* Gotta go! I'm finished here! Bye! *(etc.)*

Shanika: You know, Aimee … it's great how you're being so helpful … but … it's just …

Aimee: I can help you, too! You know how you made that resolution to be more cheerful?

Shanika: Ye-e-es.

Aimee: Well, you're not. Cheerful, I mean. That look on your face is so not cheerful. And your tone of voice … not cheerful! You're forgetting your resolution.

Shanika: Yeah, I guess I am. Well, I'll work on that. See you later. *(starts to exit)*

Aimee: *(scolding)* Shanika …

Shanika: *(forcing cheerfulness)* See you later, Aimee! *(exits)*

Scene Nine

Aimee: The afternoon went just as well as the morning had! Any time I felt that old January feeling coming upon me, I found somebody to help. I stopped Georgia from gossiping at least five more times. And every time I saw Burke I made sure he was being thoughtful. I kept an eye on Randall's temper. *(Mr. Stiller walks in eating a candy bar, but exits quickly when he sees Aimee.)* I even stopped Mr. Stiller from buying a candy bar out of the vending machine. He really appreciated that! Oh … and I kept encouraging Shanika to work on her attitude.

Shanika: *(enters, looking glum, tries to leave before Aimee sees her)*

Aimee: Hey, Shanika!

Shanika: What?

Aimee: That didn't sound very cheerful.

Shanika: So? *(exits)*

Aimee: By the end of the day, I began to notice something. The helping didn't … well … stick! It didn't stick for other people—or for me! Everybody kept doing the same things so I had to help them again and again. And the helping made me feel better for a moment, but pretty soon the blahs would be back! I was really feeling them when I went to my locker after school.

Burke: *(enters and sees Aimee)* Uh-oh! *(tries to escape)*

Aimee: Wait, Burke! Wait!

Burke: I have to go.

Aimee: You only live two blocks away. Can't you stay a minute and help me?

Burke: Gee, I would, Aimee, but you're the one with the resolution to be helpful, not me.

Aimee: You're supposed to be thoughtful. So use your brain and think for a minute.

Burke: That's not really what being thoughtful means.

Aimee: I know! Come on, Burke. I have a problem.

Burke: *(sighs)* Okay. What is it?

Aimee: *(to audience)* So I explained how I'd been helping others as a way to get rid of my January blahs. To my surprise, Burke got mad!

Burke: You're driving us all nuts just to make yourself feel better? Man! You are unbelievable!

Aimee: Hey, I was trying to be helpful! And what do you mean—driving you nuts?

Burke: You're always getting on somebody's case! It's incredibly annoying, Aimee. Nobody can stand to be around you. We can't handle any more of your help! *(starts to exit but turns back)* And by the way … maybe you'd get rid of the blahs for real if you stopped thinking about yourself and started actually caring about other people. *(exits)*

Aimee: *(calling after him)* Hey, watch that temper! *(to self)* Wait. That's Randall's resolution. *(to audience)* I tried to tell myself that Burke had it all wrong. But then I saw Georgia and Lynn, and I got the impression they were trying to avoid me.

(Georgia and Lynn enter and pull up short when they see Aimee.)

Lynn: *(to Georgia)* She's still here.

Georgia: *(to Lynn)* Do you really need your books?

Lynn: *(to Georgia)* I have homework in three subjects. How am I—

Aimee: Hi, you guys!

Georgia: Run! *(exits)*

Lynn: I'm right behind you! *(exits)*

Aimee: See what I mean? That really got me to thinking. Maybe you can help people too much. Like more than they want. And more than they need. I mean … a resolution is a way to improve yourself, right? If someone else is always helping you, then you're not improving yourself by yourself which would mean you're not really improving at all.

(Mr. Stiller enters with a bag of chips and dashes back out when Aimee looks at him.)

Aimee: *(to audience)* And is it really helping when you're just doing something for yourself? Like … isn't helping other people supposed to be about … well … other people? *(sighs)* I realized Burke was right. I had messed up! Which made me feel like it was January in the Antarctic and I was stuck in an igloo all alone in

From Diana R. Jenkins, *All Year Long! Funny Readers Theatre for Life's Special Times.* Westport, CT: Teacher Ideas Press. Copyright © 2007 by Diana R. Jenkins.

a never-ending blizzard that. … Well, I felt terrible. Worse than I had ever felt in my life!

Scene Ten

Aimee: I dragged through the next day, not talking to anyone. Which wasn't that hard since everybody avoided me. Being a social outcast, I had plenty of time to think. And I came up with an idea that I hoped would make everything right. I put my plan into action at our club meeting.

(Mr. Stiller, Shanika, Burke, Georgia, Lynn, Randall, and extra students enter.)

Mr. Stiller: Okay! Let's hear the fundraising ideas from Burke and Aimee.

Aimee: Excuse me, Mr. Stiller. There's something I need to say first.

Mr. Stiller: They were fat-free chips! I swear!

Aimee: Okay. But I need to say something about the resolutions.

Everybody: *(moans)*

Shanika: Look, Aimee. We don't want to hear it, okay? Just leave us alone, will you? Please! We can't take it anymore!

Aimee: But, Shanika … .

Shanika: And do *not* tell me to be cheerful or I am going to take you down, girl!

Aimee: Wow. Things have really gone too far. I'm so sorry about that. I didn't mean to push you guys so much. I thought I was being helpful … well … that's what I told myself. But I guess my resolution was really all about me. I'm sorry, you guys.

Mr. Stiller: That was really nice of you, Aimee. And I'd like to say that I accept your apology.

Randall: Yeah. Me, too. You were right about my temper. I just didn't like how you kept going on and on about it.

Aimee: Sorry.

Georgia: Actually you were right about all of us.

Lynn: Yeah.

Shanika: She wasn't right about me. I *am* cheerful. Cheerful is like my middle name. You can't get more cheerful than me.

Aimee: That is so true, Shanika.

Shanika: You'd better believe it. Cheerful as the day is long. That's me.

Aimee: So I'm really sorry, you guys. And I've decided to change.

Burke: You mean … you're making a new resolution?

Aimee: No, I'm going to keep the old one. But this time I'm going to do things that are really helpful. Like I'm thinking I could take charge of whatever fundraiser we decide to do.

Mr. Stiller: Thanks, Aimee. *(exits along with everybody else except Shanika and Burke)*

Aimee: *(to audience)* So that's what happened. I made mistakes, but I learned my lesson. I started helping people for real, and I got over my blahs like Burke said. And whatever you may have heard, I *didn't* ruin everybody's lives. *(to Burke)* Did I?

Burke: Naw, I guess not. It was crazy for a while there, but everything went back to normal.

Aimee: Thanks for saying that! That was really thoughtful.

Burke: Glad to help! *(They exit, laughing.)*

Shanika: *(glowers at audience a moment then starts to exit, muttering)* Cheerful as a daisy, that's me. *(whirls back and glowers a while longer, then exits, muttering)* I bring sunshine, that's what I do. Don't say I'm not cheerful …

Snow Daze

Summary

Storm convinces his friends that they don't need to study for a big science test because there's going to be a snow day tomorrow. He should know since his dad is a weather forecaster. The friends have a great time goofing off on their snow day—and on the snow days that follow. But no one can predict the weather all the time. Will Storm get the blame when his dad messes up his forecast?

Costumes, Sets, and Props

❖ All characters can wear contemporary clothing. Dad should dress in a jacket and tie. The boys can wear coats and other winter clothes, if desired, for the scenes outdoors, although just a hat or scarf might suffice.

❖ A couple of chairs or a bench can serve as Storm's bed. A few desks and chairs can be used as the classroom.

❖ If props are desired, the boys can use pretend snowballs in the outdoor scenes and school items such as books, paper, pencils, and so on could be used in the school scene.

Presentation

Storm's dad gives his forecast in a deep, announcer-style voice. He speaks normally at other times. Other characters try to imitate his tone when reporting on his forecasts.

Eddie is dense but generally enthusiastic and pleasant.

Supplemental Reading

Allaby, Michael. *Dorling Kindersley Guide to the Weather.* New York: Dorling Kindersley, 2000.

Berger, Melvin, and Gilda Berger. *Hurricanes Have Eyes but Can't See and Other Amazing Facts about Wild Weather.* New York: Scholastic, 2003.

Brotak, Ed. *Wild about Weather: 50 Wet, Windy, and Wonderful Activities.* New York: Lark Books, 2004.

Carson, Mary Kay. *Weather Projects for Young Scientists: Experiments and Science Fair Ideas.* Chicago: Chicago Review Press, 2007.

Harrison, Carol, and David Krasnow. *Weather and Climate.* Milwaukee, WI: Gareth Stevens, 2004.

Cast of Characters

Storm	JJ
Rainbow	Alan
Dad	Mrs. Pierre
Mom	Extra students (two or more)
Eddie	

Snow Day

Snow Daze

Scene One

Storm: My name is Storm. My sister is named Rainbow. We call our dog Tornado. My dad's pet name for my mom is Sunshine. And my dad's name is Ty … short for Typhoon. Can you guess what Dad does for a living? That's right! He's a TV weatherman.

Mom: *(enters with rest of family)* He's the *best* weatherman in the state.

Rainbow: No, he's the best in the whole country.

Dad: I don't know about that. I try to do a good job, but weather can take you by surprise. That's why you must always be prepared.

Mom: Take along a jacket!

Rainbow: Dress in layers!

Dad: Right! And remember—the umbrella—

Others: —can be your best friend!

Storm: *(as family, except Dad, exits)* Dad's too modest. He's right about the weather almost all the time. Like maybe 99.99999999999 percent of the time! So the morning he made this prediction …

Dad: *(in special weatherman voice)* Snow starting early this evening and continuing overnight. Heavy accumulations by tomorrow morning—six to eight inches possible. You kids better listen for the school closings. *(exits)*

Storm: I knew that nobody needed to study for the science test we were supposed to have the next day.

Eddie: *(entering with JJ and Alan)* I can't believe it! A science test! Tomorrow! How can Mrs. Pierre just spring a big test on us like this?

JJ: We always have a test at the end of the unit.

Eddie: Well, yeah, but who knew the end of the unit would come so fast?

Alan: Mrs. Pierre has been talking about that for three weeks, Eddie.

Storm: Like almost every day, she reminds us that we're getting close to the end of the unit.

Eddie: Well, yeah, but that's not the same as saying we'll be having a test soon.

JJ: She said that, too, Eddie! She said right out that we should be studying for the unit test that was coming up soon.

From Diana R. Jenkins, *All Year Long! Funny Readers Theatre for Life's Special Times.* Westport, CT: Teacher Ideas Press. Copyright © 2007 by Diana R. Jenkins.

Eddie: Well, yeah, but she didn't even mention that it was an important test.

Alan: Yes, she did! She said that like a hundred times.

Eddie: Well, yeah, but … I mean … I didn't … So have you guys been studying?

Others: *(muttering)* Not exactly. Some. Not really. *(etc.)*

Eddie: But the test is tomorrow! I can't believe it! A surprise test!

Alan: Look, Eddie—

Storm: Never mind, Alan. It doesn't matter. We won't be having the test tomorrow anyway.

JJ: What are you talking about?

Storm: Didn't you watch my dad's forecast on the early show?

JJ: *(muttering)* We … uh … watch the other channel.

Storm: What was that?

JJ: Nothing! So what did your dad say?

Storm: We're having a big snowstorm tonight. He says we won't be going to school tomorrow.

Eddie: Whoa! Are you serious?

Storm: Yep! So everybody can relax about that science test.

Alan: If we don't study and then it doesn't snow, we're going to flunk that big test. So are you sure, Storm?

Storm: You know my dad's always right.

JJ: No one can predict the weather with 100 percent accuracy.

Storm: It's going to snow. You can trust my dad. And me. You don't have to study tonight.

Eddie: Cool!

Alan: You know, we should be reviewing this stuff even if—

Storm: So everybody come over to my house tomorrow to play in the snow, okay?

JJ and Eddie: Okay!

Alan: Uh … okay.

Scene Two

Storm: And just like Dad predicted, we had tons of snow—and school was canceled. My friends all walked over to my house and we made big snow forts and had snowball fights and played in the snow all day.

(Friends enter.)

Eddie: That was fun!

JJ: But we'd better be heading home.

Alan: Yeah, we need to study for that science test.

Eddie: What science test?

Alan: The unit test! Mrs. Pierre will give it to us tomorrow.

From Diana R. Jenkins, *All Year Long! Funny Readers Theatre for Life's Special Times.* Westport, CT: Teacher Ideas Press. Copyright © 2007 by Diana R. Jenkins.

Eddie: She can't surprise us with a test after a snow day!

JJ: It's not a surprise, Eddie. It's school policy. After a snow day, everything picks right up where you left off. We'll have the test tomorrow since we were supposed to have it today.

Eddie: We were supposed to have a test today?

JJ: I sure don't feel like studying.

Storm: *(noticing as Rainbow enters and hangs around)* Wait a minute, you guys. Maybe we don't have to study after all. Hey, Rainbow!

Rainbow: What?

Storm: Did you watch Dad's latest weather report?

Rainbow: Of course! I wouldn't miss it for the world.

Storm: I figured. So what did he say?

Rainbow: *(mimicking Dad)* More snow tonight with further accumulations of six inches or more. Roads will be slick and hazardous tomorrow morning. Looks like another day off for the kiddies!

Storm: *(to friends)* See? We don't need to study. We're getting another free day tomorrow.

Eddie: Cool! Your dad is really a nice weatherman.

Storm: Uh … yeah.

Alan: You know, we're going to have that test sometime.

Storm: So?

Alan: So we really should study whether or not we're off. I mean, we can't—

Storm: Whatever! *(to JJ and Eddie)* So same time, same place tomorrow?

Eddie and JJ: Sure! *(exit)*

Alan: *(to Rainbow)* Is your dad ever wrong about the weather?

Rainbow: Of course not.

Alan: He'd better not be! *(exits)*

Scene Three

Storm: *(as Rainbow exits)* Of course, Dad's prediction was right again. School was canceled again, and my friends and I had another fun day playing outside. With all the extra snow, we were able to add onto our forts until they were humongous! And we had plenty of snow to make ammo with.

(Friends enter.)

JJ: That was the biggest snow war ever!

Storm: Too bad you lost.

Eddie: Hey, *we* won. Didn't we?

Alan: No, you and JJ lost.

Dad: *(enters)* Time to head home, boys.

Alan: Thanks for letting us come over.

From Diana R. Jenkins, *All Year Long! Funny Readers Theatre for Life's Special Times.* Westport, CT: Teacher Ideas Press. Copyright © 2007 by Diana R. Jenkins.

Dad: Storm's friends are always welcome here.

Eddie: Hey, Mr. … uh … Weatherman?

Dad: My name is Typhoon, Eddie.

Eddie: So … Mr. Phoon … Are you going to let us have another day off?

Dad: Let you?

JJ: He means: What's the weather forecast for tomorrow?

Dad: *(in weatherman voice)* Bad news, folks. Another band of snow passes through tonight. Well, I guess that's not bad news for the kids who can expect another day off from school tomorrow.

Storm and friends: *(cheer)*

Eddie: Thanks, Mr. Phoon!

Dad: Actually, Eddie, my name isn't—

Storm: Don't bother, Dad. Don't bother.

Dad: Okay then. Well, see you all tomorrow. *(exits)*

Alan: You know we're going to have to go back sometime. And when we go back, Mrs. Pierre is going to make us take that science test.

Eddie: What science test?

Storm: It's a big surprise, Eddie. We're the only ones who know about it.

Eddie: O-o-oh.

Alan: So we need to start studying right away.

Storm: Why? We're off tomorrow.

Alan: Probably, but what if we're not?

Storm: What are you talking about? My dad said we're going to have a snow day so that means we're going to have a snow day.

Alan: Yeah, but just in case, we should start studying tonight. And we're not getting out of that test forever so we should study tomorrow, too, even if we do get the day off.

JJ: I'm too tired to study tonight.

Storm: And what kind of nerd studies on a snow day?

Alan: One who doesn't want to flunk!

Storm: So go ahead, dweeb. Waste your time studying all night, if you want. And all day tomorrow, too. I mean … if you don't trust the best weatherman in the country, just go right ahead and study your brains out.

Alan: Look, I'm just saying—

Storm: And don't bother coming around here tomorrow, loser!

Alan: Whatever. *(exits)*

JJ: So … see you tomorrow, Storm. *(exits)*

Eddie: Tomorrow, dude! *(exits)*

Storm: *(calling after them)* See you! *(to audience)* Those guys are real friends. They'd never disrespect my dad—like *some* people!

Scene Four

Storm: So JJ, Eddie, and I had a great time the next day which was, of course, another snow day. Just like Dad predicted. The snow war was kind of lopsided without Alan on my side, but then we got all involved in building a big snow maze, so it didn't matter anymore. The amazing thing was, we got another snow day after that one! Then another after that! And another! It was like one big vacation. A vacation that Alan was missing. He tried calling a couple of times, but I never called him back. Why should I? He basically put down my dad—and who needs a friend like that?

(JJ and Eddie enter.)

JJ: Man, your yard is starting to look like a snow city.

Storm: I know! Hey, maybe tomorrow we should make some snow people to live in our city.

Eddie: Is your dad giving us another day off?

Storm: Eddie, he doesn't make the weather. He just predicts it.

Mom: *(enters)* JJ! Eddie! Your parents called and said for you to go home.

Eddie: Okay. Thanks, Mrs. Phoon.

Mom: Um … you're welcome. *(exits)*

JJ: Hey, what did your dad say about the weather?

Storm: *(imitating Dad)* Will it never end? *(chuckle)* Of course it will … someday! But tomorrow's not the day, folks. Yes, it looks like you'll have the kids home again!

Eddie: Great!

Storm: You know … I bet that stupid Alan has been studying all this time. He should have listened to me.

JJ: Yeah! It's a good thing we did listen. We haven't wasted a bunch of time cramming stuff into our brains.

Eddie: Yeah! Yeah?

Storm: Yeah, well … later, guys!

JJ: Bye. *(exits)*

Eddie: Tomorrow! *(exits)*

Storm: See you tomorrow! *(to audience)* And I did see the guys the next day. But it wasn't in the snow city. No. That was the day that everything fell apart. The day after the night of the freakiest weather ever!

Scene Five

Storm: I had so much faith in my dad that I'd quit setting my alarm. So I was really surprised when Rainbow woke me up before dawn had cracked.

Rainbow: *(enters)* Mom said to get up, Storm.

Storm: The guys won't be here for hours. Why should I get up now?

Rainbow: To get ready for school, you dope.

Storm: Funny, Rainbow. Now go away and leave me alone.

From Diana R. Jenkins, *All Year Long! Funny Readers Theatre for Life's Special Times.* Westport, CT: Teacher Ideas Press. Copyright © 2007 by Diana R. Jenkins.

Rainbow: We're having school today. Get up!

Storm: We're having school? But Dad said we wouldn't!

Rainbow: Even Dad can't predict the weather all the time. Get ready for school, and hurry up! *(exits)*

Storm: *(to audience)* I told myself that Rainbow was just messing with me, but when I looked out the window, I saw something so horrifying that I had to gasp. *(mimes looking out window and gasps dramatically)* What happened to the snow? There's hardly any left! Look at those humongous puddles! And is that … yes! It's raining! *(to audience)* I couldn't believe my eyes. I quickly got dressed and ran to turn on Dad's forecast.

Dad: *(enters and speaks in special weatherman voice)* Well, well, well … Mother Nature sure threw us a surprise, didn't she? The winds shifted last night and blew in warm air and heavy downpours. Much of our snow has melted already, and the rest will be gone in just a couple of days as the warm front hangs around our area. *(chuckles)* You never know whether or not the weather is going to do what you think—or not! That's why you must always be prepared. *(exits)*

Storm: Be prepared? Oh, man! The science test! I'm not ready at all! I can't even remember what this unit is about. *(to audience)* I studied as much as I could while I ate breakfast and then later on the bus. I thought I'd study some more when I got to my classroom, but I ran into my friends out in the hall.

JJ: *(entering with Eddie)* What happened, Storm? What happened?

Eddie: Yeah, what happened, dude?

Storm: Well, the wind shifted overnight, blowing in a warm front, which caused—

JJ: Never mind all that stuff! The point is that your dad was completely wrong. And now we're at school when we shouldn't be and we're going to have to take a big test we're not ready for.

Eddie: Yeah! Wait. We have a test?

Storm: Look, I'm sorry, you guys, but nobody can predict the weather all the time.

JJ: You acted like your dad could. You made us think he was some kind of weather guru or something. You said we could trust him. And you!

Eddie: Yeah, you lied to us.

Storm: No, I didn't! This is just the one time in a million that my dad has been wrong. That's a pretty good record.

JJ: Tell that to my parents when I flunk science.

Storm: Oh, you're not going to flunk, JJ. You're really good in science. I mean … you usually get good grades.

JJ: Because I study. Which I didn't have time to do. Because your dad had to make the one big mistake of his career on a day when we have a hugely important test.

Storm: But I can't help it if—

JJ: Whatever! If I fail, it's your fault, Storm. Let's go in, Eddie. *(exits)*

Eddie: Yeah. Your fault. *(exits)*

Storm: I was hoping, hoping, *hoping* that Mrs. Pierre would give us a break and reschedule the test. Sure, she was usually a very strict, stick-to-the-plan, by-the-book kind of teacher. But maybe, maybe, *maybe* she'd cut us some slack just once.

Scene Six

(Mrs. Pierre, JJ, Eddie, Alan, and extra students enter.)

Mrs. Pierre: Good morning, everyone. Did you have a lot of fun during your long vacation?

Students: Yeah. Great! Yes, ma'am. *(etc.)*

Mrs. Pierre: Good! I myself found the time off very productive. Now! I hope you did some studying during your time off in preparation for our unit test in science.

Storm, JJ, Eddie, and Some of Extra Students: *(muttering)* Kind of. Not exactly. Test? *(etc.)*

Storm: Mrs. Pierre? Could I ask you something?

Mrs. Pierre: Certainly, Storm.

Storm: Well … we've been off a long time … and I was wondering … do we have to take the science test right away? I mean … couldn't we have some time to refresh our memories?

Mrs. Pierre: Hmmm … That's a good idea, Storm.

JJ: Yes!

Eddie: Way to go, Storm!

Mrs. Pierre: Quiet! Okay, Storm. I can delay the test a bit.

Storm: Thanks, Mrs. Pierre! Thanks a lot!

Mrs. Pierre: So … I'll give the class ten minutes to study. We'll start the test at 8:45.

Storm: But I meant couldn't we take the test in a few days? Or tomorrow, at least.

Mrs. Pierre: Come now. You are quite aware of the school policy about snow days.

Storm: Yes, ma'am. But couldn't you break the rules just this once?

Mrs. Pierre: I'm sorry, but no, I can't do that. Okay, everyone! Ten minutes! Make good use of your time.

Storm: *(aside to JJ and Eddie)* Hey, I tried.

JJ: Big deal. You shouldn't have gotten us into this mess in the first place.

Eddie: Yeah. It's all your fault.

Storm: Whatever.

Alan: *(whispering to Storm)* What's going on?

Storm: None of your business.

Alan: Well, excuse me for being a friend.

Storm: *(too loudly)* Friend? Yeah, you're a great friend.

Mrs. Pierre: If people are not going to study during this time, then we may as well start the test right now.

JJ: *(hissing)* Shut up, Storm, before you mess this up, too.

Eddie: *(whispering)* Yeah, I'm trying to study.

Storm: But, listen …

Mrs. Pierre: Storm …

Storm: Sorry.

JJ: *(muttering)* You sure are.

Scene Seven

Storm: *(to audience as Mrs. Pierre and extra students exit)* I couldn't concentrate enough to study in the time Mrs. Pierre had given us. I hated it that JJ and Eddie were so mad at me. Especially since I didn't deserve it. And when Mrs. Pierre gave us the test, I did a terrible job. I could hardly answer any of the questions. I was hoping my friends did better than that so everything could go back to normal between us. But at our break, things didn't look too good. *(to friends)* So that test wasn't so bad, huh?

Alan: Not really. I knew most of the stuff, I think.

Storm: Who asked you? *(to JJ and Eddie)* So how did you guys do?

JJ: I didn't know anything!

Eddie: Me neither!

Alan: Didn't you guys ever study?

JJ: No! Storm told us we weren't having school today.

Eddie: Why did you do that to us, man? I thought we were friends.

Storm: We are! I just told you the weather forecast. That's not a crime.

JJ: We should have listened to you, Alan.

Eddie: Yeah.

JJ: You told us we should study. You were so right.

Eddie: Yeah. You're a real friend, dude. Not like some people we know.

Alan: I think you're being kind of unfair to Storm.

Storm: You do?

Alan: Yes, I do. We all had plenty of warning about the test from Mrs. Pierre.

Eddie: Dude … Ten minutes is not much warning.

Alan: I'm talking about before the snow days. When Mrs. Pierre kept telling us about the test.

Eddie: Oh.

Alan: And you said yourselves that you could have listened to me. I kept telling you guys that we'd have to take the test sometime, and we should be studying.

JJ: Yeah, I guess you did.

Alan: So you could have decided to study some of the time instead of goofing off all the time. But you didn't do that, did you?

Eddie: No, but Storm said we didn't need to.

Alan: Is he like the boss of you, Eddie? I mean … don't you have a brain of your own?

Eddie: Yeah. I guess. Probably.

Alan: So don't blame Storm.

JJ: Well … okay … I guess you're right.

Eddie: Yeah, you're right. We shouldn't be blaming Storm. We should be blaming Mr. Phoon.

JJ: No, we shouldn't! Sheesh, Eddie! Walk to the water fountain with me, and I'll try to explain it all again.

Eddie: Okay. *(exits with JJ)*

Storm: So … uh … I'm thinking … .well … thanks for … you know … .

Alan: Gee, Storm. Don't bust a gut with all that gratitude. *(starts to exit)*

Storm: Wait, Alan. *(to audience)* I'd been thinking that Alan wasn't a friend, but all he did was tell the truth. And try to get the rest of us to act like we had some sense. I knew I was the real jerk, but I hated to admit that.

Alan: So? What do you want?

Storm: I … uh … I … *(brightening)* I just wanted to tell you the weather forecast.

Alan: I already watched your dad's forecast this morning.

Storm: Yeah, but listen to *my* forecast. *(putting on weatherman voice)* Today's weather will be sorry with continuing showers of sorry followed by unseasonably sorry spells of sorry.

Alan: I get the feeling you're trying to tell me something.

Storm: I really am sorry. I just got mad that you didn't believe my dad, and I didn't handle it very well.

Alan: It's not that I didn't *believe* him, Storm. I have a lot of respect for your dad. But he can't always be right.

Storm: I know. Nobody can predict the weather all the time. That's all you were saying, and that was so true. I shouldn't have treated you the way I did.

Alan: Okay then. Thanks.

Storm: So … um … are we cool?

Alan: *(putting on weatherman voice)* I predict a 100-percent chance of … *(back to normal)* Sure! *(They exit.)*

From Diana R. Jenkins, *All Year Long! Funny Readers Theatre for Life's Special Times.* Westport, CT: Teacher Ideas Press. Copyright © 2007 by Diana R. Jenkins.

Anybody but Howard

Summary

Gina is receiving notes from a secret admirer. How romantic is that? The problem is that she can't figure out who the notes are from. And all the evidence seems to point to Howard—a pest whom she detests!

Costumes, Sets, and Props

- ❖ All actors can wear contemporary clothing.

- ❖ A few desks and chairs can serve as the classroom and cafeteria.

- ❖ Props can be mimed, but if they are desired the following can be used: folded notes, school supplies like books and pencils, trashcan, lunch trays with utensils and food, a huge valentines box, and Valentine's Day decorations.

Presentation

Gina and Howard speak sharply to each other for most of the play.

Howard and Susan speak to each other sweetly.

Maleek has a dreary, negative manner except when he's admiring Gina's deviousness.

In the classroom scenes, Gina should be seated between Howard and Maleek. Several students should be seated between Howard and Travis.

Supplemental Reading

Maguire, Gregory. *Four Stupid Cupids*. New York: Clarion Books, 2000.

Ross, Kathy. *All New Crafts for Valentine's Day*. Brookfield, CT: Millbrook Press, 2002.

Ware, Cheryl. *Venola in Love*. New York: Orchard Books, 2000.

Weeks, Sarah. *Guy Time*. New York: HarperCollins, 2000.

Cast of Characters

Gina	Travis
Susan	Mr. Brooks
Howard	Maleek
Emily	Extra Students (two or more if desired)
Joelle	

Valentine's Day

Anybody but Howard

Scene One

Gina: I didn't even notice the note. I was opening my locker with my best friend, Susan, standing beside me, and… where is she? *(calling offstage)* Susan!

Susan: *(entering)* Sorry, Gina! Go ahead.

Gina: *(to audience)* So I opened my locker…

Susan: Hey, there was something stuck in your locker door. It fell on the … I'll get it.

Gina: *(to audience)* So she gave me the note. The *mysterious* note. The note that started everything! The strange and mysterious note that started everything!

Susan: Open it already.

Gina: Okay. It says … Oh, wow!

Susan: Is that it? Just "Oh, wow"?

Gina: It doesn't say that! *I* said that because it's not an ordinary note. *(whispers)* It's romantic.

Susan: Right. Sure.

Gina: Is it so hard to believe that someone would send me a love note?

Susan: Well, it's never … No. No, of course not. What does it say?

Gina: I'll read it to you. "Dear Gina, Just wanted to tell you, I think you're beautiful. And nice, too. From: Your Secret Admirer."

Susan: Wow! I don't believe it!

Gina: Hey … .

Susan: I mean … who'd believe any of the guys around here could write something like that?

Gina: Yeah. I wonder who did it?

Howard: *(entering)* Who did what?

Gina: It's none of your business, Howard.

Howard: It is if you're accusing me. *(pleasantly to Susan)* Hi, Susan.

Susan: Hi, Howard.

Howard: *(to Gina)* So what are you accusing me of now?

Gina: Who said anything about accusing you?

Howard: *(snorts)* You're always blaming me for something. Like how about that time you told the teacher I threw water balloons on the principal?

Gina: You *did* throw water balloons on the principal.

Howard: Well, sure, but you didn't have to say anything. And then there was that time you blamed me for ruining your science fair project.

Gina: You set my volcano on fire!

Howard: I just thought a volcano should have flames.

Gina: They had to call the fire department in, and they sprayed the whole thing into smithereens so there was nothing left of it to enter in the fair.

Howard: Like that was my fault. Why not blame the firemen?

Gina: Sheesh! Just go away, Howard, and stop bothering me.

Howard: See? There you go accusing me again. *(pleasantly to Susan)* See you later, Susan.

Susan: Bye, Howard. *(waves as he exits)*

Gina: Why are you always so friendly with him?

Susan: He's nice.

Gina: To you maybe. To me he's a big pest.

Susan: Oh, he just teases you because he … likes … you … Hey!

Gina: He does not. And hey what?

Susan: Let me see that note. Hmmm … I can't tell …

Gina: What?

Susan: It could be …

Gina: What? What?

Susan: I know you won't want to hear this, but I think Howard wrote this note!

Scene Two

Gina: *(to audience)* Of course, my first reaction to Susan's theory was that she was totally, completely, utterly crazy. *(to Susan as she snatches back note)* You're totally, completely, utterly crazy.

Susan: I am not. Everybody knows that when a guy teases you a lot, it means he likes you.

Gina: *(as Emily, Joelle, and Travis enter)* For normal guys, maybe, but for Howard it just means he's a jerk. Hey, let's see if anybody saw who put the note on my locker. Hi, you guys.

Emily, Joelle, Travis: Hi.

Gina: Did any of you notice somebody hanging around my locker this morning?

Emily: Like who?

Susan: Like Howard.

Gina: No, not like Howard! Like somebody else. Anybody else.

Joelle: Well, Howard was the only person I noticed.

Susan: Ha! So he *was* hanging around Gina's locker?

Joelle: I think he was.

Gina: But you're not sure.

Joelle: No-o-o.

Gina: Ha! So maybe he wasn't there at all.

Travis: I saw him, too.

Susan: You did? Was he carrying anything? Like paper?

Travis: Sure.

Susan: Ha!

Travis: He had his science notebook.

Gina: Ha!

Travis: Stop doing that! And why are you two so interested in Howard anyway?

Gina: I am not interested in Howard. Not one little bit! And he is not interested in me.

Emily: Ha!

Travis: Stop that. Please.

Gina: *(to Emily)* And what do you mean anyway?

Joelle: Come on, Gina. It is so obvious that Howard likes you.

Emily: Really.

Gina: That is ridiculous!

Susan: No, it's not. I think he—

Gina: *(imitating bell)* BRRRRRINNNGGG! *(in normal voice)* Well, there's the bell. We'd better get going.

Susan: That was not the bell. *(Bell rings)* Ha! See?

Travis: *(as Susan, Joelle, and Emily exit)* They're just teasing you, Gina. I don't think Howard has a girl he likes. Do you?

Gina: *(snorts)* Howard? I don't think so.

Travis: Yeah, you're probably right. At least I hope you are. *(exits)*

Gina: *(opens note, rereads it, and folds it back up)* It can't be Howard. It can't!

Scene Three

Gina: *(as Mr. Brooks, Susan, Howard, Emily, Joelle, Travis, Maleek, and extra students enter)* I had to figure out who really wrote that note. I mean … I knew it wasn't Howard myself, but I had to prove that to everybody else. And when Mr. Brooks started talking about Valentine's Day, I realized it was the perfect opportunity to observe the guys in our class and figure out who my secret admirer was. He had to be someone romantic, right?

Mr. Brooks: It's very, very interesting how Valentine's Day got started.

Maleek: *(muttering)* I bet.

From Diana R. Jenkins, *All Year Long! Funny Readers Theatre for Life's Special Times.* Westport, CT: Teacher Ideas Press. Copyright © 2007 by Diana R. Jenkins.

Mr. Brooks: When young men got married, they didn't want to be soldiers any more. So the emperor of Rome made this law that young men couldn't marry.

Maleek: Sounds like he did those guys a favor.

Joelle: Oh, ha ha, Maleek.

Mr. Brooks: I'm … uh … not bothering you with my lesson, am I?

Maleek: Not too much.

Joelle: Sorry, Mr. Brooks. Go ahead.

Mr. Brooks: Thanks. A priest named Valentine thought the law wasn't right, and he decided to do something about it. He kept performing marriages for young sweethearts in secret. He knew he could get into big trouble, but he believed in love. Eventually he was found out, and the emperor had him executed.

Howard: Gee. That's pretty interesting, Mr. Brooks.

Mr. Brooks: Why, thank you, Howard.

Howard: And it's kind of *(clasps hands and flutters eyes)* romantic.

Other students except Gina and Maleek: *(laugh)*

Gina: *(to Susan as others freeze)* See? It can't be him. He's making fun of romance.

Susan: *(to Gina)* Come on! He has to act like that in front of everybody.

Gina: Whatever.

Mr. Brooks: *(as everyone unfreezes)* People started honoring Valentine on the anniversary of his death. And that day became a celebration of love. We still celebrate it today. Which brings me to our Valentine's Day party next week.

Other students except Maleek: *(cheer)*

Maleek: Whoopee. Heart decorations. Heart cookies. Heart candy with those stupid messages.

Emily: They're not stupid.

Howard: *(clasps hands and flutters eyes)* They're romantic.

Other students except Gina and Maleek: *(laugh)*

Maleek: And do we have to do those lame valentines?

Girls: Yes!

Maleek: Brother.

Howard: It's a party, dude. Who cares what kind of party it is?

Maleek: I think it's a waste of time.

Gina: *(to Susan as everyone freezes)* Well, it's not Maleek. I was really hoping it was Maleek.

Susan: *(to Gina)* I didn't know you liked him.

Gina: *(to Susan)* I don't. I just want it to be somebody besides Howard.

Susan: *(to Gina)* Too bad. It *is* Howard.

Gina: *(loudly)* It is not!

Mr. Brooks: *(as everyone unfreezes)* Did you have something to add to the discussion, Gina?

Gina: I … uh … was just saying a Valentine's Day party is not a waste of time. It's a … a tradition.

Howard: *(clasps hands and flutter eyes)* And it's so romantic!

Gina: Shut up, Howard.

Mr. Brooks: Gina!

Gina: Sorry.

Travis: I think a Valentine's Day party is a good idea. I can bring some cookies, Mr. Brooks.

Mr. Brooks: Thank you, Travis. How about making a sign-up list for the treats?

Travis: Okay.

Mr. Brooks: And would someone like to make the traditional valentines box?

Howard: I'll do it! I'll do it! Ooh! Pick me! Pick me!

Mr. Brooks: Very well, Howard.

Susan: *(to Gina)* See? Only a truly romantic person would volunteer to do that. And a truly romantic person had to write that love note.

Gina: *(to Susan)* Howard. Did. Not. Write. That. Note.

Howard: Does anybody have some lace I can put on the valentines box?

Gina: Aaaargh!

Scene Four

Gina: *(as others exit)* I tried and tried to think of some way to prove that Howard didn't send me that note, but I couldn't come up with one good idea. And things got worse the next day.

Susan: *(enters, waving a note)* Look! This was stuck in your locker door when I got here this morning. I think it's another note from your secret admirer.

Gina: *(snatches it out of her hand)* It looks like it's been opened.

Susan: Really? Hmmm … Maybe that tape wasn't very sticky … or something …

Gina: Right. *(opens note, holds it away from Susan, and reads)* "Dear Gina, You are the most gross girl in school." Hey!

Susan: That's gorgeous. I mean … I bet he meant gorgeous.

Gina: Oh, yeah. You're right.

Susan: Lucky guess! Heh-Heh.

Gina: Sure. *(reads)* "You are the most gorgeous girl in school. And brainy, too. Yours truly, Your Secret Admirer." Oh, there is no way Howard wrote this!

Susan: It sounds just like him. You know how he likes to exaggerate.

Gina: He can't be … he-e-ey!

Susan: I just mean he's not the kind of guy who would be subtle, you know? If Howard liked a girl, he would really be excited about her. He'd think she was the most fantastic person on earth.

From Diana R. Jenkins, *All Year Long! Funny Readers Theatre for Life's Special Times.* Westport, CT: Teacher Ideas Press. Copyright © 2007 by Diana R. Jenkins.

Gina: *(getting upset)* Howard doesn't even like me! And he's not my secret admirer! Okay?

Susan: Okay, then. Who is?

Gina: *(sighs)* I don't know. I just don't want it to be Howard.

Susan: Look … why don't you *ask* Howard if he sent you the notes?

Gina: Are you nuts? If he finds out about those notes, he'll tease me until he drives me insane.

Susan: Unless he already knows because he sent them. And once he knows that you know the truth, he'll have to get serious about your relationship.

Gina: *(through gritted teeth)* We don't have a relationship. And we never will.

Susan: I could ask him if he likes you.

Gina: No! Don't do that! You're my best friend. If you ask him if he likes me, he's going to think I asked you to ask him because I like him which I don't!

Susan: Then let's get somebody else to ask him. *(Travis enters.)* Like Travis. Hey, Travis!

Travis: Hi.

Susan: Could you help us out with something?

Travis: Sure.

Susan: Could you ask Howard if he likes—

Gina: Anybody! Ask him if he likes anybody.

Travis: I … uh … I don't know if I want to do that.

Susan: Come on, Travis. Please. We really want to know.

Gina: Well, I don't much care, but Susan just has to know. Heh. Heh.

Travis: Oh. Well. Okay.

Gina: But don't tell him we asked you to do it.

Travis: *(looking dejected)* Sure. *(exits)*

Susan: So now you'll have to face the truth.

Gina: No, you will! You're going to see how wrong you are. Totally wrong.

Susan: We'll see. *(exits)*

Gina: *(yelling)* Yes, we will! *(to self)* Howard doesn't like me. He does not like me. He doesn't!

Scene Five

Gina: *(to audience as other students enter, take seats, and freeze)* That morning was torture! Every time Travis passed anywhere near Howard, I was hoping he'd ask him the big question. But I was also wishing he wouldn't. I wanted to know—and I didn't. Having a secret admirer really was romantic—unless it was Howard. But then … Aaargh! I was going crazy!

Maleek: *(to Gina)* What's up with you and Howard?

Gina: Nothing! Me and Howard? Ha! Me and Howard? Sheesh! What do I care about Howard?

Maleek: Well, something's going on. You've been staring at him all morning.

Gina: I have not!

Maleek: *(lighting up)* You're planning something, aren't you? Cool! Is this like that time you glued the pages of his math book together?

Gina: *(to audience)* I only did that because he stuck gum in my speller. *(to Maleek)* Not exactly.

Maleek: Oh, man! You mean it's better than that? Is it better than the time you put that stinky cheese in his coat pocket?

Gina: *(to audience)* Well, he put a melted chocolate bar in mine! *(to Maleek)* I … uh … can't say.

Maleek: I can't wait to see what you do. You have a devious brain, Gina. I admire that in a person.

Gina: You … you do?

Mr. Brooks: *(enters)* Less talk, Gina —more work! *(Mr. Brooks and Maleek freeze.)*

Gina: *(to audience)* He said he admired my brain. Could Maleek be my secret admirer? But he's so unromantic. I guess he could be hiding his true self. Wow. Maleek.

Howard: *(unfreezes)* So what's up with you and Maleek?

Gina: Nothing! Me and Maleek? As if!

Howard: Well, you keep staring at him.

Gina: I do not. And leave me alone, will you?

Mr. Brooks: *(unfreezes)* Gina, stop all the talking and get to work.

Gina: Yes, sir. *(to audience as everybody else unfreezes and a note passes from Travis down the line to Howard)* Man! If I don't figure out what's going on soon, I'll end up with detention!

Mr. Brooks: *(taking note as Howard starts to open it)* Give me that! I don't allow note passing in my room.

Howard: Really? All the other teachers love that kind of thing.

Mr. Brooks: You're not funny, Howard. *(tosses note into trashcan as bell rings)* Everybody line up for lunch.

Gina: *(to audience as everyone else exits)* I didn't get a good look at that note, but I had the funny feeling it was addressed to me! And since it came from the other end of the room, it was just the evidence I needed to prove that Howard wasn't my secret admirer. So I dropped out of line and circled back to the classroom, planning to dig the note out of the trashcan. But when I got back to the room, I saw something interesting.

Travis: *(enters, heads for trashcan, then spots Gina)* Oh, hi, Gina.

Gina: What are you doing?

Travis: I … uh … it's just … something of mine got thrown away … .*(grabs note out of trash can)* So … see you later! *(exits)*

Gina: He wrote that note? But then … .

Howard: *(enters and looks in trash can)* Where did it go? *(notices Gina)* What are *you* doing here?

From Diana R. Jenkins, *All Year Long! Funny Readers Theatre for Life's Special Times.* Westport, CT: Teacher Ideas Press. Copyright © 2007 by Diana R. Jenkins.

Gina: I could ask you the same thing.

Howard: Go ahead.

Gina: What are you doing here?

Howard: I asked you first.

Gina: Oh, you're real funny, Howard.

Howard: That's what they say! *(exits)*

Gina: Whew! It's a good thing he didn't get hold of that note. I'd never hear the end of it if he found out I have a secret admirer. Wow. Travis. Why didn't I see it before?

Scene Six

Gina: *(to audience as Susan enters)* I was glad to finally know for sure that Howard wasn't writing those notes! And I was ecstatic to be able to prove Susan wrong. I hurried to the cafeteria and explained everything. *(to Susan)* I mean … isn't it obvious? The note came from Travis's end of the room. And Travis snuck back to get it out of the trash. And … and he acted really nervous when he saw me.

Susan: How does any of that prove anything?

Gina: It makes perfect sense.

Susan: Okay then. Why was Howard opening the note?

Gina: Well, duh … because he's Howard. He didn't care that it was addressed to me. He has to make my life miserable, you know.

Susan: Or here's an idea. The note was addressed to him!

Gina: Right. Why would Travis write Howard … oh yeah. Well, still, why would Travis write a note to ask Howard if he likes somebody? They could just talk at lunch.

Susan: Maybe Travis didn't want to ask in front of other people.

Gina: Yeah, maybe. If he did that, Howard would just make a big joke out of it, and Travis would never get a straight answer. But wait a minute! Why did Travis come back for the note?

Susan: Because … I don't know. What's your theory?

Gina: Maybe it's a really good note. Like super romantic! And he still wants to give it to me.

Susan: Or maybe there's something embarrassing in that note and he wants to destroy it.

Gina: Right. Something embarrassing. Like a bunch of romantic stuff!

Susan: Oh, come on.

Gina: And remember—he got nervous when he saw me. Why was that?

Susan: Gee, could it be because you caught him sneaking around and picking through garbage?

Gina: I'm telling you, Susan. Travis is my secret admirer. Yesterday he acted worried about Howard liking me. Oh! And he likes Valentine's Day so he's romantic. And remember how he didn't want to talk to Howard about whether he liked anybody? Yep, he's the one. I knew Howard didn't do it!

Howard: *(entering)* Didn't do what?

Gina: Nothing, Howard.

Howard: Hi, Susan.

Susan: Hi, Howard.

Howard: *(to Gina)* If you're talking about me, I have a right to know what you're saying.

Gina: No, actually, you don't. We were having a private conversation about private business.

Howard: You were talking about me! You're always talking about me! And you're always saying terrible stuff!

Gina: Hey, I just speak the truth! Maybe if you'd stop being so … so … you! I could think of something good to say about you once in a while.

Howard: *(serious)* I don't get it, Gina. Why do you hate me so much?

Gina: Because … I mean … I don't … exactly … you're always bugging me … and …

Howard: Never mind. *(exits looking dejected)*

Susan: You really made him feel bad.

Gina: Well, he's so annoying!

Susan: But he's not a bad guy, Gina. And I still think he likes you. *(exits)*

Gina: Didn't she listen to anything I said?

Scene Seven

Gina: Things were really weird in class that afternoon. Every time I looked up, somebody was giving me a strange look. Sometimes it was Howard. He acted like I really had hurt his feelings. Howard! Sometimes Susan frowned at me. I didn't understand why she was so mad. I didn't *mean* to hurt Howard. And Travis kept looking at me, too. Or maybe it was more like watching me. Was he admiring me? Was he waiting for a sign from me that I liked him, too? I always thought Travis was nice, but I didn't know if I *liked* liked him. I couldn't concentrate on my work at all. I was glad when the last bell rang and I could go home and think. I hurried to my locker and found Susan there ahead of me.

Susan: *(entering)* Look! There's another note on your locker. *(holds out note)*

Gina: *(takes note)* Did you read it already?

Susan: No. I swear. Hurry up and open it!

Gina: Okay. *(opens note and reads)* I don't get it.

Susan: Maybe I can help. What does it say?

Gina: It says, "Please ask Susan if she likes me."

Susan: What?

Gina: And it's from Travis.

Susan: WHAT? *(grabs note)*

Gina: I can't believe it. Travis likes you!

Susan: *(annoyed)* And what's so unbelievable about that? Huh?

Gina: I just meant … if Travis likes you … then who wrote *my* notes?

Susan: Oh yeah. Good question. Hey! You should talk to Travis.

From Diana R. Jenkins, *All Year Long! Funny Readers Theatre for Life's Special Times.* Westport, CT: Teacher Ideas Press. Copyright © 2007 by Diana R. Jenkins.

Gina: Right. I need to ask him about that note in class. Was that note this note? Or was that a different note? Was he writing to Howard, like you said before? Or maybe—

Susan: Yeah, yeah, talk about that stuff. But be sure to tell him … um … yes! For me, you know.

Gina: Look, Susan, I have a serious problem here … There he is! Travis!

Susan: Don't talk to him in front of me! *(exits)*

Travis: *(enters)* So? Did you ask her?

Gina: Yeah, I asked her. And she likes you.

Travis: Yes! Thanks, Gina.

Gina: And now that I helped you, you have to help me.

Travis: Okay.

Gina: What was that note you were passing in class? The one you took back out of the trash?

Travis: I … I'm sorry about that. I wrote a note to ask Howard if he liked anybody—like you and Susan said. I didn't want to do it, because … well … I liked her myself. But you said she really wanted to know so I did it anyway.

Gina: You're a nice guy, Travis.

Travis: I was trying to be nice, but after Mr. Brooks took the note, I started thinking I was a big dope. If Howard said he liked Susan, then that was it—I was out of the picture. But as long as I didn't *know* anything for sure, I still had a chance. So I decided not to do what you asked. Sorry.

Gina: That's okay. I understand.

Travis: I heard Howard telling Maleek he was going to get that note back so I had to hurry and take it out of the trash before he did. Good thing he never saw who wrote it!

Susan: *(enters and speaks in stilted voice)* Hi, Gina. Did you write down the math assignment? Oh. Hi there, Travis.

Travis: *(shy)* Hi, Susan. I wrote all the assignments down.

Susan: That's great. Could I look at your assignment book?

Travis: Sure. *(They exit.)*

Gina: Gee. Isn't that *(clasps hands and flutters eyes)* romantic? *(crabby)* Now I'm back to square one. I still don't know who my secret admirer is!

Scene Eight

Gina: *(to audience as everyone except Howard and Maleek enters, puts up some decorations, and takes seats)* After that, I didn't get any more notes. I couldn't believe it! What kind of secret admirer only admires you for two days? I was so bummed by the whole thing that I didn't even care about Valentine's Day anymore.

Maleek: *(enters)* Look at these stupid hearts and cupids. Man, this is disgusting.

Gina: It sure is.

Maleek: This has to be the dumbest holiday ever!

Gina: I know!

Maleek: Like who cares about romance?

Gina: Not me.

Maleek: And those stupid valentines!

Emily: *(to Maleek)* So you didn't bring any valentines?

Maleek: *(acting like he cares)* Come on, Emily. Of course I brought valentines! I brought valentines for everybody! But … um … *(back to usual tone)* I still think they're stupid.

Emily: Whatever.

Mr. Brooks: So where's our valentines box? Hey … and where's Howard?

Gina: *(to audience)* That's when Howard walked in with the biggest, most decorated, most romantic-looking valentines box you ever saw!

Howard: *(enters with box and sets it down)* Here it is, Mr. Brooks. What do you think?

Mr. Brooks: It's … uh … big.

Susan: It looks great, Howard.

Mr. Brooks: And big … really big.

Howard: I had to make it big enough for this! *(pulls huge envelope from hiding place behind something or just offstage)*

Gina: *(to audience)* That's when Howard pulled out the biggest valentine ever! And it had *my* name on it!

Other kids: Oooooh!

Susan: *(to Gina as Howard sticks envelope in box and takes seat)* See? I told you!

Mr. Brooks: Well, people, the party's not until this afternoon. This morning we have some work to do. Everyone take out your science books please.

Gina: *(as everyone else except Howard freezes)* So … you … you … you … .

Howard: Okay, I am so bad at this stuff! The valentine is way over the top, isn't it? I just don't know how to make you stop hating me!

Gina: I don't hate you, Howard.

Howard: But you don't like me either, do you?

Gina: *(to audience as Howard freezes)* How was I supposed to answer that? I was still stunned to find out that Howard was my secret admirer! It was like I didn't know him at all. And maybe I didn't. Maybe there was more to Howard than I realized. *(to Howard as he unfreezes)* I don't know if I *like* like you. You're always so annoying! I mean … nothing personal, you know.

Howard: *(shrugs)* I know.

Gina: Maybe we should just see if we can get along better. Then who knows?

Howard: *(grinning)* Okay. That works.

Gina: *(to audience as others exit, Maleek lingering behind, writing something)* So the mystery was solved! I don't know what's going to happen with me and Howard, but at least we're not making each other miserable anymore. If nothing else develops between us, that's an improvement. *(exits)*

From Diana R. Jenkins, *All Year Long! Funny Readers Theatre for Life's Special Times.* Westport, CT: Teacher Ideas Press. Copyright © 2007 by Diana R. Jenkins.

Maleek: *(looking at what he's written)* There! That ought to get something started. "Dear Emily, You are the nicest girl in school. And you're beautiful, too. Sincerely, Your Secret Admirer." *(folds note then looks at audience and smiles)* Just call me "Valentine"! *(exits)*

Presidents' Day

Don't Call Me Abe!

Summary

Why did Jacob's teacher have to choose him to play Abraham Lincoln in the Presidents' Day program? Like he doesn't get teased enough already! Desperate to be cool just once, Jacob does something wrong. Then he has to make a big decision. Maybe he's not Abraham Lincoln, but can he be honest like Abe?

Costumes, Sets, and Props

❖ Daniel wears a white wig while playing Washington. Jacob wears a ratty beard and oversized stovepipe hat while playing Lincoln. Other characters wear contemporary clothing.

❖ A few chairs and tables can serve as classrooms and the cafeteria.

❖ Props can be mimed, but the following props can be used if desired: school supplies, boxes to return to Mr. Yokum, big envelope, play money, and lunch trays.

Presentation

Jacob is easily upset by the teasing and obviously afraid to stand up to Anya and the others. He acts guilty about the stolen money and Daniel's trouble, but he's too concerned about being cool to do anything.

Daniel looks serious and noble as he plays Washington.

During the slow-motion portion of Scene Ten, everyone except the Narrator and Jacob moves in slow motion. Daniel moves slowly to the door. Anya slowly smirks. Others react slowly to what's going on.

Supplemental Reading

Allen, Thomas B. *George Washington, Spymaster: How the Americans Outspied the British and Won the Revolutionary War.* Washington, DC: National Geographic Society, 2004.

Bausum, Ann. *Our Country's Presidents.* Washington, DC: National Geographic Society, 2005.

Bowler, Sarah. *Abraham Lincoln, Our Sixteenth President.* Chanhassen, MN: The Child's World, 2002.

Burgan, Michael. *George Washington.* Minneapolis, MN: Compass Point Books, 2002.

Davis, Kenneth C. *Don't Know Much about Abraham Lincoln.* New York: HarperCollins, 2004.

Holzer, Harold, editor. *Abraham Lincoln, The Writer—A Treasury of His Greatest Speeches and Letters.* Honesdale, PA: Boyds Mill Press, 2000.

Roberts, Jeremy. *George Washington.* Minneapolis, MN: Lerner, 2004.

Sullivan, George. *Mr. President: A Book of U.S. Presidents.* New York: Scholastic, 2005.

Sullivan, George. *Picturing Lincoln: Famous Photographs That Popularized the President.* New York: Clarion Books, 2000.

Washington, George. *George-isms.* New York: Atheneum Books for Young Readers, 2000.

Cast of Characters

Narrator	Lily
Jacob	Extra Students (Two or more)
Mrs. Santiago	Mr. Yokum
Daniel	Coach (offstage voice)
Anya	Principal
Sam	

Presidents' Day

Don't Call Me Abe!

Scene One

Narrator: *(to audience as Jacob listens and looks embarrassed)* Jacob was not cool. Not at all. He never had been cool. Never. And it didn't look like he would ever *be* cool. Not Jacob.

Jacob: I think they have the idea.

Narrator: Right. No need to go on and on about it. I mean … you have feelings, right?

Jacob: Just move on, will you?

Narrator: Okay, sure. Now … where was I?

Jacob: *(through gritted teeth)* I was not cool.

Narrator: Right! You weren't cool and it didn't look like you ever would *be* cool. And Mrs. Santiago's plans for Presidents' Day didn't help with that problem at all.

Mrs. Santiago: *(entering along with Daniel, Anya, Sam, Lily, and extra students)* Good news, class! We've been selected to present the program at the next meeting of the parents and teachers association. Isn't that great?

Students: *(robotic)* Yes, ma'am.

Mrs. Santiago: And since the meeting takes place in February, it's the perfect time for a program about Presidents' Day. Don't you think?

Students: Yes, ma'am.

Mrs. Santiago: So I've written a special script of my very own all about President Washington and President Lincoln. And I've included a part for each and every one of you. I couldn't leave anyone out, now could I?

Students: Yes, ma'am. *(look puzzled)* No, ma'am? *(mumbling among themselves)* Yes? No? How do you answer that? *(etc.)*

Mrs. Santiago: Some of you have small parts. Some of you have big parts. But, remember, everyone is important, no matter the size of your role.

Students: Yes, ma'am.

Narrator: Mrs. Santiago assigned all the parts in the play, saving the two biggest roles for last.

Mrs. Santiago: And I'd like Daniel to play the part of George Washington.

Daniel: Thanks, Mrs. Santiago.

Mrs. Santiago: You're welcome, dear. I'm sure you'll do a good job. And, Jacob, I'm just as sure you'll be a great Abraham Lincoln.

Daniel: Way to go, Jacob. You're perfect for the part.

Narrator: But Jacob knew he'd look like a hopeless dweeb, standing on stage with a fake beard and a stovepipe hat. So not cool! I mean … even more not cool than usual.

Jacob: Couldn't I be somebody else, Mrs. Santiago?

Mrs. Santiago: Somebody else? But the parts are all filled.

Jacob: Maybe I could be … um … the usher?

Students: *(laugh)*

Sam: What an idiot!

Mrs. Santiago: That's enough. *(kindly)* Jacob, I picked you especially for the role. You have a wonderful memory, and I know you'll be a fantastic Abraham Lincoln.

Jacob: Okay. Sure. Thanks.

Narrator: But Jacob knew he was going to be sorry he had to play old Honest Abe.

Jacob: Real sorry.

Scene Two

Narrator: *(as Mrs. Santiago and extra students exit)* It didn't take long for the trouble to begin. The first time the class had a break, the teasing started.

Anya: Abraham Lincoln! Wasn't he supposed to be tall?

Sam: Yeah. He was six feet four.

Lily: Then why did Mrs. Santiago give Jacob that part? He's too short.

Daniel: I'm not very tall either.

Sam: But you're taller than Jacob. So, Jacob, are you going to stand on a box or something?

Jacob: I don't know.

Anya: Maybe you could wear stilts.

Lily: Good idea!

Jacob: It's just a school play. I don't have to actually look like Lincoln.

Daniel: That's right. You just have to act like him.

Anya: He has to look *something* like him. *(to Jacob)* I bet you'll be wearing a beard.

Jacob: Probably.

Sam: And a hat.

Jacob: I guess.

Lily: So why not stilts?

Jacob: Because that would make me look stupid!

Sam: And the beard and hat won't?

Anya: Really.

Jacob: Well, Daniel's going to have to wear a wig.

Lily: Of course. He's playing George Washington.

Daniel: So it only makes sense.

Jacob: Well, it only makes sense for me to dress like Abraham Lincoln.

Anya: Right! Now where can we get some stilts?

Jacob: I'm not using stilts!

Students except Daniel: *(laugh)*

Anya: See you later, Abe. *(exits with others)*

Jacob: *(calling)* Don't call me that!

Daniel: They're just teasing, Jacob. I know you'll do a great job playing Lincoln. *(exits)*

Jacob: *(to Narrator)* Why do people always have to tease me?

Narrator: Maybe they do it because you get so upset. If you just ignored them, they might –

Jacob: Look, I've heard all that a million times. *(mocking)* Just ignore them, Jacob. Laugh *with* them, Jacob. Don't let it bother you, Jacob. *(back to normal)* Well, none of that works. And I'm tired of being treated like a complete dweeb. Just once I want to be cool!

Mrs. Santiago: *(enters with ratty beard and too-large hat)* There you are! Let's try these on. *(puts beard and hat on Jacob)* Perfect! You look great, Jacob. Really … oh … Presidential. *(exits)*

Narrator: *(sadly)* That is so not helping, dude.

Jacob: *(looking dejected as he exits)* Four score … I'm a bore …

Scene Three

Narrator: *(as Mrs. Santiago, Sam, Lily, and extra students enter and sit to watch rehearsal)* The rehearsals only made things worse for Jacob. And Mrs. Santiago believed in rehearsing a lot.

Anya: *(enters along with Daniel who is wearing wig and looking noble)* … So that's why he was called "The Father of Our Country."

Students: *(applaud)*

Mrs. Santiago: Excellent! Good job, Anya! And, Daniel … *(hand to heart)* That was amazing. Wasn't it, class?

Students: *(applaud)*

Mrs. Santiago: Okay, now let's do the part about Lincoln.

(Daniel and Anya join others, Lily stands.)

Lily: He was born in extreme poverty, and he lived a hard life. But he became one of our greatest presidents. *(pauses then repeats loudly)* But he became one of our greatest presidents. *(pauses and looks offstage)* Yo! Abe! Get out here!

Jacob: *(offstage)* Don't call me "Abe"!

Mrs. Santiago: Get ready to enter on your cue, Jacob.

Jacob: *(offstage)* Yes, ma'am.

Lily: But he became one of our greatest presidents.

Narrator: Jacob stumbled into the room with his stovepipe hat falling over his eyes.

Sam: And one of our clumsiest, too.

Students except Daniel: *(laugh)*

Mrs. Santiago: That's enough of that. Are you okay, Jacob?

Narrator: Then he knocked the hat completely off his own head.

Jacob: Yes … oops!

Students: *(laugh)*

Mrs. Santiago: Quiet! Pick it up, Jacob, and go ahead with your lines.

Jacob: These are troubling *(sniffs)* times for our country. *(sniffs)* Every decision I make … *(sneezes)*

Students except Daniel: *(laugh)*

Mrs. Santiago: Go on, Jacob.

Jacob: Every decision *(sneeze)* I make *(sneeze)* must be … *(several sneezes)*

Students except Daniel: *(laugh)*

Daniel: What's wrong, Jacob?

Jacob: I think *(sneeze)* I'm allergic *(sneeze)* to this beard. *(several sneezes)*

Mrs. Santiago: Oh, dear. I hope not.

Anya: He's faking, Mrs. Santiago.

Sam: Yeah.

Jacob: I am not!

Anya: That's not very honest, Abe. *(to friends)* Get it? Honest Abe?

Lily: Good one!

Jacob: I'm not faking, okay? And stop calling me "Abe"!

Lily: Why don't you try it without the beard?

Mrs. Santiago: That's a good idea.

Narrator: So Jacob removed the beard … .

Jacob: These are troubling times for our country. Every decision I make must be carefully weighed. See? It's the beard. I can't be Abraham Lincoln.

Mrs. Santiago: That's a shame. I just knew you—

Jacob: *(sneezes repeatedly)*

Anya: Aha! So it wasn't the beard.

Sam: He can still play Lincoln.

Daniel: That's good.

Mrs. Santiago: Wonderful!

Jacob: *(muttering)* Yeah. Wonderful.

Scene Four

Narrator: *(as all except Jacob, Anya, Sam, and Lily exit)* It looked like playing Abraham Lincoln was sealing Jacob's fate. He was never going to be part of the popular group.

Jacob: Never.

Narrator: But one day an opportunity came along—an opportunity Jacob couldn't pass up! Mrs. Santiago sent Jacob and a few other students to the art room to return some things she'd borrowed from the art teacher.

Anya: Mr. Yokum's not here.

Sam: Let's just leave the stuff on the table.

Lily: Look—something's sticking out of his desk drawer. Hey, isn't that the envelope with the field trip money?

Anya: Yeah, it is. I'm going to see how much is in there. Whoa! That is a lot of money!

Sam: It sure is.

Jacob: Come on, you guys. Let's get back to class.

Lily: You are such a dweeb, Jacob. Nobody hurries back to class from an errand.

Sam: Really.

Anya: You know … I bet Mr. Yokum thought he closed that drawer. If I just push it shut … yep! It locks!

Lily: What did you do that for? Now we can't put the envelope back inside.

Anya: *(grinning)* Isn't that too bad? Gee, what are we going to do with all this money?

Lily: *(grinning)* Gosh. I don't know.

Sam: *(grinning)* I guess we'll just have to take it with us.

Anya: And split it up three ways.

Lily: And spend it!

Jacob: Hey, wait a minute!

Anya: Oh, yeah. I forgot about Honest Abe here.

Lily: Are you going to rat us out?

Sam: I bet he is.

Jacob: No, I'm not. I wouldn't do that. I'm just … uh … wondering about my cut.

Lily: Your cut? Man, you have a lot of nerve asking for a cut.

Anya: I didn't know you had that kind of guts. *(looks at others then back)* Okay. You're in!

Sam: Let's get out of here. We can stop in the alcove and divide things up. Then we'd better get back to class.

Anya: *(to Jacob)* You're okay, Jacob. *(others exit)*

Jacob: I … I'm in!

From Diana R. Jenkins, *All Year Long! Funny Readers Theatre for Life's Special Times.* Westport, CT: Teacher Ideas Press. Copyright © 2007 by Diana R. Jenkins.

Scene Five

Narrator: So they split up the loot and headed back to class. As soon as Jacob stuffed that money in his pockets, he started to feel kind of funny.

Jacob: It's not like I actually stole anything. The others did that. And if they want to share with me ... well, why would I say no? That wouldn't be cool at all. Or friendly.

Narrator: *(as Mrs. Santiago and students enter and take seats to watch rehearsal and Jacob puts on beard and hat)* So he pushed away the guilty feeling and concentrated on how his life had changed. Now he was friends with the popular people which was a completely new experience.

Jacob: Four score and seven years ago ... *(hat falls off as he gestures)*

Extra students: *(laugh until they notice others aren't laughing)*

Mrs. Santiago: Try it again, Jacob.

Jacob: *(puts hat back on)* Four score and seven years ago, our fathers brought forth on this continent ... *(hat falls off as he gestures)*

Extra students: *(laugh until they notice others aren't laughing)*

Jacob: Sorry! *(puts hat back on and stands stiffly)* Four score and seven years ago, our fathers brought forth on this continent a new nation.

Anya: *(applauding)* You rock!

Others: *(applaud)*

Mrs. Santiago: Very good, Jacob.

Sam: You-da-man!

Daniel: Good job, Jacob.

Jacob: Thanks. I mean ... like ... four score and seven thanks.

Anya, Sam, Lily: *(laugh loudly)*

Extra students: *(look puzzled but join in)*

Narrator: *(as Mrs. Santiago and extra students exit)* Things were different at lunch, too.

Anya: You can sit with us, Jacob.

Jacob: Okay, thanks.

Lily: I'm going shopping after school.

Anya: Hey, maybe I'll go with you. I have some spare change to spend.

Lily and Sam: *(laugh)*

Jacob: *(gives a fake laugh)*

Daniel: What's so funny?

Anya, Lily, Sam, and Jacob: *(laugh)*

Sam: Never mind, Daniel.

Anya: It's like a private joke. Right, Jacob?

Jacob: Right!

Daniel: Oh. Okay.

Narrator: *(as others except Jacob exit)* So it looked like Jacob had finally gotten what he wanted.

Jacob: *(swaggering)* I'm cool. That's right. Uh-huh. I'm cool. Uh-huh.

Narrator: Yes, Jacob's life was perfect now. Or so it seemed.

Scene Six

Narrator: *(as other students enter and take seats)* Jacob had managed to forget all about the stolen money stinking up his pockets. But when he got to art class that afternoon, he had to remember everything.

Mr. Yokum: *(enters)* Sorry I'm late. I'm afraid we have a big problem. Someone stole all the field trip money.

Daniel: Does that mean we don't get to go?

Mr. Yokum: I'm afraid it does.

Daniel and extra students: *(moan)*

Mr. Yokum: It wouldn't be right to ask all your parents to pay again. And I don't think we can come up with the money in time for the trip anyway.

Lily: That's really disappointing.

Anya: Yeah. Disappointing.

Mr. Yokum: I'm sorry. I locked the money in my desk, but someone got to it anyway.

Anya: I didn't see anybody around when we brought that stuff back this morning, did you guys?

Sam: No.

Lily: Nobody.

Jacob: Right. Nobody.

Mr. Yokum: I've been taking all my classes down to the pottery studio. I guess someone picked the lock on my desk some time when the room was empty.

Daniel: How can anybody be that selfish? They took money that doesn't belong to them, and they ruined things for everybody. *(to Jacob)* They could learn a lesson from us.

Jacob: From us?

Daniel: Well, from George Washington and Abraham Lincoln.

Jacob: Oh. Yeah. Sure. Honesty and all that.

Daniel: Right.

Anya: People just aren't like that anymore. That whole Honest Abe thing is so back-in-the-day.

Mr. Yokum: Some people are dishonest. But I think a lot of folks try to do the right thing. Maybe the thief will have a change of conscience and give the money back.

Anya: I doubt it.

Sam: Me, too.

Lily: It'll never happen. Right, Jacob?

From Diana R. Jenkins, *All Year Long! Funny Readers Theatre for Life's Special Times.* Westport, CT: Teacher Ideas Press. Copyright © 2007 by Diana R. Jenkins.

Jacob: I don't know.

Anya: *(intensely)* You think somebody's going to return the money?

Jacob: Uh … no … of course not. There's no way that will happen.

Anya: Right.

Mr. Yokum: I really wanted you kids to see the museum. I feel like I've let you all down. I'm sorry.

Daniel: It's okay, Mr. Yokum. Don't blame yourself. It's the thief's fault—not yours.

Anya: Yeah.

Lily: Right.

Mr. Yokum: Thanks. Well, let's head down to the pottery studio. Don't leave anything valuable here.

Narrator: *(as others exit)* Jacob didn't get much work done in that class because he was too busy feeling like a worm.

Jacob: I really feel bad about the field trip. And Mr. Yokum! That money isn't mine, and I shouldn't have taken any of it. But … what can I do about it now? I can't tell on my friends! That would be a rotten thing to do. And if I gave back my share … well, that would be like saying those guys did something wrong.

Narrator: Uh … excuse me, but—

Jacob: I know! I know! They *did* do something wrong, but I'm their friend so I shouldn't do anything to point that out. I mean … what kind of friend would I be if I went around making them feel bad about themselves?

Narrator: Jacob worked hard to convince himself he shouldn't do anything about the stolen money. But he had a thing or two to learn about honesty—and friendship.

Scene Seven

Narrator: *(as Anya, Lily, and Sam enter)* In P.E., Jacob's new friends cornered him behind the bleachers.

Anya: You're not going to tell, are you?

Jacob: No, of course not! No! No way!

Sam: Good.

Jacob: It's just …

Lily: What?

Jacob: Everybody was really looking forward to that field trip.

Anya: To the art museum? I don't think so. Only the true dorks wanted to go.

Lily: Right.

Sam: You didn't want to go, did you, Jacob?

Jacob: *(snorts)* No. Museums are so boring. But … you know … Mr. Yokum felt so bad …

Lily: So? He'll get over it.

Anya: And who cares how a teacher feels anyway?

Jacob: I don't! I was just saying … you know … He felt bad and that's just too darn bad! Yeah. Too bad for him.

Sam: So we're cool then?

Jacob: You bet.

Anya: And you're not going to pull some Honest Abe thing on us?

Jacob: Of course not. I wouldn't do that to you guys. I know you have plans for that money—

Daniel: *(entering)* What money? Did you … oh, man! You guys stole the field trip money?

Sam: *(to Jacob)* Way to go, big mouth!

Daniel: I can't believe you did that! You … you have to give it back.

Anya: Well … okay.

Lily: What?

Sam: We're giving it back?

Anya: It's the right thing to do. George Washington says so.

Jacob: But I said that, too, and … never mind.

Anya: Just give us some time, Daniel. We have to figure out a way to give the money back without getting caught, okay?

Daniel: Okay. I won't say anything.

Anya: Thanks!

Daniel: Oh, the coach sent me to look for you. You'd better get out there. *(exits)*

Jacob: Man! Busted! Darn! I can't believe we have to give that money back.

Anya: *(laughs)* We're not giving the money back, you dope.

Jacob: We're not?

Lily: Good!

Sam: Ha! You scared me for a minute there.

Jacob: I don't understand.

Anya: We're keeping the money. And we're not getting blamed for stealing it either.

Jacob: But … but how can that happen?

Lily: Yeah. Daniel will tell on us.

Anya: Don't worry. I have a plan. That money envelope should still be in the trashcan in the alcove. All I have to do is—

Coach: *(offstage)* Everybody on the gym floor! Now!

Anya: You guys go ahead. I'll be back soon. *(exits)*

Jacob: *(as others exit)* I wonder what she's planning. I have a bad feeling about this, but that's probably stupid. I mean … she's going to save us all, right? That's a real friend.

Scene Eight

Narrator: *(as Sam, Lily, Daniel, and extra students enter and take seats)* Anya slipped back into the gym later, but after P.E., she disappeared again.

Jacob: *(to Sam and Lily)* Where's Anya?

Sam: I don't know.

Lily: *(as Anya and Mrs. Santiago enter)* There she is—out in the hall with Mrs. Santiago.

Mrs. Santiago: *(to Anya)* Are you sure?

Anya: *(acting upset)* Yes, ma'am. I just hated to say anything, but I felt like I had to.

Mrs. Santiago: *(to Anya)* You did the right thing. Go ahead and take your seat. *(coming closer to class)* I know you've all heard about the stolen money. I have reason to suspect the thief is in this class.

Sam: No!

Lily: You're kidding!

Mrs. Santiago: I'm afraid not. I'd like to give the thief a chance to come clean. If you own up to what you've done—and return the money—things will go easier on you. And, more importantly, you'll be doing the right thing. *(pause)* Well?

Jacob: Mrs. Santiago—

Anya: I don't think the thief is going to confess.

Mrs. Santiago: I think you're right, Anya. Very well then.

Narrator: Mrs. Santiago walked across the room and stood by Daniel's desk.

Mrs. Santiago: Daniel, please open your desk for me.

Daniel: Yes, ma'am.

Anya: There it is! Right by his math book! It's Mr. Yokum's money envelope!

Others (except Jacob and Daniel): *(gasp)*

Daniel: How did that get there?

Mrs. Santiago: Let me see that … It's empty. Where's the money, Daniel?

Daniel: I … I … I …

Sam: Man. You sure aren't like George Washington. He was an honest guy.

Lily: This is unbelievable.

Anya: It's like we don't know you at all. Right, Jacob?

Jacob: Yeah. Right. We don't know you.

Daniel: *(to Jacob)* And I don't know you. *(to Mrs. Santiago)* I didn't take that money, Mrs. Santiago. Somebody else stole it.

Anya: Can you prove that?

Daniel: No. But an envelope isn't really proof either.

Anya: It's evidence!

Mrs. Santiago: All right. That's enough. Daniel, you're right that the envelope doesn't prove anything, but it doesn't look good. I'm going to take you to the principal's office.

Maybe he can sort this problem out. Everybody, get out your library books and read until I return. Come along, Daniel. *(exits)*

Daniel: *(to Jacob)* I can't believe you're going along with this. *(exits)*

Anya: *(to Lily, Sam, and Jacob)* Well, that solves that problem.

Lily: Man! Thanks for taking care of things.

Sam: Yeah, thanks.

Anya: What do you say, Abe?

Jacob: *(upset)* Don't call me that! I'm not Honest Abe, okay?

Anya: Okay, okay. Just relax.

Jacob: *(to self)* I'm nothing like Honest Abe. Not at all.

Scene Nine

Narrator: *(as everyone except Jacob exits)* Jacob had never felt more confused. In one day, he had become a part of the in group—and lost a friend.

Jacob: Daniel and I aren't really friends.

Narrator: Whatever. You're friendly, right? In fact, Daniel's the closest thing you have to a friend.

Jacob: *(muttering)* I have plenty of other friends.

Narrator: Right. Friends. Sure. So where was I?

Jacob: I was confused.

Narrator: Right. So Jacob was confused. He had committed a crime—

Jacob: I did not! I didn't steal the money!

Narrator: Okay. He was the accomplice to a crime—and he let somebody else take the blame.

Jacob: I didn't have anything to do with that!

Narrator: You didn't plant the evidence, but you also didn't speak up for Daniel.

Jacob: Are you kidding? And rat out my friends? That wouldn't be right.

Narrator: *(snorts)* Which is so important to you, huh, Honest Abe?

Jacob: *(through gritted teeth)* Don't call me that.

Narrator: *(sighs)* So Jacob was confused. He finally had what he wanted, but he felt terrible anyway.

Jacob: Yeah. Why is that?

Narrator: Come on. You know why. You're not going to feel right until you make things right.

Jacob: Look … I keep telling everybody … I. Am. Not. Abraham. Lincoln. Nobody is, okay? All that stuff about being honest no matter how tough it is … that's like ancient history, okay? Anya's right about that.

Narrator: I don't think Anya's right about much of anything, but let's go on with our story, shall we?

Jacob: Whatever.

From Diana R. Jenkins, *All Year Long! Funny Readers Theatre for Life's Special Times.* Westport, CT: Teacher Ideas Press. Copyright © 2007 by Diana R. Jenkins.

Narrator: Mrs. Santiago came back without Daniel and started English. Jacob was worried about Daniel, but he told himself that nobody could prove Daniel was guilty so he'd be okay. The mystery of the stolen money would never be solved, no one would be punished, and Jacob would keep his new position and his new friends. Of course, Daniel would probably never forgive him, but so what?

Jacob: Can we move on?

Narrator: *(as Anya, Sam, Lily, and extra students enter)* During the afternoon break, Daniel finally returned. He went right to his desk and started gathering his things.

Lily: So what happened, Daniel?

Daniel: The principal didn't believe me. I'm suspended.

Scene Ten

Narrator: Jacob was really confused now.

Jacob: What? But didn't you say that thing about how the envelope didn't prove anything?

Daniel: What do you care what I said? You're safe—isn't that all that matters to you?

Anya: Yep. Sure is. *(laughs)*

Sam and Lily: *(laugh)*

Jacob: It's not funny! He's being punished for something he didn't do. It isn't right!

Mrs. Santiago: *(enters with principal)* Do you have everything, Daniel?

Daniel: Yes, ma'am.

Principal: Then let's go. Your parents will be here soon to pick you up.

Daniel: *(to extra students)* Bye, you guys.

Extra students: Bye! Later! *(etc.)*

Narrator: *(as Daniel starts to exit in slow motion)* Jacob just stood there and watched Daniel head for the door. He felt awful—just awful. He felt even worse when he saw Anya smirking at him. *She* didn't care about what they were doing to Daniel. She didn't feel bad at all. Was that the kind of person he wanted for a friend? Someone who was that selfish and cold? So what if she was cool—and could make him cool, too? Was it really worth it? And who cared what she thought about old-fashioned ideas like honesty? Was she somebody whose opinion—

Jacob: Okay, okay! *(to Daniel)* Wait! *(to Mrs. Santiago and Principal)* Daniel didn't steal the money. We did—Anya and Sam and Lily and me.

Extra Students: What? Oh, man! *(etc.)*

Anya: That's ridiculous!

Jacob: It's the truth. I have my share of the money right here in my pocket. Here. *(gives Mrs. Santiago the money)*

Mrs. Santiago: Well. This changes everything.

Principal: It certainly does.

Anya: *(nervous)* But it doesn't prove anything … Just because he has money … I mean … I tried to stop them! I told them it was wrong—so wrong—but they wouldn't listen.

Sam: Hey!

Lily: You're lying!

Sam: It was her idea!

Lily: Yeah!

Principal: We're going to get to the bottom of this right now. I want to see all the involved parties in my office. *(exits)*

Lily: *(as she exits)* Gee, thanks, Jacob.

Sam: *(as he exits)* Yeah.

Anya: *(as she exits)* I hate you … you … Abe!

Daniel: *(to Jacob)* Thanks for telling the truth.

Jacob: I should have done that before. Sorry! I guess there's a reason people still admire Washington and Lincoln. It's not easy to do the right thing, and I—

Principal: *(enters)* Let's go, Jacob! Office! Now!

Jacob: Yes, sir. (ma'am)

Narrator: *(as everyone exits)* Everything got settled pretty quickly after that. The money was returned, apologies were made to Mr. Yokum, and the field trip was back on. Not that Jacob, Anya, Lily, or Sam got to go. They were all suspended for a while. Luckily, they returned to school in time for the Presidents' Day program.

Jacob: *(enters wearing hat and beard)* People call me "Honest Abe." I try to live up to that name, but it's not easy. Still, I believe honesty is important. Maybe I explained my philosophy best in the speech I gave in 1854. *(clears throat)* "Stand with anybody that stands RIGHT. Stand with him while he is right and PART with him when he goes wrong."

Narrator: Cool.

Jacob: Not really. I'm not cool, remember?

Narrator: *(grinning)* So? At least you're honest … Abe.

Jacob: Thanks. *(They exit.)*

St. Patrick's Day

The Luck of the Irish

Summary

Arizona doesn't believe in good luck charms, but her friend Shannon does. Shannon's grandmother gave her a necklace with a shamrock charm, and now she thinks she has the luck of the Irish! Arizona decides to convince her there's no such thing by stealing the necklace. But then Arizona starts getting lucky herself!

Costumes, Sets, and Props

❖ All characters can wear contemporary clothing. Mr. Barrymore could dress like a coach with a cap, whistle, and clipboard.

❖ A few chairs or desks can serve as the classrooms.

❖ Props can be mimed, but if props are desired, the following can be used: necklace with shamrock charm; school supplies such as books, pencils, and notebooks; and cafeteria trays.

Presentation

Arizona becomes more and more frustrated with Shannon as the play goes on.
Mr. Barrymore acts more like a coach than a director.

Supplemental Reading

Gnojewski, Carol. *St. Patrick's Day Crafts.* Berkeley Heights, NJ: Enslow, 2004.

Krull, Kathleen (adapter). *A Pot o' Gold: A Treasury of Irish Stories, Poetry, Folklore, and (of Course) Blarney.* New York: Hyperion Books for Children, 2004.

Richardson, Charisse K. *The Real Lucky Charm.* New York: Puffin Books, 2005.

Riordan, James, editor. *The Kingfisher Treasury of Irish Stories.* Boston: Kingfisher, 1995.

Cast of Characters

Narrator

Arizona

Arizona's friends: Shannon, Pamela, Brody, Raoul, and Chris

Mrs. (Mr.) Everwood, art teacher

Mr. (Mrs.) Barrymore, play director

Extra students (two or more)

Ms. (Mr.) James, math teacher

St. Patrick's Day

The Luck of the Irish

Scene One

Narrator: A rabbit's foot … lucky socks … a four leaf clover … Some people believe in good-luck charms like that. But Arizona always thought the idea of some thing bringing luck was ridiculous. So when Shannon became obsessed with the "luck of the Irish," Arizona just couldn't handle it. The whole thing started with a gold necklace that had a shamrock charm.

(Arizona, Shannon, Pamela, Brody, Raoul, and Chris enter.)

Shannon: Hey, you guys! Look at this necklace my grandmother gave me.

Arizona: Cute. So is anybody auditioning out for the spring play? I was thinking of trying out for the princess. I love how she gets all worried about her big feet. Talk about funny!

Shannon: It's a special necklace. That's what Grandma says. The shamrock will bring me the luck of the Irish, and I'll have good fortune whenever I wear it.

Pamela: It's nice, Shannon.

Arizona: Yeah. Now about the play …

Chris: Have you had any good luck yet?

Shannon: Not yet. But I'm sure I will soon.

Arizona: Wearing that necklace won't do anything. Good luck charms don't work, you know.

Raoul: I always wear my lucky socks when I play basketball. I haven't washed them since we won the championship last year.

Arizona: Ew! That's disgusting!

Raoul: But it works, Arizona.

Arizona: No, it doesn't. You've lost three games in a row.

Raoul: Well … it works a lot of the time.

Brody: I have a lucky rock that works. I carry it in my pocket when we're going to have a test.

Chris: He-e-ey … and you always get As.

Arizona: Because he studies all the time. Not because of the rock!

Shannon: Well, I believe in charms. I can't wait for all the good luck this necklace will bring.

Arizona: Then you're going to be waiting a long time, Shannon. A long, long time.

Scene Two

Narrator: *(as Arizona, friends, and extra students take seats)* But it wasn't long at all before things began to happen to Shannon. *Lucky* things. Like in art class …

Mrs. Everwood: *(enters)* I have some big news, everybody. Remember the painting contest you entered back in January?

Chris: The one sponsored by the new nature center?

Brody: With the fifty-dollar prize?

Mrs. Everwood: That's it! I'm delighted to announce that one of my art students won.

Students: Wow! Yay! Great! *(etc.)*

Mrs. Everwood: And the winner is … Shannon!

Brody: What?

Chris: Seriously?

Mrs. Everwood: Yep! Congratulations, Shannon.

Shannon: Thanks. Wow! Fifty dollars!

Arizona: But her painting was so … I mean … It was just the sun.

Brody: Yeah. Just a yellow circle. With orange rays.

Mrs. Everwood: Shannon's painting was beautiful in its simplicity.

Arizona: It was simple all right.

Mrs. Everwood: That's enough, Arizona.

Shannon: Oh, it's okay, Mrs. Everwood. My picture wasn't very good at all. I don't understand how I won … Wait a minute. Maybe I do. It was my lucky necklace!

Arizona: That doesn't make sense, Shannon. You didn't have the necklace back in January.

Shannon: But I wore it all weekend. Maybe that's when the judges picked the winner.

Arizona: That's ridiculous!

Chris: You just don't want to believe good-luck charms work.

Arizona: Well, they *don't* work. Do they, Mrs. Everwood?

Mrs. Everwood: Hmmm … I don't know, Arizona. I once had this penny I thought was lucky. Every time I carried it, something good happened to me.

Arizona: Where's the penny now?

Mrs. Everwood: Oh, I lost it years ago.

Arizona: Gee. That was kind of unlucky, wasn't it?

Mrs. Everwood: Yes, I guess it was. Well, let's get started on today's project.

Narrator: But Arizona couldn't concentrate on her work. All she could think about was how wrong it was for Shannon to win the contest.

Arizona: They must have mixed her painting up with somebody else's. Like mine.

Scene Three

Narrator: (*as everyone except Arizona and Shannon exits*) Shannon's good luck continued throughout the day.

Shannon: Ms. James didn't give us any math homework. I really do have the luck of the Irish!

Arizona: Duh, Shannon. None of us has math homework.

Shannon: Man! This shamrock charm is powerful. It worked for everyone around me.

Narrator: At lunch, the cafeteria ladies served Shannon's favorite food.

Shannon: Veggie pizza! How lucky is that?

Arizona: It's not like it's the first time they ever had veggie pizza.

Shannon: I know, but they don't have it very often. I'm so lucky they have it today.

Narrator: And in science class …

Shannon: I got the best Bunsen burner!

Arizona: So?

Narrator: All day long, everything went Shannon's way.

Shannon: Wow! The luck of the Irish is making my life wonderful.

Arizona: Aaargh! There's no such thing as luck. That stupid necklace isn't doing anything.

Shannon: Yes, it is! And I'm feeling so lucky, I think I'll try out for the play this afternoon.

Narrator: Arizona had seen Shannon perform in a few plays in elementary school. She knew she had no acting talent whatsoever.

Arizona: Good idea! That'll be a real test of your good luck charm.

Shannon: Yes, it will. You'll see, Arizona. It really works.

Arizona: Sure it does. Sure.

Scene Four

Narrator: (*as Mr. Barrymore, friends, and extra students enter*) Arizona had starred in lots of plays, and she was confident she would soon be playing the princess with the big feet. Of course, she'd have to audition like everybody else, but she figured that was just a formality.

Mr. Barrymore: (*blows whistle*) Listen up! We're going to hit these auditions fast, and we're going to hit 'em hard.

Chris: I don't understand. What does that mean?

Mr. Barrymore: Look, I don't need any attitude from you. Are you a part of this team or not?

Chris: Team?

Mr. Barrymore: Okay. That's ten laps.

Chris: But … but …

Mr. Barrymore: Make it twenty.

(*Chris runs offstage.*)

Mr. Barrymore: (*blows whistle*) Princesses first!

From Diana R. Jenkins, *All Year Long! Funny Readers Theatre for Life's Special Times.* Westport, CT: Teacher Ideas Press. Copyright © 2007 by Diana R. Jenkins.

Narrator: Of course all the girls tried out for the princess. Finally, it was Arizona's turn onstage.

Mr. Barrymore: Okay, Arizona. Hit the ground running.

Arizona: Uh … yes, sir. *(pauses to get into character, then overacts)* Why was I cursed with these humongous clodhoppers? These flapping flippers? These huge, stinking tootsies? If only I could be a normal princess! Oh, boo-hoo-hoo!

Mr. Barrymore: Good effort, good effort. Your turn, Shannon.

Shannon: *(flatly)* Why was I cursed with these humongous clodhoppers these flapping flippers these huge stinking tootsies if only I could be a normal *(takes a breath)* princess.

Mr. Barrymore: Shannon—

Shannon: Oops! I forgot something. *(flatly)* Oh. Boo. Hoo. Hoo.

Mr. Barrymore: Shannon. That was absolutely unbelievable.

Arizona: *(to friends)* No kidding! She's terrible.

Mr. Barrymore: Your performance was beautifully understated and yet so moving. You're going to be the star of our play.

Arizona: WHAT? But she's … but I … I thought … This isn't right!

Mr. Barrymore: Settle down there. I'm going to play you, too. You can be the maid.

Arizona: But the maid doesn't have any lines!

Mr. Barrymore: Can the attitude, Arizona. Unless you want to *(Chris enters)* drop and give me fifty push-ups. *(Chris collapses to floor and attempts push-ups.)* Okay, Shannon. Get right to work on memorizing your lines.

Shannon: Yes, sir. And thanks! I feel so lucky to get this role.

Arizona: Brother.

Scene Five

Narrator: *(as everyone exits except Arizona, Pamela, and Raoul)* After the tryouts, Arizona stomped towards home with Pamela and Raoul. She had never been so upset in her life.

Arizona: The luck of the Irish! How ridiculous is that? *(pauses)* Well? How ridiculous is that?

Pamela: Very!

Raoul: A lot!

Pamela: Incredibly a lot.

Raoul: Very incredibly a lot.

Arizona: You're telling me! She actually believes that shamrock necklace brings her luck. Hasn't she ever heard of coincidences? *(pauses)* Well? Hasn't she?

Pamela: Apparently not.

Raoul: Doesn't look like it.

Arizona: No kidding! So she had one good day.

Pamela: Probably one of the best days of her life.

Arizona: The necklace didn't have anything to do with that. A lucky necklace! That's just dumb.

Raoul: *(snorts)* It's not like lucky socks.

Arizona: I'm going to prove to her that necklace is worthless.

Pamela: How are you going to do that?

Arizona: Easy! I'll take it.

Raoul: You're going to steal it?

Arizona: No, of course not. I'm going to borrow it awhile. When her life goes on just fine without it, she'll realize the necklace has no powers at all.

Pamela: I don't know, Arizona. … You're not doing this just because you're jealous, are you?

Arizona: Jealous? What are you talking about?

Raoul: Well, you seemed pretty mad when Shannon won the art contest and you didn't.

Pamela: And now she has the lead in the play, too.

Arizona: She didn't *deserve* any of that, but it's no big deal. Really. The important thing is Shannon can't go through life relying on some stupid good luck charm instead of standing on her own two feet. Right?

Pamela: Right.

Raoul: Yeah. Sure.

Arizona: So this is for Shannon's own good. I have to. … What's that awful smell?

Pamela: There's a basketball game tonight.

Arizona: Ew, Raoul! Are you wearing those nasty socks?

Raoul: Sorry. It works better if I wear them all day. I guess the luck has to kind of build up.

Arizona: Along with the smell. See you guys tomorrow! *(They exit.)* Now I have to figure out a way to get my hands on that necklace.

Scene Six

Narrator: Luckily...

Arizona: *(clears throat)*

Narrator: Or maybe it had nothing to do with luck at all. Whatever! The next day they had swimming in P.E. So Shannon took off her necklace and left it in her gym locker. Then Arizona lingered behind while everyone else went to the pool. Since she and Shannon were friends, she knew Shannon's combination which made it easy to steal her most prized possession.

Arizona: It's not stealing! I'm trying to teach her an important lesson. Because I care, you know.

Narrator: Right. Arizona hid the necklace in her own locker and went to the pool. After class, she slipped the necklace into a pocket and headed for Math.

Arizona: *(to self as friends and extra students enter)* Shannon will have to give up her idiotic superstition as soon as something good happens to her.

From Diana R. Jenkins, *All Year Long! Funny Readers Theatre for Life's Special Times.* Westport, CT: Teacher Ideas Press. Copyright © 2007 by Diana R. Jenkins.

Shannon: *(entering)* I can't find my shamrock necklace! I wore it to school, but now it's gone.

Brody: Did you have it when you went to P.E.?

Shannon: I … I think so. It seems like I remember taking it off and putting it in my locker.

Arizona: Sometimes the clasp will break on a necklace and it'll fall off.

Pamela: Yeah. And sometimes people steal things like that.

Arizona: And sometimes people borrow stuff awhile and then return it so it's not really stealing.

Pamela: Whatever.

Ms. James: *(enters)* Please clear your desks for a pop quiz.

Students: *(groan)*

Shannon: *(to Arizona)* I'm going to flunk without my lucky necklace.

Arizona: You are not. That necklace is not lucky!

Ms. James: Arizona, you've aced every pop quiz so far. I'm giving you something else to do.

Arizona: I don't have to take the quiz?

Ms. James: Not this time. Instead, could you return some books to the office for me?

Arizona: Okay. Sure!

Shannon: Man! I wish I had your kind of luck.

Arizona: It's not luck, Shannon.

Mr. James: Quiet, people! Let's get started on the quiz.

Shannon: I am so going to flunk.

Scene Seven

Narrator: *(as others except Arizona and Shannon exit)* The rest of Arizona's day went just as well. In English class, Arizona got picked to edit the new school newspaper.

Shannon: Lucky dog!

Arizona: It's not luck, Shannon. I'm a good writer.

Shannon: Me, too. But I'm not lucky anymore so I wasn't chosen.

Narrator: And at lunch …

Arizona: I can't believe I got the last piece of chocolate cake.

Shannon: See? You *are* lucky.

Arizona: No, I'm not. It's just a coincidence.

Shannon: No, it's not. You're lucky, and I'm unlucky. I got stuck with this green gelatin goop. Are those peas floating inside?

Narrator: In science …

Shannon: You got the good Bunsen burner? Man! It's like you have the luck of the Irish now.

Arizona: Give me a break.

From Diana R. Jenkins, *All Year Long! Funny Readers Theatre for Life's Special Times.* Westport, CT: Teacher Ideas Press. Copyright © 2007 by Diana R. Jenkins.

Narrator: *(as Shannon exits in a mope)* It did seem strange that good things started happening to Arizona after she got the shamrock necklace, but she told herself it didn't mean anything.

Arizona: Nothing at all.

Raoul: *(entering with Pamela)* Where's Shannon's necklace?

Arizona: It's safe. I have it in my pocket.

Pamela: You have to give it back.

Arizona: Later. If I give it back to her now, she won't learn anything.

Raoul: But everything's going wrong for her. It's making her feel terrible.

Arizona: That's just part of the learning process.

Pamela: Don't you care about how she feels?

Arizona: Of course I do! She's my friend. But something will go right soon. Then she'll have to admit good luck charms don't work.

Pamela: Hmmm … so charms don't work, huh? It seems to me you're having a pretty good day.

Raoul: Yeah. Everything's going great for you—while you're carrying around that necklace.

Arizona: Maybe this is a good lesson for you guys, too. Soon something bad will happen to me even though I have the necklace. That will be even more proof that charms don't work.

Pamela: Whatever. That necklace doesn't belong to you and you have to give it back.

Arizona: I will.

Raoul: Well, do it soon. Or we'll have to tell Shannon you took it. *(They exit.)*

Arizona: Things will all work out at play practice. After all, Shannon has the lead so something good is bound to happen to her there.

Scene Eight

Narrator: *(as all students enter and take seats)* But losing the necklace had really affected Shannon. She was depressed and discouraged, and *that* affected her performance.

Mr. Barrymore: *(enters, blowing whistle)* I hope you all brought winning attitudes today because we're going to hustle. Right? I said, "Right?"

Students: Right!

Mr. Barrymore: *(to Chris)* Right?

Chris: Right!

Mr. Barrymore: *(to Chris)* Look, I don't want any of your lip. Got it?

Chris: Yes, sir! Got it! You bet!

Mr. Barrymore: Okay, then. Shannon, let's start with your speech from page three.

Shannon: *(with great emotion)* My life is ruined—just ruined! Everything is going totally wrong for me—and things will never get better. Never! I can't—

Mr. Barrymore: Cut! Cut! Cut, cut, cut! What are you doing, Shannon?

Shannon: The speech from page three.

From Diana R. Jenkins, *All Year Long! Funny Readers Theatre for Life's Special Times.* Westport, CT: Teacher Ideas Press. Copyright © 2007 by Diana R. Jenkins.

Mr. Barrymore: But what happened to the character you showed me yesterday? Where's all the poignant subtlety?

Shannon: I don't know.

Mr. Barrymore: Try your speech from the audition. Maybe that'll get you back in the groove.

Shannon: Okay. *(with great emotion)* Why was I cursed with these humongous clodhoppers? These flapping flippers? These huge, stinking tootsies? If only I could be a normal—

Mr. Barrymore: CUT! What is the matter with you, Shannon?

Shannon: I … I don't think I can handle playing the princess, Mr. Barrymore. I'm sorry. *(exits)*

Mr. Barrymore: You see that, team? That's a quitter. There's nothing worse than a quitter. Nothing! Well, Arizona, you'll have to be our princess.

Arizona: Really? Me? The princess?

Mr. Barrymore: Yep. I guess this is your lucky day.

Pamela: Yeah. Lucky.

Raoul: Real lucky.

Arizona: It is not! I mean … thanks, Mr. Barrymore. Thanks.

Scene Nine

Narrator: *(as everyone exits except Arizona)* Arizona figured Pamela and Raoul would have plenty to say about the good luck charm that seemed to work—and she didn't want to hear it! After rehearsal, she let them get a good head start on the walk home, but they waited for her along the way.

Pamela: *(entering with Raoul)* Okay, you have to admit it now. That necklace *is* lucky.

Arizona: No, it's not.

Raoul: Then how do you explain what happened today? Shannon was actually good.

Pamela: But Mr. Barrymore got on her case about her acting.

Raoul: Yet he loved her terrible acting when she had the shamrock necklace.

Pamela: Isn't that proof enough for you?

Arizona: All that proves is that Mr. Barrymore isn't a very good director.

Pamela: *(to Raoul)* He's not really.

Raoul: *(to Pamela)* Not at all.

Pamela: *(to Arizona)* Okay, maybe you're right. But even if the necklace doesn't have any powers, Shannon thinks it does.

Raoul: Yeah. And her life is a train wreck without it. So you have to give it back.

Arizona: I will, but I think I should hold onto it a while longer.

Pamela: Like until the play is over, maybe?

Raoul: Ri-i-ight. In case the necklace got you the lead?

Arizona: Don't be ridiculous. It's just that I think my plan can still work. If one good thing would happen then … hey … I have an idea. Why wait around? Let's *make* good stuff happen. Yeah … let's make tomorrow a great day for Shannon.

Pamela: How?

Arizona: For one thing, we can be extra nice to her. And … and … and … well, let me think about it and come up with a plan. You guys will help me, right?

Raoul: Couldn't you just return the necklace now?

Arizona: We have to help Shannon face reality. We're her friends. If we don't do it, who will?

Raoul: I don't know …

Arizona: *(intensely)* Just imagine it! She has a fantastic day … and then BAM! I whip out the necklace and make her admit that I was right all along! *(mildly)* What a great life lesson, huh?

Pamela: Okay. I'll help.

Raoul: I'm in, too. But this better work.

Arizona: It will … it will. *(They exit.)*

Scene Ten

Narrator: The next morning, Arizona explained her plan to Raoul and Pamela as they walked to school. When they got inside the building, they hurried around the school and talked to all Shannon's teachers. When the teachers heard that Shannon was feeling down on herself, they agreed to give her some extra attention.

Arizona: *(entering with Raoul and Pamela)* There! Now we have to do our part, too. We're going to say nice stuff to Shannon and let her go first in the lunch line and … who has a dollar?

Raoul: What for?

Arizona: I'll put the dollar where Shannon can find it. That will make her feel lucky, see?

Pamela: Why don't you use your own money?

Arizona: Oh, all right. I just thought you guys wanted to help, but if you don't care …

Narrator: Arizona dug a dollar out of her pocket and slid it through a slot in Shannon's locker.

Arizona: Shannon is going to have a great day while her good luck charm is safe in my pocket.

Raoul: And once she's convinced, you're going to give it back, right?

Arizona: Yes! How many times do I have to tell you guys that? *(pauses)* Well? How many?

Pamela: Lots.

Raoul: Lots and lots.

Pamela: Lots and lots and—

Arizona: Funny. *(They exit.)*

From Diana R. Jenkins, *All Year Long! Funny Readers Theatre for Life's Special Times.* Westport, CT: Teacher Ideas Press. Copyright © 2007 by Diana R. Jenkins.

Scene Eleven

Narrator: Shannon *did* have a great day. Teachers picked her to do special jobs. Her friends praised everything she did. The cafeteria served veggie lasagna for lunch, and she bought an extra helping with the dollar she found in her locker.

Shannon: *(enters, talking to self)* Luck sure is funny. It can change like that! *(snaps fingers)* One minute you have no luck. Then suddenly you find your luck again. Who would have thought—

Arizona: *(enters)* We're starting rehearsals in a few minutes.

Shannon: I know.

Arizona: So what are you doing here? You're not in the play anymore.

Shannon: I'm going to ask Mr. Barrymore to give me another chance. I have the feeling he's going to say yes. I have the luck of the Irish back! I think I'll wait for him out in the hall. *(exits as Pamela and Raoul enter)*

Arizona: This is terrible! She thinks she's lucky again!

Pamela: Isn't that what you wanted?

Arizona: But she's going to ask if she can have her part back. *My* part! I have to convince her she's unlucky again before Mr. Barrymore gets here! Hey, isn't breaking a mirror supposed to be bad luck? Now where can I get a mirror? Quick! Help me!

Raoul: Wait a minute. I thought you were doing all this because you cared about Shannon.

Pamela: Yeah. You wanted to help her learn an important lesson. Are you her friend or not?

Arizona: Sure, but … but … but … *(in a tiny, pouty voice)* I want to be the princess.

Raoul: *(to Pamela)* She just did all this to get back at Shannon.

Pamela: *(to Raoul)* Yeah, she couldn't stand it that Shannon won the contest.

Raoul: *(to Pamela)* Right. And she *really* hated it when Shannon got the lead in the play.

Pamela: *(to Raoul)* So she decided to make Shannon suffer. She stole her necklace and—

Arizona: Yoo-hoo. I'm standing right here.

Raoul: Oh. Yeah.

Arizona: Look, you guys. Maybe you're kind of, a little bit, partially right. I *was* slightly jealous. And a teensy bit mad.

Pamela: A teensy bit?

Arizona: And maybe I started all this for the wrong reasons. But … I am Shannon's friend. And I do want her to quit believing in good luck charms. Getting her part back without the necklace will be really convincing proof. So … *(sighs)* I won't try to stop her.

Raoul: That's great, Arizona.

Pamela: Yeah. Shannon's really going to learn an important lesson because you cared.

Arizona: *(sighing)* Yeah.

Raoul: You know … Mr. Barrymore might not let her come back. He did say she was a quitter.

Arizona: *(brightening)* Yeah!

Scene Twelve

Narrator: *(as other students, except Shannon, enter)* So Arizona did the right thing. It killed her to see Shannon talking to Mr. Barrymore out in the hall, but she didn't interfere.

Mr. Barrymore: *(enters blowing whistle)* Okay, listen up, everybody! I've decided to give Shannon one more chance so welcome her back to our team.

Chris: *(clapping and shouting as Shannon enters)* Welcome back, Shannon! Way to go! Woo … *(realizes everyone is staring)* hoo.

Mr. Barrymore: *(to Chris)* That's ten laps, funny guy.

Chris: But I … Yes, sir. *(exits running)*

Shannon: Thanks so much, Mr. Barrymore. I won't let you down this time.

Mr. Barrymore: Of course not. Now let's practice the banquet scene. On the double, people! *(exits along with everyone except Shannon and Arizona)*

Shannon: Wow! This has been my lucky day!

Arizona: It wasn't luck. How can it be luck when you don't have your shamrock necklace?

Shannon: But I—

Arizona: Wait! I'll show you. I have it … I mean … wait a minute … it's here somewhere …

Shannon: Did you lose something? Maybe I can help you find it now that I have my lucky necklace back. *(takes out necklace)*

Arizona: *(shocked)* Where did you get that?

Shannon: I found it when I got here this morning. It was on the floor right in front of my locker. Wasn't that lucky? Then I found a dollar that I didn't know I had and Mrs. Everwood said that nice stuff about my sculpture in Art and … well … the whole day was fantastic! *(exits)*

Arizona: I … I can't believe it. It works! It's a good luck charm that really works! Why didn't I believe that before? Now Shannon has the luck of the Irish and the starring role in the play, and I'm the unlucky one! I have to find a lucky penny … or a … a … chicken bone … yeah … one of those wishbones … or a four leaf clover …

Shannon: *(enters)* Mr. Barrymore says to get the lead out of your britches and get in here because we can't do the banquet scene without the princess.

Arizona: Huh? I thought you were the princess.

Shannon: Me? After what I did, I'm lucky I get to come back and play the maid. *(exits)*

Narrator: *(to Arizona)* So what were you saying? About the chicken bone and the four leaf clover and all that?

Arizona: Nothing. Never mind. Just joking. Well … I have a play to rehearse. *(starts to exit)*

Narrator: Hey, good luck with that!

Arizona: *(smiling)* Thanks! *(exits)*

(Chris runs a lap through the audience during curtain call.)

Spring Break

Hos-key-wow-wow!

Summary

Reese's family always takes boring, educational vacations. This spring break, they're visiting Museum Kingdom! Reese figures he'll be bored to death, like usual, but then he meets Lorelei. She teaches him a secret game that changes everything!

Costumes, Sets, and Props

❖ All characters can wear contemporary clothing.

❖ Some chairs can serve as the family car. A table and a few chairs will do for the rest of the scenes. Museum exhibits can be left to the imagination.

❖ If props are desired, Reese can use index cards and a pencil, and Lorelei can use a notebook and a pencil. Reese and Lorelei can drink from large measuring cups in Scene Five. Dishes, silverware, cups, trays, and food can be used in the snack bar.

Presentation

Reese's and Lorelei's families are enthusiastic about everything no matter how dull.

The offstage voice should sound dreary and boring.

Reese and Lorelei hang on their parents' words when they're playing the game and act disappointed when they don't say anything that counts.

Supplemental Reading

Kraft, Erik P. *Lenny and Mel's Summer Vacation.* New York: Simon & Schuster Books for Young Readers, 2003.

Smith, Anne Warren. *Tails of Spring Break.* Morton Grove, IL: Albert Whitman, 2005.

Cast of Characters

Reese

Mom, Dad, Amber, and Will—Reese's family

Offstage voice

Lorelei

Mother and Father—Lorelei's parents

Spring Break

Hos-key-wow-wow!

Scene One

Reese: What comes to your mind when you hear the words "spring break"? Do you think of warm, sunny beaches? Or fun in the snow? Does spring break mean fishing … or hiking … or just relaxing at home? Well then … you're normal. Unlike my family! Don't get me wrong. They're regular, ordinary people—except for their ideas about vacations. When my family hears the words "spring break," they think of boring stuff like …

Dad: *(entering with Mom, Amber, and Will)* The Museum of Rulers and Measurement Devices!

Mom: The World's Largest Collection of Historical Buttons!

Amber: The City of Miniature Dolls!

Will: Rice-a-Rama!

Reese: But couldn't we do something … what's Rice-a-Rama?

Will: Get this: it's an entire building covered with rice, inside and out. Doesn't that sound cool?

Reese: Not really.

Will: Listen! All the furniture and appliances and other stuff are covered with rice.

Reese: Dude, that sounds really … I don't know … white?

Will: Right.

Reese: Look, couldn't we just go someplace fun for once?

Mom: We are going someplace fun, Reese. Super fun!

Reese: *(snorts)* You mean we're going to spend our whole break touring the button museum?

Dad: Not really.

Reese: The Land of Dolls?

Amber: That's the *City* of Dolls.

Reese: Whatever. Is that what we're doing with our vacation? Visiting the City of Dolls?

Mom: Not exactly.

Dad: And it's not … oh, let's just tell him. We're vacationing at Museum Kingdom.

Will: It's all there, Reese. It's not *just* the Museum of Rulers and Measurement Devices.

Amber: Or *just* The City of Miniature Dolls.

Mom: Or *just* the World's Largest Collection of Historical Buttons.

Dad: Museum Kingdom is all that—and more. Lots more!

Reese: Wait a minute. Are you saying we're going someplace that's nothing but museums?

Amber: Isn't it great?

Will: They have a corn house, too.

Reese: *(to audience)* Is it possible to die of boredom?

Scene Two

Reese: *(to audience)* So we packed up our suitcases …

Mom: Don't forget to bring plenty of index cards.

Reese: You know, it's not much of a vacation if you have to take notes.

Dad: But how else are you going to remember everything you've learned?

Reese: *(to audience)* And we loaded up the car …

Dad: I bought a very special book on tape for us to listen to on our way to Museum Kingdom.

Reese: How about if we listen to some music?

Mom: But we always listen to a book on tape when we're traveling. It's fun.

Dad: Especially when it's … ta-da! The encyclopedia!

Mom, Amber, and Will: *(cheer)*

Will: We're going to learn so much on this trip.

Reese: But we shouldn't have to learn anything! It's a vacation!

Mom: There's nothing wrong with an educational vacation, son.

Dad: They're the best kind. Remember our trip to the amusement park? Wasn't that fun?

Reese: All we did was watch them repair that broken merry-go-round.

Dad: Talk about educational!

Mom: And fun.

Amber: Who knew a merry-go-round had so many parts?

Reese: *(to audience, getting frustrated)* Aaargh! And then we … And then we … *(takes a deep breath)* I'm okay now. Then we got in the car and headed across the country to the magical world of museums.

Will: That's the Museum Kingdom.

Reese: Whatever.

Scene Three

Reese: *(to audience)* After a long ride …

Offstage Voice: *(gradually fading)* The abacus was used by ancient peoples to solve arithmetic problems. The device consists of a simple frame, wires, and beads. With an abacus, one …

Reese: *(to audience)* A long, long, long ride …

Offstage Voice: *(gradually fading)* The zucchini is a cucumber-like squash that is easily grown in the home garden. Its greenish-white flesh can be eaten raw or cooked in a variety of …

Reese: *(to audience)* We finally reached our hotel which was right next to Museum Kingdom.

Mom: I can't wait to see our rooms. They're sure to be something special.

Reese: *(alarmed)* What do you mean?

Amber: The rooms here are just as educational as the museums.

Reese: Great. Just great. *(to audience)* So … lucky us … we got the Pioneer Suite.

Will: This is so cool!

Reese: You won't think it's cool when you have to go to the outhouse in the middle of the night.

Mom: That just makes the experience authentic, Reese.

Reese: Yeah. Authentically boring. *(to audience)* We unpacked, chopped some firewood, and milked our authentic cows. Then it was time to go to bed.

Dad: We don't want to waste our candles.

Reese: *(to audience)* After a terrible night lying on a burlap bag and an awful morning slopping hogs, I was dragged off to the Museum of Rulers and Measurement Devices. We were looking at a display of thermometers that had been used by doctors who took care of the presidents, and I felt hopelessly bored. I was never going to have a fun vacation. Never!

Amber: So were these thermometers ever in the actual mouths of the presidents?

Dad: Nobody knows for sure, but it is possible.

Will: Wow. Like that one could have Woodrow Wilson's slobber on it?

Reese: Not anymore, you dope. It's all dried up. Or they wiped it off with alcohol or something.

Will: Cool!

Reese: *(to audience)* I felt like screaming, but this girl and her parents came along so I controlled myself. *(Lorelei, Mother, and Father enter.)* The girl had a notebook and a pencil. I figured her parents believed in educational vacations, too, and they were making her take notes.

Mother: Oh, look! Thermometers that were used by the presidents' physicians.

Lorelei: I see.

Will: They used to have presidential slobber on them.

Reese: *(through gritted teeth)* Shut up.

From Diana R. Jenkins, *All Year Long! Funny Readers Theatre for Life's Special Times.* Westport, CT: Teacher Ideas Press. Copyright © 2007 by Diana R. Jenkins.

Father: That's very interesting, young man. Isn't it, Lorelei?

Lorelei: Sure, Father.

Reese: *(to audience)* I couldn't tell how this Lorelei felt about things. Was she actually interested? Or was she just as bored as I was? *(aside to Lorelei)* So is this lame or what?

Lorelei: Shhhh …

Mother: What an educational exhibit!

Lorelei: Hos-key-wow-wow!

Father: *(to Reese's family)* That's the special word she uses when something's really wonderful.

Reese: *(to Lorelei as their families exit, heading for next display)* You like this boring stuff?

Lorelei: Of course not. Do I look like a complete weirdo?

Reese: Well … no … not exactly …

Lorelei: Thanks. Look … I get stuck on a vacation like this every year.

Reese: Yeah. Me, too.

Lorelei: I learned a long time ago that I don't have to be bored out of my gourd.

Reese: You don't?

Lorelei: No, I don't. Thanks to Hos-key-wow-wow.

Reese: Okay. Sure.

Lorelei: Just let me explain it to you.

Scene Four

Reese: *(to audience)* Lorelei showed me her notebook.

Lorelei: Read this list of words.

Reese: Okay. "Interesting. Exhibit. History. Educational." Do I have to keep going?

Lorelei: No. That's enough for you to get the idea. Before we leave on one of these boring family vacations, I make a list like this. A nice long list of words I think my parents might say.

Reese: And the point would be … ?

Lorelei: To make things fun. When they say one of the words, I check it off and say, "Hos-key-wow-wow!" They think that means something is great.

Reese: What does it really mean?

Lorelei: Nothing. It's just a made-up word that I thought sounded cool when I was a little kid. I've been suffering through these boring trips for a long time, you know.

Reese: Me, too. Me, too.

Lorelei: If I get all the words checked off before we get back home, I win.

Reese: What do you win?

Lorelei: Just personal satisfaction, I guess.

Reese: Gee. There's a great prize.

Lorelei: Hey, playing the game helps me enjoy our vacations. And it makes things better for my parents, too, because I'm not moping around the whole time.

Reese: You know, moping is an important communication skill.

Lorelei: Funny. You should try Hos-key-wow-wow, too.

Reese: Maybe that works for you, but I don't think a game can save me. I'm drowning in boredom. And now you want me to pay special attention to the boring stuff my parents say?

Lorelei: You know, a lot of boredom is just a matter of attitude.

Reese: Whatever. I'd better catch up with my family.

Lorelei: Wait! How long are you going to be here?

Reese: All this week.

Lorelei: Us, too. How about if we play Hos-key-wow-wow *against* each other?

Reese: What do you mean? How would we do that?

Lorelei: We make up a list of words together. Then we both use the same list and whoever checks everything off first wins.

Reese: I don't know …

Lorelei: And we'll have a real prize. Like on our last day, the winner gets to pick something from that big souvenir store on the square and the loser has to buy it.

Reese: It might be worth playing your boring game for one of the cool models they sell there.

Lorelei: It's not boring … you'll see!

Reese: Right.

Lorelei: So are you in or not?

Reese: Yeah, I'm in. And I'm going to win.

Scene Five

Reese: *(to audience)* We got permission to go to the snack bar where we ordered two sodas.

Lorelei: Man! Whoever heard of serving pop in measuring cups?

Reese: *(to audience)* Then we sat down and made a new list for Hos-key-wow-wow. We used some of the words Lorelei already had in her notebook, and we came up with some new ones, too. *(to Lorelei)* I think "pickle" should be one of our words.

Lorelei: Come on! What are the chances that anybody's going to say "pickle"?

Reese: Not great, but that's what will make it interesting. Don't you see? If we put in some unlikely words, the game won't be so boring.

Lorelei: It's not boring!

Reese: Look at this list. "Fascinating." "Educational." "Dawn of time." Sounds boring to me!

Lorelei: Of course, the *words* are boring. That's the point! We're turning something boring into … Oh, never mind. Go ahead and put it on the list. But let's not use too many strange words.

Reese: *(to audience)* So we completed our list, and I copied it onto my index cards. Then we made sure we were both clear on the rules. Like it only counted if parents said the words. And whoever said "Hos-key-wow-wow!" first checked the word off and scored a point.

Lorelei: We'll just have to trust each other whenever we're apart.

Reese: Yeah. No cheating!

Lorelei: I don't need to cheat to win.

Reese: Me neither. Okay, let's get started.

Lorelei: Wait, there's one more thing. Be careful. Our parents can't find out what we're doing.

Reese: Well, duh. We'll get in big trouble.

Lorelei: That's not the worst thing. We won't be able to play the game ever again.

Reese: Yeah. And that would be so tragic.

Lorelei: Think about it, Reese. Without Hos-key-wow-wow, all our future vacations will be boring. Hopelessly, torturously boring! Like the boredom would go on and on and—

Reese: Got it. It would be like this conversation. Let's catch up with everybody. The sooner we start playing, the sooner it will be over—and the sooner you lose!

Lorelei: Dream on.

Scene Six

Reese: *(as families enter)* We found our families in front of the measuring tapes display.

Will: So the guy who laid the carpet on the thirty-seventh story of the Empire State Building measured the floors with that tape?

Mom: *(choking up)* Yes, son. Isn't that amazing?

Reese: Hos-key-wow-wow!

Dad: I see you're moved, too, Reese.

Reese: Huh? I mean … right.

Father: I have the feeling that visiting this museum is an experience we'll—

Reese: Hos-key-wow-wow!

Amber: This is really an interesting—

Lorelei: Hos-key-wow-wow!

Reese: I don't think so.

Lorelei: *(aside to Reese)* She said "interesting."

Reese: *(aside to Lorelei)* My brother and sister don't count, remember?

Lorelei: Oh. Oh, yeah.

Dad: Look! Here's the measuring tape that a carpenter who worked on Edison's house in Florida used while making a bookcase for the Madison, Wisconsin library. That's just … *(voice trails off)*

Reese: Just what, Dad? Just what?

Dad: Oh. I was just thinking …

Lorelei: Thinking what? I'm so interested in your thoughts, sir.

Dad: Oh, it's just that …

Reese, Lorelei: What? What?

Dad: How great is it that they've gathered all this stuff in one place?

Reese: *(disappointed)* Really great, Dad.

Lorelei: *(disappointed)* Isn't it though?

Mother: I love it that there's a place like this—a place where a family can go and learn together.

Reese, Lorelei: Hos-key-wow-wow!

Father: It certainly is, kids. It certainly is.

Scene Seven

Reese: *(to audience)* Our families hung together almost all day. We did split up for a little while when my family went outside to eat our authentic picnic lunch of dried-up … something … on dried-up pieces of … something else. But other than that, we spent all day together in that boring place. At least, Hos-key-wow-wow helped pass the time. At five o'clock, Lorelei and I were tied.

Offstage Voice: Attention, please. The museum is now closing. Please visit us again tomorrow.

Will: Can we, Dad? Can we?

Dad: You know, your mother has her heart set on seeing the World's Largest Collection of Historical Buttons.

Will: Okay!

Amber: Cool!

Mother: We're going there tomorrow, too. Maybe we'll meet up again.

Mom: That would be wonderful. Well, ciao!

Reese: Hos-key-wow-wow! *(to Lorelei)* Now I'm winning.

Dad: Ciao, everybody.

Father: Good-bye.

Mother: See you tomorrow.

Lorelei: *(as families exit)* Hey, wait a minute Reese. What's up with this "ciao" stuff?

Reese: That's Italian for "good-bye."

Lorelei: I know that! What I want to know is, do your parents say it a lot?

Reese: A lot? Not really. No. Not much at all.

Lorelei: So you didn't put it on the list because you knew they would say it sometime and get you a point or anything devious like that, huh?

Reese: No! I told you: I don't have to cheat to win.

Lorelei: Well … okay. See you tomorrow. *(exits)*

Reese: *(calling after her)* Ciao!

From Diana R. Jenkins, *All Year Long! Funny Readers Theatre for Life's Special Times.* Westport, CT: Teacher Ideas Press. Copyright © 2007 by Diana R. Jenkins.

Scene Eight

Reese: *(as family enters)* The next morning—after chores, of course—we headed for the World's Largest Collection of Historical Buttons. In just fifteen minutes I scored four points.

Mom: Wow! Think of the skill it—

Reese: Hos-key-wow-wow!

Dad: Why, in olden days they—

Reese: Hos-key-wow-wow!

Mom: I'm amazed by the ingenuity of—

Reese: Hos-key-wow-wow!

Will: Look at that funny button. It's shaped like a pickle.

Reese: Hos-key … oh, yeah. What the heck! Hos-key-wow-wow!

Amber: You're really into this stuff, aren't you?

Reese: Sure. It's kind of … uh …

Amber: Hos-key-wow-wow?

Reese: That's the word! *(to audience)* Soon we ran into Lorelei and her parents.

Everybody: Hello. Hi. Good morning. *(etc.)*

Lorelei: So what does everybody think of this button that was found in a drawer at the shop of the tailor who knew the guy who made Teddy Roosevelt's shirts?

Mom: Amazing!

Reese: You said that about the world's skinniest yardstick.

Mom: Well, that was amazing, too.

Dad: And so is this button. Truly amazing!

Father: I think that's the most amazing button I've seen so far.

Amber: Well, I think—

Reese: Put a lid on it, Amber. I mean … have some manners. The adults were talking.

Will: *(pointing offstage)* Look at that!

Everyone except Reese and Lorelei: *(exiting)* Oooooooooooooooh!

Lorelei: I got three points this morning. "Artistic." "Impressive." "Dawn of time."

Reese: Well, I got four. "Skill." "Olden days." "Ingenuity." "Pickle."

Lorelei: Somebody actually said pickle?

Reese: Yep! I think it was … um … my dad.

Mom: *(entering)* Come on. You need to keep up, kids.

Dad: *(entering)* There you all are! Everybody, look carefully at this next display. *(to wife as they exit)* You're going to love this, Petunia.

Reese: Hos-key-wow-wow!

Lorelei: Hey, is your mom's name "Petunia"?

Reese: No. Of course not.

Lorelei: But your dad just called her that.

Reese: I guess it's a pet name. Like "dear" or "darling" or something like that.

Lorelei: Uh-huh. Something like a pet name that he calls her all the time so you decided to put it on our list to give yourself an advantage?

Reese: Don't be ridiculous. I just picked that word to make this boring game a little more interesting. And it worked, didn't it?

Lorelei: I guess. You just better not be cheating! *(exits)*

Scene Nine

Reese: *(to audience)* Things went back and forth all morning long. Sometimes I surged ahead by two or even three points. Then Lorelei would catch up and pass me. Then I'd move ahead. Then she'd catch me. At noon we were tied again.

Dad: *(as everyone enters)* How about some lunch, everybody?

Others: Yeah! Sure! *(etc.)*

Mom: We could have packed another picnic, but I thought it might be fun to eat at the snack bar.

Reese: Yes! Great idea! But what should we eat? What do you want, Mom?

Mom: Anything but chick-

Reese: Hos-key-wow-wow!

Mom: -en.

Lorelei: Hey …

Reese: I wonder if they take credit cards at the snack bar.

Dad: Now, Reese, you know we only use ca—

Reese: Hos-key-wow-wow!

Dad: —sh.

Lorelei: *(aside to Reese)* You *are* cheating!

Reese: *(aside to Lorelei)* I am not! *(to others)* Gee, I hope they serve something with their sandwiches. Like maybe chips. Or something brown and twisty, you know. And salty.

Father: You mean—

Reese, Lorelei: Hos-key-wow-wow!

Father: —pre—

Reese, Lorelei: Hos-key-wow-wow!

Father: —tz—

Reese, Lorelei: Hos-key-wow-wow!

Father: —els?

Reese, Lorelei: Hos-key-wow-wow! I said it first! No, you didn't! Yes, I did! *(turning to own parents)* I said it first, didn't I?

Mom: Oh, my! What's the problem, kids?

Reese: Nothing.

Lorelei: Yeah. Nothing.

Mother: Well, it doesn't look like nothing to me. You two seem upset.

Lorelei: We're fine, Mother.

Reese: Yeah. Fine.

Will: Good! Let's go eat. *(Families exit.)*

Reese: *(to audience)* But things weren't fine. They weren't fine at all.

Scene Ten

Lorelei: You rigged the list so you would win.

Reese: I did not!

Lorelei: Liar, liar, pants on fire!

Reese: It's not nice to call someone a liar.

Lorelei: Okay then. Cheater, cheater, eat a skeeter!

Reese: I did not cheat!

Lorelei: Right. Like you never noticed your parents like to say "ciao"!

Reese: I didn't! They don't!

Lorelei: Sure. I bet your mom says "anything but chicken" every time you eat out. And you knew you could make your dad say "cash." You stacked the deck in your favor, you cheater!

Reese: You're just accusing me because you can't stand to lose. I feel sorry for you, Lorelei.

Lorelei: Well, I feel sorry for you, too, Reese.

Reese: *(snorting)* Why?

Lorelei: Because … because … because I'm not playing Hos-key-wow-wow with you anymore.

Reese: So? Who cares about your stupid game? It's boring. And so are you.

Lorelei: I can't believe you said that! *(exits)*

Reese: *(to audience, looking ashamed)* I couldn't believe I said it either. I mean … I was just mad because she called me on the cheating. Yeah … I was cheating. How lame was that? It was just a game! And the really bad thing was that I didn't just ruin Hos-key-wow-wow. I ruined what could have been a pretty good friendship, too. If only I could have a do-over!

Scene Eleven

Reese: *(to audience as families enter, sit, and eat)* At lunch, I got an idea I hoped would fix everything. If I could get Lorelei involved in Hos-key-wow-wow again, maybe she'd start having fun and stop being mad, and we could work things out. It was worth a try anyway.

Mom: Now, Will, remember to chew your food thoroughly. It's better for your digestion.

Reese: Yeah. *Digestion.*

Dad: Listen to your mother, son. She is a veritable fount of knowledge.

Reese: Did you hear that, Lorelei?

Lorelei: Yeah. Fount of knowledge. I heard.

Amber: Which display should we see after lunch?

Mom: Hmmm...Let's look at the buttons found in historical cisterns.

Reese: Where did you say they found the buttons?

Mom: In cisterns.

Reese: Cisterns, huh? *Cisterns.* Hmmm … cisterns.

Lorelei: I heard, I heard.

Father: I love this museum. It's so … so mind-expanding!

Reese: *(to audience)* "Mind-expanding" was on the list along with "digestion," "knowledge," and "cisterns." Lorelei knew that! *(to Lorelei)* Your dad said this place is "mind-expanding."

Lorelei: So?

Reese: Well … don't you think he's right? I mean … isn't it really … you know?

Lorelei: *(dully)* It's great. The museum's great.

Reese: Yeah, it's really … something … .You know … .Hos … Hos-key …

Lorelei: Say it if you want. I don't care. I'm not playing, remember?

Reese: *(dully)* Hos-key-wow-wow.

Lorelei: *(to parents)* Can we get out of here?

Mother: But you've hardly touched your lunch. Nothing's more important than good nutrition.

Reese: *(dully)* Hos-key-wow-wow.

Lorelei: I'd really like to see the corn house today. Couldn't we go there next?

Father: Well … all right. We can't fit everything into this week anyway.

Mother: Maybe we *should* be covering ground more quickly. *(to Reese's family)* Good-bye!

Father: Hope to see you later!

Reese's family: *(as Lorelei's mother and father exit)* Good-bye! Ciao! *(etc.)*

Reese: Wait, Lorelei! You left your notebook on the table.

Lorelei: I don't want it anymore. *(exits)*

Scene Twelve

Reese: *(to audience as family exits)* My family spent all afternoon looking at buttons. I didn't pay attention to the displays. And I didn't listen to anything anybody said either. I just walked around like a zombie carrying Lorelei's notebook in my undead hands like … like whatever zombies like to carry around. I felt like I was smothering in boredom—*and* I felt terrible for making Lorelei feel bad. This was the worst vacation ever! And it was my own fault, wasn't it?

Amber: *(entering with Will)* Come on, Reese! We're going to see the world's largest button.

Will: It's really hos-key-wow-wow!

Reese: No, it's not.

Amber: But you haven't even seen it yet.

Reese: And yet I'm absolutely certain it's boring.

Amber: Never mind, Will. *(exits)*

Will: Believe me, dude. You *want* to see that button. *(exits)*

Reese: *(to audience as Lorelei enters)* I dragged myself over to the world's largest button and got a big surprise. *(to Lorelei)* Lorelei! I thought you were going to the corn house.

Lorelei: It's closed for repairs. The sun got too hot, and the roof popped off. So my parents decided we'd come back here for the afternoon.

Reese: Listen, Lorelei … I … uh … that is … I mean …

Lorelei: What do you want, Reese?

Reese: I … uh … want to give you your Hos-key-wow-wow notebook.

Lorelei: I told you: I don't want it. Why would I want to play such a "boring" game?

Reese: It's not boring, Lorelei. It's genius! Come on. Let's make a new list and start over.

Lorelei: But you don't want to play with somebody like me—somebody "boring"—do you?

Reese: I'm sorry I said that, okay? I just didn't want to admit that I *had* been cheating. I don't really think you're boring.

Lorelei: Right.

Reese: You're not! Look … you dreamed up Hos-key-wow-wow, didn't you? I never thought an educational vacation with my family could be fun, but you showed me that it could be. I mean … you saved my life! You are so *not* boring, Lorelei.

Lorelei: Well … thanks.

Reese: So can we go back to the way things were? Without the cheating, I mean.

Lorelei: Yeah. Okay. We can do that.

Reese: Great! Here's your notebook back. I'll get out some new note cards. It's a good thing Mom made me bring so many of them. He-e-ey … you know what?

Lorelei: What?

Reese: My parents wanted me to learn something on this vacation and I did! Now I know that I can make something boring not so boring by changing my attitude about it. That is so … so …

Lorelei: I think the word you're looking for is "Hos-key-wow-wow."

Reese: *(grinning)* Yeah. That's it! *(They exit.)*

From Diana R. Jenkins, *All Year Long! Funny Readers Theatre for Life's Special Times.* Westport, CT: Teacher Ideas Press. Copyright © 2007 by Diana R. Jenkins.

Scrambled!

Summary

Jordan and her friends have always loved Easter egg hunts, but Jordan just can't get excited about the hunts this year. She has plenty of reasons for her new attitude, and she convinces her friends they should create their own hunts. But she makes everyone miserable with her desperate need to make the new idea work! Wouldn't you feel desperate, too, after a run-in with a killer bunny?

Costumes, Sets, and Props

- ❖ All actors can wear contemporary clothing.

- ❖ Furniture is not required, but a couple of chairs and a shelf could represent the kitchen, Jordan's and Rosemarie's bedrooms, and the family room.

- ❖ All props can be mimed, but if props are desired, the following can be used: Easter eggs and baskets, notes (clues), a lamp, a coffee cup, a pot of lip gloss, and some coins.

Presentation

The "eggs" syllable should be emphasized in the "ex" words.

Other characters roll their eyes at Fox's puns.

If space allows, clues could be hung at different points around the room, and characters could move from one to another during hunts.

Supplemental Reading

Hort, Lenny. *Treasure Hunts! Treasure Hunts!* New York: HarperCollins, 2000.

Ross, Kathy. *All New Crafts for Easter.* Brookfield, CT: Millbrook Press, 2004.

Cast of Characters

Narrator	Fox
Jordan	Tucker
Owen, Jordan's brother	Kristin
Rosemarie	Mom

Easter

Scrambled!

Scene One

Narrator: Jordan and her friends always spend the week before Easter hunting eggs. In fact, they hit every Easter egg hunt in town.

Jordan: Yeah, we've always gotten into the frenzied rush of competition … the challenge of the hunt … the thrill of discovery … the victory of winning and the joy of gloating afterwards. Man … I really used to love those hunts. But this year … I don't know … they just don't sound that fun.

Owen: *(enters)* Gee. I wonder why.

Jordan: Go away, Owen.

Owen: Could it be that a bad experience last year is affecting your attitude this year?

Jordan: Go away, Owen.

Owen: Like maybe you're still upset about the attack of—

Jordan: Go away, Owen!

Owen: Okay, okay! But you really need to face your fears—

Jordan: GO AWAY, OWEN!

Owen: I'm going, I'm going. *(exits)*

Jordan: Brothers can be such a pain.

Narrator: So … Jordan wasn't feeling excited at all about the Easter egg hunts.

Jordan: Not one bit.

Narrator: *(as friends enter)* And the first hunt of the year was a real letdown.

Rosemarie: Hey, I found eight eggs.

Fox: I found nine so I *beat* your eggs. Get it? Get it?

Rosemarie: Funny.

Tucker: I found an even dozen.

Kristin: No, you didn't. You found eleven. You stole one from a little kid.

Tucker: I did not. He dropped it so it was fair game.

Kristin: Whatever. How many did you find, Jordan?

Jordan: Um … uh … One.

From Diana R. Jenkins, *All Year Long! Funny Readers Theatre for Life's Special Times.* Westport, CT: Teacher Ideas Press. Copyright © 2007 by Diana R. Jenkins.

Rosemarie: That's all?

Tucker: Even the little kids found more than that.

Jordan: So? What's the big deal? I don't know if you've noticed, but all we found was a bunch of hard-boiled eggs. I mean … they're just eggs. I can find plenty of those in my own refrigerator.

Rosemarie: They're not much of a prize, but hunting for them is fun.

Kristin: Let's go to the hunt at the park. They use those plastic eggs filled with stuff.

Fox: Yeah, that's better.

Narrator: So they tried that egg hunt, too. Even though the prizes weren't as lame, Jordan still couldn't get into it.

Rosemarie: I found eight eggs. And they're full of candy!

Fox: I found nine. My eggs have candy and some little cars, too.

Tucker: I found a dozen. And I didn't—

Jordan: This is just as bad as the last time, you guys.

Kristin: At least we got some candy and toys.

Fox: But Jordan didn't get anything. She didn't even try!

Kristin: I noticed. Why did you do that, Jordan?

Jordan: *(shrugs)* It just wasn't worth the trouble.

Fox: What do you mean?

Jordan: Well, for one thing, there's not any real hunting. The eggs are too easy to find.

Rosemarie: They have to make it simple enough for the little kids.

Jordan: I know, but it's not challenging for us. And the prizes are dinky! We need a different kind of hunt, you guys. Something we make up ourselves. Something more like a treasure hunt.

Kristin: You mean with maps and buried gold?

Fox: We can't do anything like that. For one thing, we don't have any gold.

Tucker: And if we do it ourselves, it won't be much of a hunt, will it? We'll already know where the treasure is.

Jordan: I'm not talking about actual treasure. We can use those plastic eggs, too. We'll just put something more interesting inside of them. And we can have our hunts indoors. Yeah … that way it doesn't matter if it rains or if it's hot or if there's any … um … wildlife or anything. And since it will just be us, we can make the hunt a real challenge.

Fox: And how are we going to do that?

Jordan: Just let me think a bit! I'm sure there's some way to work it out.

Kristin: Well, good luck with that. Let's go to the hunt at Evans Woods next.

Fox: Yeah!

Jordan: Go ahead, but let's meet at my house afterwards. I'll have things figured out by then.

Fox: So you're going to *hatch* a plan? Get it? Get it?

Rosemarie: Brother. Let's go. *(Friends exit.)*

From Diana R. Jenkins, *All Year Long! Funny Readers Theatre for Life's Special Times.* Westport, CT: Teacher Ideas Press. Copyright © 2007 by Diana R. Jenkins.

Scene Two

Narrator: Jordan hurried home and went to her room to think.

Owen: *(entering)* What are you doing?

Jordan: Leave me alone.

Owen: Why aren't you out hunting eggs with your friends?

Jordan: Not that it's any business of yours, but my friends and I aren't really interested in Easter egg hunts anymore.

Owen: Oh, really? Your *friends* don't like egg hunts?

Jordan: Right. We're getting a little too old for Easter egg hunts, really. Instead, we're going to make up our own hunts that will be a lot more fun. And more … indoorsy.

Owen: Uh-huh. So where is everybody?

Jordan: You ask too many stupid questions. Get out of here, Owen.

Owen: Jordan, Jordan, Jordan. You can't just bury your feelings, you know. That leads to—

Jordan: OUT!

Owen: I'm just trying to help. *(exits)*

Narrator: Jordan was determined to come up with a new kind of hunt. She thought long and hard, and finally inspiration hit.

Jordan: Yes! That's it! Now I need to set up a demonstration for everybody.

Narrator: She quickly arranged everything then waited for her friends to return.

Jordan: *(waiting to one side as friends enter)* First, they'll find the clue on the front door … .

Rosemarie: What's this? *(reads)* "Enter here. Hang a right. Take three steps, and hit the light."

Tucker: That's strange. Like we need directions to her room.

Kristin: Let's do it.

Jordan: Then they'll get to my room and find another clue hanging on the lamp …

Kristin: So where is she?

Fox: There's another note.

Tucker: *(reads)* "Down the hall, then through the door. Find a clue … on the floor."

Rosemarie: A clue? I get it! This is some kind of treasure hunt.

Fox: Yeah! Let's go!

Jordan: Then they'll reach the kitchen …

Kristin: Here's the clue under the rug! *(reads)* "Look up, look up, and find the cup."

Tucker: There's a coffee cup on that shelf. With a plastic egg inside! Let me get it.

Rosemarie: What's inside the egg?

Tucker: *(disappointed)* Nothing.

Jordan: *(joining friends)* But there could have been a treasure.

Fox: But there's not.

Rosemarie: There's nothing at all.

Jordan: Look, you guys. I was just trying to show you how we could make our own hunts. See? One person hides something in a plastic egg and then leaves clues that lead us to the treasure.

Kristin: That could be fun.

Tucker: Hey, we can all take turns hiding stuff and setting up the hunt.

Jordan: Exactly!

Fox: *(laughing)* Eggs-actly!

Jordan: I wasn't trying to … oh, forget it.

Rosemarie: I don't know … We have so much fun at the regular Easter egg hunts.

Jordan: Trust me. Our own hunts will be a lot better.

Kristin: I guess we could try it. And if it's not more fun, then we'll just go back to the old way.

Rosemarie: That sounds okay. Hey, can I do the first hunt?

Jordan: Okay. But just remember to make the clues challenging.

Tucker: Your clues weren't that hard.

Jordan: That was just an example, okay?

Fox: *(laughing)* An eggs-ample! Good one, Jordan.

Jordan: No, it's not. I wasn't. … Listen, I didn't have much time to fix up this hunt. We'll make the real hunts more complicated. Be sure to put a good prize in the egg, Rosemarie.

Rosemarie: Okay.

Fox: This is going to be so cool.

Tucker: Maybe.

Kristin: We'll see.

Jordan: So how about if we meet at Rosemarie's house in an hour? That will give her time to set up her treasure hunt.

Others: *(exiting)* Sure! Okay! Later! (*etc.*)

Scene Three

Narrator: Jordan had high hopes for the treasure hunts.

Jordan: Not to brag, but it really is an excellent idea.

Fox: *(offstage)* Egg-cellent! *(laughs)* Good one!

Jordan: Whatever.

Narrator: But things didn't work out the way Jordan had planned.

Rosemarie: *(entering with friends)* Okay, you guys. Everything's set up. Good luck!

Jordan: Where's the first clue?

Rosemarie: Right there on my bedroom door.

From Diana R. Jenkins, *All Year Long! Funny Readers Theatre for Life's Special Times.* Westport, CT: Teacher Ideas Press. Copyright © 2007 by Diana R. Jenkins.

Fox: I'll read it. "Come in."

Jordan: What kind of clue is that?

Rosemarie: It means to go on into my room.

Jordan: No kidding.

Kristin: There's the next clue on the bed. It says, "Look around."

Jordan: Brother.

Tucker: I see an egg behind the computer!

Rosemarie: Look inside.

Tucker: Okay. It's a … it's a … what is this?

Rosemarie: It's my favorite lip gloss.

Tucker: Goody.

Fox: It's half empty!

Jordan: That's not a good treasure, Rosemarie.

Rosemarie: I really like that lip gloss. It's good lip gloss. The best!

Kristin: I'll take it.

Tucker: But what am I supposed to do for a prize?

Jordan: See, Rosemarie? You need a good treasure that anybody would like.

Rosemarie: Oh. Sorry. Maybe we should stick to the real Easter egg hunts.

Jordan: No, no. It's just the first time. Now everybody knows to hide a good treasure. And I guess you all realize you need to use interesting clues. Make your clues mysterious. And challenging. Okay? Everybody understand?

Tucker: We get it.

Kristin: Yeah.

Rosemarie: You could have explained all that before.

Fox: Don't feel bad, Rosemarie. Your hunt was egg-citing while it lasted. Get it? Egg-citing!

Jordan: So who wants to go next?

Tucker: I'll do it. But I have to go home now. How about if everybody meets at my house tomorrow morning?

Jordan: Okay. That should give you plenty of time to set up a really great treasure hunt.

Tucker: Okay. See you guys tomorrow. *(exits)*

Other friends: Bye! See you tomorrow! *(etc.)*

Jordan: I hope he comes up with something good. I don't want everyone to give up on this idea.

Scene Four

Narrator: *(as Tucker and Fox enter)* But Tucker's egg hunt turned out to be disappointing, too.

Jordan: Sheesh, Tucker! Don't you know what a clue is?

Tucker: Of course I do.

Jordan: I don't think so. All you did was put up signs with arrows on them.

Tucker: Those *were* the clues.

Jordan: Arrows are not clues! And talk about a lame treasure. Three postage stamps?

Tucker: Well … that was the best thing I could find.

Jordan: It was not! You could have come up with a lot better treasure than that.

Fox: I thought Tucker's hunt was fun. And I didn't mind winning some stamps. You're being too hard on him, Jordan.

Jordan: Well, excuse me.

Fox: *(laughing)* Ha! Eggs—

Jordan: Don't say it! Just go on home and set up a decent treasure hunt, will you?

Fox: Well … okay. I'll try. *(exits with Tucker)*

Jordan: Man, this is totally exasperating! I mean … frustrating. I've explained … I mean … told everybody how to do this. Is it too much to expect … I mean … This is driving me nuts!

Fox: *(sticking head in)* I think you're *cracking* up, Jordan. Get it? Like an egg. Get it?

Jordan: *(intensely)* Go home and get busy.

Fox: Okay! *(exits)*

Scene Five

Narrator: But Fox's hunt was a bust, too.

Jordan: *(reading as Fox enters)* "Eat three crackers and whistle 'Peter Cottontail.' Then stick out your tongue and touch your nose. Rub your belly and … " These are stunts, not clues.

Fox: But at the end I said to look under my bed.

Jordan: And you thought a rock would be a good treasure?

Fox: Hey, that's real-life, genuine, authentic fool's gold. *(exits)*

Jordan: It sure is. Man! Everyone's going to go back to the old Easter egg hunts, if things don't improve soon. Maybe Kristin can do this right.

Narrator: Nope. Not a chance.

Jordan: *(reading as Kristin enters)* "Walk four steps. Turn left. Walk seven steps. Turn right. Walk five steps. Turn left. Walk ten steps Turn left. Walk … ." Aargh! This is totally stupid, Kristin. We ended up in the broom closet!

Kristin: I don't understand. I counted the steps carefully. Maybe I mixed up a right and a left.

Jordan: And please. … You put a hard-boiled egg inside of a plastic egg for your prize?

Kristin: I thought it was funny. And it wasn't hard-boiled.

Rosemarie: *(offstage)* Oops! Oh, man! Where's a mop?

Jordan: *(calling offstage)* Just follow Kristin's stupid clues to the broom closet!

Kristin: *(angry)* Hey, I did my best. This is supposed to be fun, you know.

Jordan: I know.

Kristin: Well, it's not. You're making such a big deal about these hunts that you're ruining everything. What is your problem?

Jordan: You guys are my problem. I come up with this great idea, and you just don't get it.

Kristin: Why don't you show us how to do it? I mean … you're the big expert.

Fox: *(laughing offstage)* Eggs-pert!

Jordan: Okay, I will. Everybody can come to my house tomorrow for the best hunt ever.

Kristin: Right. It better be. *(exits)*

Scene Six

Narrator: But thinking up a really amazing hunt wasn't easy. Jordan worked and worked and worked on her clues.

Jordan: Aargh! These stupid clues are just not challenging enough. And what am I going to use for a stupid treasure? Why did I ever start this whole stupid thing? I'm so … so …

Owen: *(entering)* Stupid?

Jordan: Don't bother me right now, Owen.

Owen: Oh, sorry. Are you busy with your treasure hunt?

Jordan: How did you know about that?

Owen: I'm smarter than you think. I can figure stuff out … reason things through … My mind is like a steel trap.

Jordan: Right.

Owen: And Fox told me.

Jordan: That bigmouth.

Owen: He also told me that *you're* the one who doesn't want to do the Easter egg hunts anymore. Everybody else still likes them. And they don't understand why you're so obsessed with making this treasure hunt thing work.

Jordan: I'm not obsessed! I'm just frustrated, that's all. You would not believe the kind of so-called hunts those guys came up with—and the lousy treasures they made us hunt for. It's … so … .Hey! You didn't say anything to Fox, did you? I mean … about … you know … what happened at the family egg hunt last year?

Owen: No, of course not. Mom and Dad made me promise not to tell, and I keep my promises.

Jordan: Good. Not that it's a big deal or anything. I practically forgot all about it, you know.

Owen: Come on, Jordan! It's still eating away at you. Ha! Get it? *Eating* away at you?

Jordan: You've been spending too much time with Fox. And it's not bothering me at all.

Owen: I don't believe you. You're scared.

Jordan: I am not! That's ridiculous! Sheesh! Nobody's afraid of rabbits.

Owen: Except you, Jordan. You're afraid you'll meet up with another killer bunny.

From Diana R. Jenkins, *All Year Long! Funny Readers Theatre for Life's Special Times.* Westport, CT: Teacher Ideas Press. Copyright © 2007 by Diana R. Jenkins.

Jordan: There's no such thing as a killer bunny!

Mom: *(entering)* What are you kids fighting about?

Jordan: Mom, there's no such thing as a killer bunny, is there?

Mom: Is this about last year's egg hunt? Goodness, Jordan! I can't believe you're still worrying over that.

Owen: Me neither, Mom. She's totally freaked about it, you know.

Jordan: I am not!

Owen: Gosh. I guess I misunderstood. So you'll be having your treasure hunt outside then? I mean … since you're not scared of being around rabbits?

Jordan: Sure.

Mom: What's this treasure hunt?

Owen: It's a great idea, Mom. Jordan is making up a hunt for her friends. They have to follow clues that lead them to a prize.

Mom: That sounds fun. You know, you could set it up in the corner park like we did for our hunt last year.

Owen: I was just about to suggest that. The park is perfect, what with all the bushes and trees and little furry animals. Don't you think, Jordan?

Jordan: Yeah. Perfect.

Mom: Well … it's almost time for supper. Go get washed up. *(exits)*

Owen: Hey, good luck with the treasure hunt. And be careful. Be. Very. Careful.

Jordan: Oh, ha, ha, ha. You don't scare me, you know.

Owen: Yes, I do. *(exits)*

Jordan: *(calling after him)* No, you don't! *(to self)* No, he doesn't. But killer bunnies do!

Scene Seven

Narrator: After supper, Jordan tore up the clues she'd already written and started over. The whole time she was writing clues for a hunt in the park, she thought about her bad experience at last year's family Easter egg hunt. The idea of walking through the trees at the park tomorrow or reaching under the bushes or just seeing something brown and furry made her heart pound in her chest. But now she *had* to have her hunt outside to prove to her brother that she wasn't afraid.

Jordan: And Mom will be asking about how the hunt went. That's why Owen got her involved. Just to put more pressure on me!

Narrator: When she finished the clues, she looked around for a treasure.

Jordan: I have something to prove to my friends, too. So I have to have a really good prize.

Narrator: But nothing in Jordan's room seemed that great.

Jordan: The boys won't want my heart necklace. And the girls don't like pepper gum. I can't fit a game into the egg. Or anything else good. I'll have to raid my piggy bank.

Narrator: Jordan filled the egg with coins and taped it shut. Then she went to bed and lay there worrying all night except for the times when she fell asleep and dreamed she was being attacked by a giant rabbit with long fangs and an evil gleam in its eyes. The next morning she set up her hunt, then waited for her friends to arrive. She didn't know Owen was waiting, too.

Jordan: *(as friends enter)* First, they'll find the clue on the front door …

Tucker: Look! There's her first clue.

Owen: *(entering)* Hi, you guys.

Others: Hi, Owen.

Owen: What are you doing?

Kristin: We're on a treasure hunt.

Owen: Can I watch?

Fox: Okay.

Rosemarie: But don't bother us.

Kristin: I'll read the note. "A treasure awaits you … a treasure of value. What you must do … is follow each clue. And when you are through … the prize belongs to you."

Rosemarie: That's pretty good.

Tucker: Better than my arrows. What else does it say?

Kristin: "Go to the park."

Fox: That doesn't rhyme.

Rosemarie: And aren't we supposed to be doing this stuff inside?

Fox: It will be more fun hunting in the park. Let's go!

Jordan: Then they'll find the next clue on the park's entrance gate …

Fox: I'll read this one. "Don't be dense. Don't feel tense. Work your way around the fence. Find a clue that makes some sense. And follow it to the treasure."

Tucker: That doesn't rhyme either!

Kristin: And what does it mean anyway?

Owen: Maybe you should go around to the other entrance.

Rosemarie: Good idea! And, hey, you stay out of this.

Jordan: Then they'll find a clue on the other gate … .

Tucker: Here it is. "You're there almost. … Count down four posts. … Watch out for ghosts. … Don't get lost." Lost? Did she think that rhymed?

Rosemarie: There's another clue on that fence post. I got it! "Home again, home again. … Come on, friends. … You're near the end. … Go see Jordan. … " This clue is so lame.

Owen: Sheesh! She was too scared to go into the park at all.

Kristin: What's that, Owen?

Owen: Nothing.

From Diana R. Jenkins, *All Year Long! Funny Readers Theatre for Life's Special Times.* Westport, CT: Teacher Ideas Press. Copyright © 2007 by Diana R. Jenkins.

Scene Eight

Narrator: So everyone hurried back to the house and searched for Jordan.

Jordan: Then they'll come back here and someone will find me hiding in the family room with the treasure egg in my hand …

Fox: There she is!

Jordan: And here's your reward, Fox.

Fox: Wow! An egg filled with money! That's a real treasure, Jordan.

Rosemarie: It's just some loose change. What's so great about that?

Tucker: Yeah … I can find that in my own pocket.

Jordan: Well, it's better than the prizes you guys came up with.

Kristin: And where were those challenging clues you promised us?

Tucker: Yeah. Your clues were strange.

Kristin: "Lost" does not rhyme with "post," you know.

Rosemarie: And all we did was walk around a fence. That wasn't fun.

Owen: We didn't even get to go into the park.

Tucker: Yeah! How lame was that?

Owen: Really lame. Really, really lame.

Rosemarie: This isn't working out at all. Let's just go back to the regular Easter egg hunts.

Jordan: No! We can't do that!

Tucker: Why not?

Jordan: Because … because … because …

Owen: Because she thinks—

Jordan: I'll tell them myself, Owen.

Owen: But I was—

Jordan: Let me talk! *(to others)* I didn't want to tell you guys this, but if I don't do it, *he* will. I don't think I can keep it a secret anymore anyway.

Owen: I wasn't going to—

Jordan: Zip it, Owen! *(to others)* I'm … I'm afraid of Easter egg hunts.

Kristin: You're joking, right?

Jordan: No. I'm one big chicken.

Fox: *(laughing)* Chicken! Ha! Good one! *(laughter fades)* You're serious, aren't you?

Jordan: Dead serious. You see … something really … traumatic, I guess you'd say … happened at our family egg hunt last year. I never told you guys about it, but I guess you need to know.

Rosemarie: Oh, no! What happened?

Jordan: I was reaching for this egg … under a bush, you know … and it rolled away … so I had to reach in further … and then … and then …

Owen: Something nibbled her finger.

From Diana R. Jenkins, *All Year Long! Funny Readers Theatre for Life's Special Times.* Westport, CT: Teacher Ideas Press. Copyright © 2007 by Diana R. Jenkins.

Jordan: Something bit me, Owen. And it hurt! It really hurt! And then this killer rabbit jumped out and started chasing me across the grass!

Owen: It did not! The poor thing was scared to death, and it was trying to run into the woods.

Jordan: It was after me, I tell you!

Others: *(laugh)*

Jordan: It's not funny!

Others: *(laugh)*

Jordan: This is why I didn't want to tell you. *(stomps off to one side)*

Scene Nine

Narrator: Everybody felt bad that Jordan's feelings got hurt.

Owen: *(muttering)* Not everybody.

Tucker: We're sorry, Jordan.

Kristin: Yeah. Really sorry.

Jordan: You're supposed to be my friends.

Fox: *(angry)* And you're supposed to be *our* friend. Why didn't you just tell us the truth?

Jordan: Isn't that obvious? Look at how you guys laughed at me.

Fox: And we're sorry about that. But it really was kind of a funny story. And so what if we laughed for a minute? Don't we always support you?

Jordan: Well … yeah … I guess …

Fox: So you should have told us! Keeping it a secret … making us give up something we all like … .That is so messed up, Jordan.

Others: *(belligerent)* Yeah.

Jordan: I … I know. I guess my thinking was kind of scrambled, huh? Heh heh.

Fox: *(seriously)* Yes, it was. We could have helped you through it, you know.

Others: *(kindly)* Yeah.

Jordan: I'm sorry. I should have trusted you guys. The treasure hunts were pretty bad, huh?

Tucker: They would have been pretty fun without … well … without you criticizing everything.

Kristin: I liked them … except for … you know …

Rosemarie: Me, too.

Fox: Hey, we should do the treasure hunts at other times of the year. Like when there aren't any Easter egg hunts.

Tucker: Good idea!

Rosemarie: But let's go back to the regular egg hunts while there's still time, okay?

Kristin: Yeah! Hey, there's a big hunt at the baseball field this afternoon.

Fox: Are you up for that, Jordan?

From Diana R. Jenkins, *All Year Long! Funny Readers Theatre for Life's Special Times.* Westport, CT: Teacher Ideas Press. Copyright © 2007 by Diana R. Jenkins.

Tucker: We'll keep the rabbits away from you.

Rosemarie: Don't worry.

Jordan: Okay. Thanks, you guys. I'll give it a try.

Fox: So let's all meet at the field at one o'clock, okay?

Others except Owen: *(exiting)* Okay. See you later. *(etc.)*

Scene Ten

Narrator: So Jordan learned to have a little more faith in her friends. And her brother, too.

Owen: Don't you feel better now?

Jordan: Yeah. I guess you were right about keeping it all inside.

Owen: Of course. But I wasn't going to tell them, you know.

Jordan: You weren't?

Owen: No! I told you I wouldn't break a promise. I was getting ready to say that you thought you guys were too old for Easter egg hunts.

Jordan: You were going to cover for me?

Owen: Yep!

Jordan: Thanks. That's really … I guess the only word is … extraordinary!

Fox: *(laughs offstage)* Eggs-traordinary! Ha! You crack me up! Ha! Crack! Get it? Get it?

Jordan: *(calling offstage as all exit)* We get it! We get it!

From Diana R. Jenkins, *All Year Long! Funny Readers Theatre for Life's Special Times.* Westport, CT: Teacher Ideas Press. Copyright © 2007 by Diana R. Jenkins.

Mother's Day

Mom Swap

Summary

Troy can't believe it when his mother wants to participate in a family exchange program in which the mothers of two families swap lives for a week. After all, his mom never does anything fun—and she always squashes everyone else's fun, too. Luckily, his "new" mother is fun and free-spirited. But can a person be too much fun? Like how many times does anybody want to eat Garbage Pizza? And would a few rules be so bad?

Costumes, Sets, and Props

❖ All characters can wear contemporary clothing, but Jackie should wear something unusual and colorful. Her hair should be styled in a wild way.

❖ A few chairs and a table can be used to represent the living room and the kitchen.

❖ If props are desired, the following can be used: brochure, basketball, schoolbooks, napkins, Mom's and Jackie's luggage, pizza pan, plates, television remote, glasses, and games.

Presentation

The other actors can freeze when Troy narrates or mime what he's describing.

Mom acts hurt whenever Troy seems eager to get rid of her.

Jackie is loud, friendly, and enthusiastic.

Dad acts uncomfortable with Jackie but for much of the play is too polite to say anything.

Supplemental Reading

Blacker, Terence. *Parent Swap.* New York: Farrar, Straus & Giroux, 2005.

Hicks, Betty. *Busted!* Brookfield, CT: Roaring Brook Press, 2004.

McDonough, Alison. *Do the Hokey Pokey.* Chicago: Front Street, 2001.

Williams, Carol Lynch. *A Mother to Embarrass Me.* New York: Delacorte Press, 2002.

Cast of Characters

Troy

Mom

Dad

Annie, Troy's younger sister

Leonard, Troy's younger brother

Kellie and Nick, Troy's friends

Jackie

Mother's Day

Mom Swap

Scene One

Troy: When my parents started talking about swapping mothers with another family, I thought they were joking. Like my mom would do anything fun like that!

Mom: *(entering with rest of family)* The brochure certainly makes this Family Swap Program sound interesting.

Dad: It sure does. Listen to this, kids. Somebody from one family trades places with somebody in another family. They live in each other's houses for a week, just like a member of the family.

Annie: Somebody like who?

Dad: Actually, we were thinking of swapping moms with another family.

Troy: *(laughing)* Sure. Right. Good one, Dad.

Mom: He's not joking, Troy.

Troy: *You're* going to travel somewhere and live with another family?

Mom: I'm thinking about it. It sounds like a fun experience.

Troy: Fun? Did you say, "Fun"?

Mom: Yes. I think it would be a lot of fun.

Troy: *(to audience)* I couldn't believe it! "Fun" had never been a major factor in my mother's life. She was the most un-fun parent in the world. In fact, she liked to squash fun like a bug!

Mom: *(as Annie jumps)* Annie, stop jumping on your bed before you break it down.

Annie: *(sighs and stops)* Yes, ma'am.

Mom: *(as Leonard pretends to play basketball)* Don't you have homework, Leonard?

Leonard: *(sighs and stops)* Yes, ma'am.

Mom: *(whirling on Troy)* And what do you think you're doing, young man?

Troy: I … um … was going to watch TV.

Mom: Isn't it your turn to do the dishes?

Troy: Oh, yeah. I forgot.

Mom: And did you take out the garbage?

Troy: Not yet.

Mom: Have you cleaned your room, made your bed, swept the walk, straightened the garage, washed the car, vacuumed the family room, and established peace throughout the world?

Troy: I was going to get to all that after my program.

Mom: Responsibilities come first, Troy. Then you can have your fun.

Troy: *(muttering)* Like when I'm a hundred years old.

Mom: What was that?

Troy: Yes, ma'am.

Mom: Good.

Troy: *(to audience)* And this was the woman who wanted to swap lives with another mother because it might be "fun"? Unbelievable! *(to Mom)* So you guys are serious about this?

Dad: We're really considering it. It will be a good experience for all of us. Why, having a different mother for a while might make you guys appreciate the one you have.

Annie: We appreciate you, Mom. Don't go!

Leonard: Yeah. Don't leave us, Mom.

Mom: It's only for a week, kids. *(to Troy)* What do you think, Troy?

Troy: *(to audience)* It sounded great to me! Maybe we'd get a new mother who was more fun than Mom—which would be just about anybody! Don't get me wrong—I love my mom. I just needed a little break. *(to Mom)* I say you should go for it, Mom.

Mom: Thanks for your support, Troy. You know … I just might do it!

Troy: *(to self)* Yes!

Scene Two

Troy: *(to audience as family exits)* It took a while to work everything out. First, my parents had to make sure Annie and Leonard could handle Mom leaving for a week. Mom and Dad explained how she wouldn't be gone that long … it would be a great experience … she wasn't leaving forever … that kind of stuff. Annie and Leonard just weren't convinced.

Annie: *(offstage)* Don't go, Mom!

Leonard: *(offstage)* Don't leave us!

Troy: *(as Annie and Leonard enter)* But after I had a little talk with them, they were onboard with the swap. *(to Annie and Leonard)* This will be fun! Don't you want to have some fun?

Annie: Ye-es.

Troy: Well, a new mother will be so fun. She has to be less strict than Mom, doesn't she?

Leonard: That's for sure.

Troy: Having a new mom will be like a vacation for us. Like why should she care if we do all our chores? It's not her house.

Annie: Will she let us jump on the beds?

Troy: Well … probably.

Annie: Cool.

Leonard: I don't know …

Troy: I bet she won't even ask about our homework.

Leonard: Really?

Troy: I doubt it. Man! This is going to be great!

Annie: Yeah.

Leonard: Yeah! Let's go talk to Mom and Dad.

Troy: Wait! Don't say anything about how fun the new mom is going to be, you guys. I mean … you don't want to make Mom feel bad, right?

Annie and Leonard: Okay. *(exit)*

Troy: *(to audience)* Once that was all settled, Mom and Dad applied for the Family Swap Program. And we waited.

Scene Three

Troy: *(as Kellie and Nick enter)* Weeks and weeks and weeks went by. I was beginning to think my dream of a new mom was never going to become a reality. Unfortunately, my friends weren't very sympathetic about that. *(to friends)* It's been six weeks since we applied for that stupid swap! Six whole weeks! Can you believe it?

Kellie: Six weeks. Wow. That is so amazing.

Nick: Why, just last week it was … let's see … five whole weeks since you applied.

Kellie: And here it is a week later. And now six weeks have gone by.

Nick: Gee, in another week—

Troy: Okay, okay! You guys just don't understand how important this is to me.

Kellie: Of course we do. You talk about it all the time!

Nick: What we don't get is why you're so desperate to get rid of your mom.

Kellie: Yeah. She's really nice.

Troy: I'm not desperate! And, yes, she *is* nice. She just so darned strict … and picky … and demanding … and she never lets me have any fun!

Kellie: Oh, come on! She drives you to all your practices and games. Those are fun.

Troy: But she's always getting on my case about leaving the house on time.

Nick: Man! I had no idea she was so cruel.

Troy: Funny.

Nick: Hey, didn't she throw you a big birthday party last year? That was fun!

Troy: But before the party, she gave me a huge lecture about being polite to everybody.

Kellie: You're kidding! She wouldn't let you be a rude jerk at your own party?

From Diana R. Jenkins, *All Year Long! Funny Readers Theatre for Life's Special Times.* Westport, CT: Teacher Ideas Press. Copyright © 2007 by Diana R. Jenkins.

Troy: Look, I'd just like some freedom for once. I want to enjoy life without getting harassed about rules and chores and responsibility and manners. Is there anything wrong with that?

Kellie: I guess not.

Nick: Not exactly. It's just … well, life is like that, you know.

Troy: That's what I'm saying! It's so unfair! And I'm hoping, hoping, hoping the new mom will change my life for the better. At least for a while.

Kellie: Yeah. Good luck with that. *(exits)*

Nick: See you later, prisoner dude. *(exits)*

Troy: Why do I try to explain anything to them? Anyway … so much time went by that I almost gave up hope. Then one day …

Mom: *(enters)* We're in, Troy! They accepted us in the program!

Troy: That's great, Mom. When do you leave?

Mom: *(joking)* Are you trying to get rid of me?

Troy: No. Uh-huh. Of course not. Nosirree. No way.

Mom: Okay then.

Troy: So when *do* you leave?

Mom: *(hurt)* Don't worry. It won't be too long now. *(exits)*

Scene Four

Troy: *(to audience)* Finally … *finally* … the big day arrived. Mom was going to travel to the other end of the state and become the new mom for another family. And *our* new mom would be arriving at our house later in the day. *(as family enters and sits at table)* Before Mom left, we had one of our special waffle breakfasts, which should have been fun, right?

Mom: *(as family mimes)* Napkins in your laps please. Elbows off the table. Cut up your food into small pieces. Chew with your mouths closed.

Troy: *(to audience)* Not fun. Not fun at all. And then there was the lecture.

Mom: Remember … the new mom is a guest in our house.

Kids: Yes, ma'am.

Mom: You need to be on your best behavior.

Kids: Yes, ma'am.

Mom: Do your chores without being asked.

Kids: Yes, ma'am.

Mom: And follow the rules.

Kids: Yes, ma'am.

Dad: They're going to do fine. You should just go and have a good time.

Mom: You're right.

Troy: *(to audience)* I kept imagining the new mom sitting there instead of our real mom. She would laugh and joke around with us. And she wouldn't gripe us out

From Diana R. Jenkins, *All Year Long! Funny Readers Theatre for Life's Special Times.* Westport, CT: Teacher Ideas Press. Copyright © 2007 by Diana R. Jenkins.

all the time! *(to Mom)* Man. Look at the time. Shouldn't you be hitting the road, Mom?

Mom: I guess I should.

Dad: We'll walk you to your car. *(family exits)*

Troy: *(to audience)* Finally! We all hugged Mom good-bye and watched her drive off. Then we waited for our new mom to arrive.

Scene Five

Troy: *(to audience)* At one o'clock, the new mom pulled up outside and hopped out of her car. As soon as I laid eyes on her, I knew she was going to be the fun person I'd imagined. She had wild hair and colorful clothes and a huge smile. *(calling offstage)* Hey, everybody! She's here!

Leonard: *(entering)* Oh, boy!

Annie: *(entering)* Does she look nice?

Dad: *(entering)* Remember what your mother said. Everybody be on your best behavior.

Jackie: *(enters bellowing)* Hello! I'm your new mommy!

Dad: Nice to meet you. I'm Edward.

Annie: Hi. I'm Annie.

Leonard: And I'm Leonard.

Troy: Hello. I'm Troy.

Jackie: What a great family! What a great family! What. A. Great. Family! You can call me "Jackie." So how about some help with my luggage?

Dad: Sure.

Troy: *(to audience)* Jackie's car was full of … stuff. She had several suitcases plus a stack of games, a big box of chocolates, some fluffy pillows … and bags … and boxes … and I don't know what all. There wasn't much space left in the guest room by the time we got everything in there, but Jackie didn't seem to care. That was the kind of fun, relaxed type of person she was!

Jackie: Isn't this cozy? I just love it! Hey, isn't it time for lunch?

Dad: Sure. We could make some sandwiches.

Jackie: Sandwiches? That doesn't sound like much fun, does it, kids?

Annie: Um … .

Leonard: I don't know …

Troy: No, it doesn't. Not at all.

Dad: *(scolding)* Troy …

Jackie: I know! Let's have Garbage Pizza!

Leonard: Ew!

Annie: Garbage? Yuck!

Dad: *(scolding)* Now, kids …

Troy: Sounds great!

Jackie: You're all going to love it! Come on—let's hit the kitchen!

Troy: *(to audience)* I had no idea what Garbage Pizza was. But I knew it was something different—something that Mom would never make. And I wanted to try it!

Scene Six

Troy: *(as Jackie mimes)* So we all went to the kitchen and watched as Jackie made some dough. She acted like she was having a great time. She smushed that dough and punched it and twisted it and even threw it up in the air like they do at a real pizza place. Then she spread it in the pan and gave us a big smile.

Jackie: And now for the garbage!

Troy: *(to audience)* Okay, that's when things got kind of strange. Jackie went to the fridge and took out canned peaches, grape jelly, radishes, bologna, and shredded cheese. I thought she was just being funny—until she spread the jelly on the dough like tomato sauce. Then she chopped up the peaches, radishes, and—yuck!—bologna and spread the pieces over the jelly!

Jackie: A little cheese on top … and TA-DA! Garbage pizza!

Dad: That looks … interesting.

Jackie: Just wait until you taste it!

Troy: *(to audience)* Once the pizza was baked, it looked like any ordinary pizza. Jackie gave us each a big slice on a plate then led us out to the living room.

Dad: Listen, my wife—

Troy: Wait! *(everyone freezes)* I knew what Dad was going to say. Mom didn't allow us to eat anywhere except the kitchen. But I was tired of Mom's rules. I wanted to live wild … and … and free! So I interrupted before he could finish what he was saying. *(as everyone unfreezes)* Man! This pizza looks great! Just great! I can't wait to try it, can you, Dad? Go ahead. Try it, Dad!

Dad: All right. Hmmm … that's pretty good.

Troy: Let me try it. He-e-ey, it *is* good!

Jackie: See? Didn't I tell you?

Troy: *(to audience)* Annie and Leonard liked the Garbage Pizza, too. We all dug in, and Jackie picked up the remote and switched on the television.

Dad: We don't usually—

Troy: Wait! *(everyone freezes)* Before he could say we don't watch TV at meals. I jumped right in. *(everyone unfreezes)* This is so much fun! This is the most fun we've had in a long time!

Annie: Yeah!

Leonard: Thanks, Jackie.

Troy: Thanks, Jackie. Thanks a million!

Jackie: You're welcome. *(to Dad)* What a nice bunch of kids. What. A. Nice. Bunch. Of. Kids!

Dad: Well, thanks.

Jackie: Oooh! *The Attack of the Caterpillar Eaters* is on! Let's watch this!

Troy: Cool!

Dad: But—

Jackie: I LOVE this movie!

Dad: Oh.

Scene Seven

Troy: *(as everyone else exits)* That day is going to go down in history as the most fun day of my life! We sat around and watched stuff on television that Mom would not have approved of. Oh, nothing bad, you know. But if a show isn't historical or educational or incredibly boring, Mom always says it's not worth watching and makes us go do something else. Jackie didn't care about that kind of thing at all. And after the pizza, she gave us popcorn and sodas and cookies and chips without ever once saying we were going to spoil our appetites eating junk. I was afraid Dad would put an end to all the fun, but I guess he didn't want to say anything to Jackie since she was a guest. He even made a special supper that night in Jackie's honor.

Dad: *(enters)* Supper's ready, everybody!

Troy: *(to audience as family enters)* Dad had made my favorite meal: meatloaf, mashed potatoes, and green beans. Too bad I was too full to eat it! So were Annie and Leonard. Of course, we didn't admit that. *(with pretended enthusiasm)* That meatloaf looks delicious, Dad.

Leonard: Yeah. Delicious.

Annie: Like so delicious. Mm.

Jackie: Wow, Edward! Wow! You are quite the chef!

Dad: Thank you, Jackie.

Jackie: Quite the chef!

Dad: Thanks.

Jackie: Yep! A real chef!

Dad: Thanks again.

Troy: *(to audience)* Jackie ate like a starving person! Annie, Leonard, and I had a hard time forcing down that food, but at least Jackie made our meal fun. She used catsup to write her name on her meatloaf. She made green bean fangs. She pretended her mashed potatoes were a volcano and her gravy was lava. And she let us do all that stuff, too. Dad didn't say anything, but he looked worried like he was afraid Mom might walk in at any time and catch us goofing around.

Jackie: Edward, that was the best meal I ever ate!

Dad: Thank you, Jackie. And now—if you'll excuse me—I need to work in my study awhile.

Jackie: Go right ahead. I'll hold down the fort out here!

Dad: Thanks. *(exits)*

Troy: *(to audience)* Mom and Dad have this deal worked out. One of them prepares supper, and the other does the cleaning up—with the help of us kids. I guess Dad was assuming Jackie was going to do the usual thing. But Jackie had other ideas.

From Diana R. Jenkins, *All Year Long! Funny Readers Theatre for Life's Special Times.* Westport, CT: Teacher Ideas Press. Copyright © 2007 by Diana R. Jenkins.

Jackie: Okay, kids! It's Game Time!

Annie: Goody!

Jackie: Troy, would you go to my room and get that stack of games I brought with me? Take them to the living room, okay? We can watch TV and play at the same time.

Troy: Sure … but what about all this mess?

Jackie: What mess? I don't see any mess. Do you see any mess, Annie?

Annie: *(giggling)* No.

Jackie: Do you see any mess, Leonard?

Leonard: *(laughing)* No mess here!

Jackie: Now what were you saying about a mess, Troy?

Troy: *(laughing)* What mess? I don't see a mess!

Jackie: Good! *(exits along with Annie and Leonard)*

Troy: *(to audience)* So we finished up the most fun day of my life playing games and watching TV until late. I think Jackie would have let us stay up all night, but Dad finally came in and made us go to bed. I went to sleep thinking about what a great mother Jackie was.

Scene Eight

Troy: *(to audience)* It was hard to get up the next morning. Dad goes to work early, so Jackie had to take care of things. She woke Leonard and me so late that we had to skip breakfast and run for the bus. There wasn't a clear spot anywhere in the kitchen to make anything anyway, but still … I hated going to school hungry. Luckily, I was able to borrow an energy bar from Kellie and an apple from Nick. I told them all about Jackie and the fantastic time we had.

Kellie: *(entering with Nick)* That Garbage Pizza is a very creative idea!

Troy: I know! And it was really good, too.

Nick: And she allowed you to watch anything you wanted on TV?

Troy: Yep! And she never once said that a program was going to rot our brains.

Kellie: And she let you stay up late! You know, this is working out even better than you hoped.

Troy: No kidding! I wonder if they'd let us keep her for a whole month. Or two.

Nick: You don't really want your mom to be gone that long, do you?

Troy: I don't know … I could get used to this kind of life.

Kellie: *(scolding)* Troy!

Troy: Hey, you've never tasted freedom, Kellie. If you ever do, then you'll understand how I feel. It's like … it's like … the wind in your hair!

Kellie: Uh-huh. Freedom tastes like the wind in your hair? That doesn't make sense, Troy.

Troy: Look, I'm just saying I like the freedom of having a mother who's fun. It's a nice change. *(sighs)* And it's going to be rough to go back to the old ways. Real rough.

Nick: Can we come over to your house sometime and taste the freedom in our hair, too?

Troy: Okay! We'll do that before Jackie goes back home.

Kellie: I hope she makes that Garbage Pizza.

Nick: Me, too!

Troy: Me, three!

Scene Nine

Troy: *(as friends exit)* When Leonard and I got home that afternoon, Jackie didn't even ask if we had homework. She gave us a snack of chocolates from the big box she'd brought with her, and then we all watched TV for a while. When it was almost time for Dad to get home, Jackie headed to the kitchen and I followed. Things were even messier than the night before. Jackie cleared off a spot and made another Garbage Pizza. This time she used barbeque sauce, pickles, and raisins.

Jackie: *(enters)* What a great combination, huh? This is going to be the best Garbage Pizza ever!

Troy: I can't wait to try it!

Dad: *(enters)* I'm home! Hello … oh my! This kitchen! I mean … um …

Jackie: Hello, Edward! Supper's almost ready!

Troy: We're having Garbage Pizza again. It's going to be even better than last night's pizza.

Dad: Oh. Great. I'll go wash up. *(exits)*

Jackie: Darn! I left the potato chips off the pizza! Oh, well. We'll eat them for a snack later.

Troy: Sounds good to me!

Jackie: Me, too! *(moves to living room)*

Troy: *(to audience as Annie and Leonard enter and sit in living room)* We had a good time again that night. Jackie let us eat the Garbage Pizza in front of the TV, and afterward we snacked on the chips and some pop. We played a few games, and then we started to watch this cool movie about a blobby monster that could squeeze through the tiniest crack. Dad didn't spend much time with us. Instead he cleaned up the kitchen, which I guess was only fair since Jackie made supper.

Dad: *(enters)* Time for bed!

Troy: But we're right in the middle of this movie, Dad.

Dad: I'm sorry, but it's bedtime. You boys have school tomorrow, and Annie needs her rest, too.

Jackie: Oh, come on, Edward. They don't want to miss the ending.

Troy: Yeah!

Dad: Jackie can tell you how it turns out. Right, Jackie?

Jackie: I'd be glad to!

Dad: So off to bed, kids.

Jackie: Come on, Annie. I'll tuck you in.

From Diana R. Jenkins, *All Year Long! Funny Readers Theatre for Life's Special Times.* Westport, CT: Teacher Ideas Press. Copyright © 2007 by Diana R. Jenkins.

Annie: Good night! *(exits with Jackie)*

Dad: Good night, Annie. And Leonard …

Leonard: Night. *(exits)*

Dad: Let's go, Troy. *(exits)*

Troy: You're no fun.

Dad: *(offstage)* I heard that!

Troy: *(calling offstage)* Sorry, Dad! Just joking! *(to audience)* Actually, I *was* kind of tired. At least it was the good kind of tired that comes from doing a lot of fun stuff instead of the bad kind of tired that comes from working too hard. This mom swap thing was fantastic!

Scene Ten

Troy: *(to audience)* We slept so late the next morning that we didn't get to eat breakfast, *and* we missed the bus. Jackie tried to make the drive to school fun by telling jokes and singing songs, but I was too sleepy and crabby to get into it. Just as I got out of the car, I remembered to ask Jackie if my friends could come over some day. My mom would have made a big deal about that, setting up a special time and calling their parents, but Jackie said any time would be fine. So I brought Kellie and Nick home that afternoon. *(as they enter)* Come on in, you guys.

Kellie: Man! What happened to your carpet?

Troy: What do you mean?

Nick: Look at all those stains!

Troy: Oh, yeah. I guess we spilled some pop out here. And maybe some other stuff, too.

Kellie: Why are Annie's toys all over the place?

Troy: What does that matter? Come on. Let's see if Jackie's in the kitchen.

Jackie: *(enters)* Hello there!

Kellie: Hello.

Nick: Hi. What are you doing?

Jackie: I'm making my specialty—Garbage Pizza!

Kellie: Cool! Troy told us about that!

Jackie: This one is going to be a gourmet feast! I'm starting with mustard.

Troy: *(to audience)* The pizzas were fun, but … I don't know … another Garbage Pizza didn't sound that good to me. *(to Jackie)* Maybe we should have something … um … different.

Jackie: *(laughing)* Nothing could be more "different" than Garbage Pizza!

Troy: Yeah … and it's great. But shouldn't we be eating some vegetables? For nutrition, I mean? *(to audience)* I know! I know! I couldn't believe I was saying that either.

Jackie: You are so right, Troy. That's why I'm putting corn on tonight's pizza!

Kellie and Nick: *(laughing)* Ew!

Jackie: You're going to love it! Troy, why don't you pick out something else to go on the pizza?

Troy: *(to audience)* Like what goes with mustard and corn? *(to Jackie)* Maybe Kellie and Nick want to choose something.

Kellie and Nick: Yeah!

Troy: *(to audience as Jackie exits)* So we had another fun evening eating pizza in front of the television— except for Dad who ate in his study then cleaned up the kitchen. After he finished, he offered to drive my friends home. *(to Kellie and Nick)* See you guys tomorrow.

Kellie: Thanks for having us over, Troy. That was fun!

Nick: Now I get what you were saying. This freedom stuff is great!

Troy: Yeah. Great.

Kellie: Bye! *(exits)*

Nick: Later! *(exits)*

Troy: *(to audience)* After that, something really crazy happened. I went to my room and caught up on my homework! Wouldn't that have surprised Mom? It surprised me, too. But there wasn't really anything worth watching on television, and I didn't want any of the snacks Jackie had put out on the coffee table. To tell you the truth, the Garbage Pizza wasn't sitting too well in my stomach. I could have gone back to the living room after I finished my work, but instead I just read awhile then went to bed. I guess I had had enough fun for one day.

Scene Eleven

Troy: *(to audience)* The next few days of Jackie's visit were pretty much the same, except that … I don't know … I kept telling myself everything was great, but things just didn't seem as fun as they had at the beginning of the week.

Kellie: *(enters with Nick)* Hey, Troy! How are things at home?

Troy: Fine. I mean—great! Fun, you know. Really fun.

Nick: Can we come over again?

Kellie: Yeah. Let us taste the freedom one more time!

Troy: Right. The freedom.

Kellie: What's the matter?

Troy: Nothing. I'm fine.

Nick: You don't seem fine.

Troy: Well, I am, okay? I'm having the time of my life! I'm having the kind of fun you only dream of! Yeah, fun!

Kellie: But something is bothering you—I can tell.

Nick: Me, too. Wait a minute! I get it! Poor Troy! Him miss his mamma!

Troy: I've just been thinking, that's all. Like do you think a person can be too much fun?

Kellie: You mean a person like Jackie?

From Diana R. Jenkins, *All Year Long! Funny Readers Theatre for Life's Special Times.* Westport, CT: Teacher Ideas Press. Copyright © 2007 by Diana R. Jenkins.

Troy: Yeah. All she *does* is have fun. Don't get me wrong. She's really nice. And she tries to make stuff fun for everybody else, too. But, gee, how many times can a person eat Garbage Pizza? And all we do is lie around watching TV and playing the same old games. And that's great! Yeah, great. But … I don't know … the house looks like a tornado hit it!

Kellie: Okay. Who are you and what have you done with Troy?

Troy: I can't believe I said that. I sound like Mom.

Nick: Scary, man.

Troy: Yeah. What's the matter with me?

Kellie: Maybe it's the stress. The mom swap isn't really working out, is it?

Troy: I didn't say that! It's not perfect, but it's been a great experience. Just great! And fun? We're talking super-fun!

Nick: Mm-hmm.

Kellie: Right.

Troy: It is! *(snorts)* Stress! How could I be stressed when I'm having so much fun? Brother!

Nick: Mm-hmm.

Kellie: Right.

Scene Twelve

Troy: *(as friends exit and Leonard enters and sits)* I stayed after school a while that day to help set up for the book fair. When I got home, Leonard was already there, sitting on the couch, watching TV, and eating the last of Jackie's chocolates. To my surprise, these words exploded right out of my mouth: *(to Leonard)* Don't you have homework to do?

Leonard: Maybe.

Troy: Well, get to work on it!

Leonard: You're not the boss of me.

Troy: Look, Leonard. Homework is important. It helps you learn.

Leonard: So?

Troy: And you get graded on it. You don't want a bunch of zeroes, do you?

Leonard: Maybe.

Troy: Oh, you do not! Come on. Do your work.

Leonard: Oh, all right. *(exits)*

Troy: *(to audience as Annie enters and starts jumping)* I hated to get on his case like that, but somebody had to do it. I mean … he could flunk the whole grade. I decided to check on Annie after that. I found her jumping on her bed. Without even thinking, I told her to stop. *(to Annie)* Get down from there, Annie! Right now!

Annie: *(still jumping)* Jackie doesn't care if I jump on the bed.

From Diana R. Jenkins, *All Year Long! Funny Readers Theatre for Life's Special Times.* Westport, CT: Teacher Ideas Press. Copyright © 2007 by Diana R. Jenkins.

Troy: Well, I do. I mean … it's not safe. You could fall and get hurt. And you could break the bed and get into big trouble.

Annie: *(stops)* You're no fun. *(exits)*

Troy: I can't believe she said that. I was just trying to help. After all, I only want what's best for those kids. Aargh! That's sounds like something Mom would say, too. *(looks offstage)* You put that down this instant, young lady! Right now! *(to self)* Man! I can't stop myself!

Jackie: *(entering)* I heard yelling. Is everything all right?

Troy: *(to audience)* I really liked Jackie. But I realized she wasn't the mom for me and my family. I just couldn't take that much fun! And neither could Annie and Leonard. They were starting to have bad attitudes, and they weren't behaving like they should. I realized I had to get Jackie to change or our lives would be a complete mess by the end of the week!

Scene Thirteen

Troy: Could I talk to you about something?

Jackie: Sure, you can! Anything! Why, you're practically my own son. My. Own. Son!

Troy: Thanks. I … uh … don't know how to say this … .

Jackie: Just say it, Troy. Let it all out, kid!

Troy: Well …

Jackie: Is this about the Garbage Pizza?

Troy: Kind of …

Jackie: Sorry, Troy. We won't be having Garbage Pizza tonight.

Troy: We won't?

Jackie: No. I know you love the Garbage Pizza—my kids do, too. But it's not good for you to eat like that all the time.

Troy: No. No, it's not.

Jackie: And you kids snack too much.

Troy: We … we do?

Jackie: It's probably such a habit that you don't even realize you're doing it. Being a visitor, I can see things more clearly. Like I've noticed you kids never do any homework. And you spend way too much time sitting around. You need to turn off that TV and get active!

Troy: Yes, we do.

Jackie: And this house! It looks like—

Jackie and Troy: A tornado went through it.

Jackie: I like to have fun, Troy. And I … I wanted to be a really fun mother for you kids. But I just can't go on like this. There's more to life than fun, and I should be teaching you about that. That's what a good mother does.

Troy: Wow.

Jackie: I think it's time your father and I had a talk.

From Diana R. Jenkins, *All Year Long! Funny Readers Theatre for Life's Special Times.* Westport, CT: Teacher Ideas Press. Copyright © 2007 by Diana R. Jenkins.

Troy: Me, too!

Jackie: There are going to be some changes around here, young man. *(exits)*

Troy: Yes!

Scene Fourteen

Troy: *(to audience)* I guess Dad was ready for some changes, too, because he came home with a bunch of nutritious groceries and asked Jackie if they could have a talk. It didn't take long for them to realize they were pretty much on the same page, and the rest of the week was different. Less fun, I guess, but better. We straightened up the house and got back to a more normal routine. Jackie never was as tough as Mom, but she kept on top of us better and enforced most of our rules. *(as Dad, Jackie, Annie, and Leonard enter)* I'm glad to say she still played around sometimes and let us taste the freedom in our hair now and then.

Dad: We're really sorry to see you go, Jackie.

Jackie: And I hate to leave. This has been a great experience. A. Great. Experience!

Annie: Don't leave us!

Jackie: I have to go, honey. I really miss my family, and I need to get back home.

Leonard: Thanks for everything.

Jackie: You're welcome. And thank you all for making me a part of your family.

Troy: We'll never forget you.

Jackie: Oh, now you're going to make me cry! Let's get the car loaded up before I spring a leak.

Troy: *(as others exit)* We got everything into the car, and then Jackie gave each of us one last, bone-crushing hug. She drove off tooting the horn and waving.

Kellie: *(entering)* Are we too late?

Nick: *(entering)* Did Jackie leave?

Troy: Yeah. Just a couple of minutes ago.

Kellie: We wanted to say good-bye!

Troy: You know, I'm really sorry to see Jackie go, but I'm glad the swap is over.

Nick: Why? Did him miss his mamma?

Troy: Yes, I did. A lot worse than I thought I would. I really should appreciate her more. Sure, she can be hard on us, but sometimes we need that. And she just does it because she cares.

Kellie: It sounds like you really learned something, Troy.

Troy: Yeah. I hate to admit it, but yeah.

Nick: Well … tell your mom hi for us. *(exits)*

Kellie: Bye! *(exits)*

Troy: *(to audience)* I *had* learned a lot from the mom swap. But I had one more lesson to come.

Scene Fifteen

Annie: *(enters)* Mom's home!

Leonard: *(enters)* It's Mom!

Dad: *(enters)* I'm so glad to see her!

Mom: *(enters)* Hi, everybody!

Rest of family: *(as they hug her)* Hi! Welcome back! Mom! Mom! *(etc.)*

Troy: We really missed you. Really, really missed you. I mean … really!

Annie: Yeah.

Mom: Well, I missed you guys, too.

Dad: How did things go with the other family?

Mom: They were so nice. And talk about fun! They were always playing around and joking and trying interesting foods and … oh, they were really fun people.

Troy: We're glad you had a good time, Mom, but we're happy to have you back.

Mom: *(surprised)* Thank you, Troy.

Troy: I mean … we really, really missed you!

Leonard: We sure did!

Troy: *I* really missed you.

Mom: *(moved)* Thank you, Troy.

Dad: Let's get your mother's things out of the car. *(exits with Annie and Leonard)*

Troy: Uh … Mom … I just want you to know I've learned my lesson. I mean … I'm going to really appreciate you now, okay?

Mom: That's nice! You know what? I learned a few things, too.

Troy: You did?

Mom: Yep.

Troy: *You* did?

Mom: Uh-huh.

Troy: You *did?*

Mom: *(laughing)* Yes! *(serious)* I learned that I'm probably a little hard on you kids. I don't have to be after you all the time. I could loosen up a little, give you some freedom, and let you play around more.

Troy: Wow.

Mom: So … are you ready for some fun?

Troy: Yeah! But … um … just not *too* much fun, okay?

Mom: *(laughing)* Okay. Let's go help with the luggage. Oh, I have a fantastic new recipe I want you guys to try. *(exits)*

Troy: New recipe? Not … oh, no! Please, Mom, no! *(exits)*

From Diana R. Jenkins, *All Year Long! Funny Readers Theatre for Life's Special Times.* Westport, CT: Teacher Ideas Press. Copyright © 2007 by Diana R. Jenkins.

The End

Summary

As the end of the school year approaches, Rio receives a notice that she could fail the grade! She decides the only way to save herself is to kiss up to the teacher. It can't hurt, right? Or is it too late to escape her doom?

Costumes, Sets, and Props

❖ All characters can wear contemporary clothing.

❖ A few desks or chairs can serve as the classroom and Rio's house.

❖ If props are desired, the following can be used: books and other school supplies, worksheets, a poetry book, an apple, and an envelope for Mrs. Bradbury.

Presentation

Local terminology can be substituted for "progress report."

Rio becomes belligerent when anyone even tries to mention she might be at fault for her problems, and her friends always back down. Selah is especially nice to Rio until she finally gets mad in Scene Nine.

Supplemental Reading

Butler, Dori Hillestad. *Tank Talbott's Guide to Girls.* Morton Grove, IL: Albert Whitman and Company, 2006.

Schumm, Jeanne Shay. *School Power—Study Skill Strategies for Succeeding in School.* Minneapolis, MN: Free Spirit, 2001.

Winkler, Henry, and Lin Oliver. *Help! Somebody Get Me Out of Fourth Grade!* New York: Grosset and Dunlap, 2004.

Yee, Lisa. *Stanford Wong Flunks Big-Time.* New York: Arthur A. Levine Books, 2005.

Cast of Characters

Narrator

Rio

Caitlin, Malone, Darius, and Selah—Rio's friends

Mrs. Bradbury

Mom and Dad—Rio's parents

End of School Year

The End

Scene One

Narrator: *(to audience)* The end. Thanks for coming, everybody! Ha! Just joking. Let me start over. *(serious)* The end. Sometimes we're sorry to reach the end. Like when we're finished reading a really good book. Sometimes we're glad to reach the end. Like when we've hiked for miles and miles to get home. And sometimes the end scares us to death. Like when the school year is almost over and we're in serious danger of flunking. That's the way Rio felt.

Rio: I can't believe it. How can this be happening to me?

Caitlin: What's the matter, Rio?

Rio: Oh, nothing. Except that I'm doomed. Doomed, doomed, doomed.

Malone: So … you're saying you're doomed?

Rio: Funny, Malone. Yes, I'm doomed. And it is so unfair!

Darius: What's the problem now?

Rio: Well, I … what do you mean by that?

Darius: Never mind. What's wrong?

Rio: I'm going to flunk!

Selah: Oh, no! Are you sure?

Rio: Well, no, but Mrs. Bradbury sent home a progress report about my terrible grades.

Malone: You get those reports every grading period.

Caitlin: And then your parents ground you until you improve.

Darius: Well … she improves *some*. It's not like her grades are ever really—

Rio: Let's stick to the subject. This report said I might be held back. And there are only a few weeks of school left to fix things! Why don't they give you a little warning about this stuff?

Darius: That's what all those progress reports were for, Rio. To warn you!

Rio: Yeah … well … they didn't really sound that serious.

Caitlin: But they always said you were getting poor grades. That's pretty serious.

From Diana R. Jenkins, *All Year Long! Funny Readers Theatre for Life's Special Times.* Westport, CT: Teacher Ideas Press. Copyright © 2007 by Diana R. Jenkins.

Rio: I guess … but I … Oh, what difference does it make now? The end is near, and I'm doomed!

Selah: No, you're not. There's still time left.

Malone: Yeah. You just have to work hard and show Mrs. Bradbury you're ready to move on.

Rio: Do you think I really have a chance?

Selah: Sure!

Malone and Caitlin: Yeah!

Darius: No way.

Selah: Darius!

Darius: I mean … no way you can fail!

Rio: Okay then. I'll try.

Scene Two

Narrator: So Rio set out to save herself.

Rio: I guess the first thing I'd better do is get all my work in.

Selah: Good idea!

Malone: Yeah. Why don't you do all those worksheets you threw in the bottom of your locker?

Rio: Hey, I *dropped* them, okay? They kind of slipped out of my hands and landed down there.

Malone: Whatever.

Caitlin: Of course, Mrs. Bradbury doesn't have to accept late papers.

Rio: What? Then why should I do them at all?

Selah: So you can learn the stuff you need to know to go to the next grade.

Darius: And so you can show Mrs. Bradbury that you're serious.

Rio: Oh, all right. But it just seems so unfair that I have to do all that work at once.

Darius: Hey, you're the one who let the stuff pile up!

Rio: I didn't know I had that much unfinished work! I'm not the person with the grade book that shows what is and isn't turned in. Mrs. Bradbury should have told me how bad things were.

Malone: Yeah. That Mrs. Bradbury is so irresponsible.

Rio: No kidding!

Caitlin: You must be joking.

Rio: What's that supposed to mean?

Caitlin: Nothing, nothing. See you later. *(Friends exit.)*

Narrator: So Rio worked really hard for the next few days and finished all the papers from her locker plus the ones she found under her bed and the big batch of worksheets in her backpack.

Rio: There's no way Mrs. Bradbury can flunk me now!

Scene Three

Narrator: Rio gathered all the makeup work in a folder and presented it to her teacher.

Rio: I know this work is a little late, but I've been … um … busy. But now I'm all caught up!

Mrs. Bradbury: I appreciate your good intentions, but a lot of these papers are too late to count.

Rio: Couldn't you give me a break?

Mrs. Bradbury: I'm sorry, but I can't count any work from previous grading periods. Those report cards are finished. But I'll look through all this and consider what I can.

Rio: *(sighing)* Okay.

Mrs. Bradbury: Does this new effort has something to do with the progress report I sent home?

Rio: Yes, ma'am.

Mrs. Bradbury: So your parents were upset by the report?

Rio: Upset? Oh, yeah. Yeah, they hate getting stuff like that. They always say that education is very important. Very, very important. They're always saying that.

Mrs. Bradbury: They are quite right. A good education is essential to a successful future.

Rio: Yeah. They say that, too. So … um … I'm not going to be held back, am I?

Mrs. Bradbury: I can't tell you that right now, Rio. *(exits)*

Rio: Did she mean she *is* going to flunk me, but she's not saying so? Or did she mean she hasn't decided yet so she can't tell me anything? How can she just leave me hanging like that?

Scene Four

Narrator: Rio was stuck in a bad position. If Mrs. Bradbury had already made up her mind to hold her back, then why bother to do anything?

Rio: Yeah, I might as well quit knocking myself out. At least until my parents get the bad news.

Narrator: But if Mrs. Bradbury hadn't made a decision, then Rio could still influence her.

Rio: I'm going to be in big trouble if I flunk. Big, big trouble!

Narrator: Rio decided she couldn't take any chances. She did all her work that day. And she actually took her books home so she could do her homework and study up in her subjects.

Mom: *(entering with Dad)* I'm glad to see you working so hard.

Dad: It's about time you took your education seriously.

Rio: Oh, I do, Dad. I really do.

Mom: I know you feel like we were rough on you this year, but you understand now, don't you?

Rio: Sure, Mom.

Dad: We're really proud that you didn't get a progress report this period.

Mom: Very proud.

From Diana R. Jenkins, *All Year Long! Funny Readers Theatre for Life's Special Times.* Westport, CT: Teacher Ideas Press. Copyright © 2007 by Diana R. Jenkins.

Rio: Thanks. I … um … better get back to studying.

Dad: All right. Keep up the good work. *(exits with Mom)*

Narrator: So now you know the truth. Rio's parents never got that last progress report—the one that said she was in danger of failing. Gee. I wonder what happened to it. I wonder …

Rio: Okay, so I took it out of the mailbox and opened it. It's about *my* life, isn't it? And when I read it … well … I couldn't let them see that, could I? They'd just blame me for the whole thing!

Narrator: Imagine that.

Rio: As long as I pass, the progress report won't matter anyway. They'll never even know I took it. So it'll be like it never happened. Yeah. I just can't flunk, that's all.

Narrator: Right.

Scene Five

Narrator: Rio had been coasting along all through the year, and she didn't know her subjects as well as she should. So she failed a unit test in social studies.

Rio: How am I supposed to remember the stuff from *three* chapters? That is so unreasonable!

Narrator: She got a D on a pop quiz in science.

Rio: Pop quizzes should be illegal. It just isn't right to make us learn stuff before the real test.

Narrator: And her English essay had so many mistakes, Mrs. Bradbury made her do it over.

Rio: What's the big deal about spelling and punctuation? And who cares about complete sentences? I mean … it's not like.

Narrator: *(pauses)* It's not like what?

Rio: It's not like any of it matters!

Narrator: Uh-huh. *(to audience)* The end was rapidly approaching, and Rio was still in danger.

Rio: *(as friends enter)* I'm still going to flunk. I can feel it. I'm going to flunk!

Selah: Oh, no!

Rio: You guys have to help me. Please, please, please help me!

Malone: So … you're saying you want our help?

Rio: This isn't a joke, Malone. This is my life!

Malone: Yeah, but what can *we* do?

Rio: I don't know! You're all passing, right? Couldn't you share your secrets with me?

Friends: *(laugh)*

Caitlin: There aren't any secrets, Rio.

Darius: Yeah. We just do all the normal stuff. Like complete our homework and study and—

Rio: Come on. There has to be more to it than that!

Friends: Uh-uh. Not really. Nope. (*etc.*)

Rio: But I already do that stuff!

Malone: Right.

Rio: Well … I'm doing it now. Well … last night at least.

Selah: Maybe it would help if we studied with you.

Caitlin: Yeah. Like we could quiz you on your science vocabulary cards.

Malone: And social studies notes.

Darius: She doesn't have any cards or notes! She never even reads the chapters.

Rio: Yes, I do! Sometimes.

Malone: Rio! You can't expect us to help you when you're not doing your part.

Rio: Gee, thanks. Something terrible is happening to me, and you guys don't even care.

Selah: Of course we care! It's just—

Rio: Never mind. I'll handle this myself.

Darius: Great plan. You're doing a bang-up job so far.

Rio: Well, I have a new idea that's going to change everything. I just thought of it. A great, great idea. So you guys can forget I even mentioned anything.

Caitlin: Okay, we will. (*exits along with others, except Selah*)

Selah: If you change your mind, I'd be glad to help you study.

Rio: (*coldly*) No, thanks.

Selah: Okay. (*exits sadly*)

Rio: I don't need *their* help. (*sighs*) All I need is a great, great idea that could change everything.

Scene Six

Narrator: The great idea she needed hit Rio when she was walking past the teachers' lounge. The door opened for a moment as someone left the room, and Rio caught a glimpse of Mrs. Bradbury lying on a sofa with her shoes off and her feet up.

Rio: She looks really tired. I guess I forget sometimes that teachers are just people, too. Hey … Mrs. Bradbury is only human! Couldn't I use that to my advantage? Let's see … I know! Everybody likes to be admired. (*as Mrs. Bradbury and other kids enter*) If I make her think I really like her, she won't be able to hold me back. Yeah … What kind of mean teacher would flunk a kid who worships the ground she walks on?

Narrator: Rio put her plan into action during social studies that afternoon.

Mrs. Bradbury: We don't have much time left, class, but I want to be sure to discuss—

Rio: (*waving hand*) Mrs. Bradbury! Mrs. Bradbury!

Mrs. Bradbury: Yes?

Rio: I just wanted to say thanks for making social studies so interesting this year.

Malone: (*muttering*) Brother!

Mrs. Bradbury: Why … thank you, Rio. Now let's get on with our lesson.

Narrator: And in English class …

Mrs. Bradbury: "And so it goes that, in the end, we often make a brand-new friend." Wasn't that a lovely poem, class?

Rio: It was great! And you read it with such good expression, Mrs. Bradbury.

Caitlin: *(muttering)* Oh, come on!

Mrs. Bradbury: Um … thank you, Rio. Now let's discuss the theme of the poem.

Narrator: Then in math … .

Mrs. Bradbury: Who has solved the problem?

Rio: *(waving hand)* I have!

Mrs. Bradbury: Okay, Rio. What is your answer?

Rio: One hundred thirty-seven.

Mrs. Bradbury: No, that's not correct.

Rio: Oh! I forgot my decimal point. One hundred thirty *point* seven.

Mrs. Bradbury: No, that's not right either.

Darius: Not even close!

Rio: Oh. I'm sorry about that. But I want you to know, Mrs. Bradbury, that my mistake is totally my own fault and no reflection whatsoever on your excellent teaching.

Malone: You must be joking!

Mrs. Bradbury: I beg your pardon.

Malone: That didn't come out right. I didn't mean … I was just trying to say … I mean … Sorry.

Mrs. Bradbury: That's all right, Malone. And thank you, Rio.

Rio: Sure! I meant every word! You're the best teacher ever.

Mrs. Bradbury: Thanks. Let's get back to the problem.

Darius: *(to Rio)* It's not going to work, you know. If Mrs. Bradbury thinks you should be held back, she'd going to do it. Getting on her good side won't change anything.

Rio: *(to Darius)* We'll see.

Darius: We sure will. *(Everyone exits.)*

Scene Seven

Narrator: Over the next week, Rio tried to make it look like she deserved to pass. She did a lot of her work. She studied now and then. She took some notes and made some vocabulary cards. But mostly she worked on kissing up to Mrs. Bradbury.

Rio: *(holding apple, enters with friends)* Hi, you guys!

Selah: Good morning, Rio.

Darius: You brought *another* apple for Mrs. Bradbury?

Caitlin: That is so lame.

From Diana R. Jenkins, *All Year Long! Funny Readers Theatre for Life's Special Times.* Westport, CT: Teacher Ideas Press. Copyright © 2007 by Diana R. Jenkins.

Selah: I think it's nice.

Rio: So does Mrs. Bradbury. She always eats my apples at lunch.

Darius: That doesn't mean you're fooling her. She knows you're just trying to save yourself.

Caitlin: And all the compliments are really getting sickening, Rio.

Malone: Yeah. You're totally ridiculous.

Rio: I am not!

Darius: Right. It's not ridiculous to tell your teacher she has the handwriting of an angel.

Caitlin: And that stuff about her being a mathematical genius? Way over the top!

Rio: Hey, you guys wouldn't help me so I was forced to take drastic measures, okay?

Selah: We offered to study with you.

Rio: The end is near, Selah! I don't have time for that to work!

Malone: Well, it's a better idea than putting on a big act with the teacher. You're such a fake—and Mrs. Bradbury knows it!

Darius: Really! You are so going to flunk.

Rio: No, I'm not. Mrs. Bradbury is liking me more and more every day—too much to do something mean like flunking me.

Selah: I hope you're right.

Rio: Don't worry. I have everything under control. *(Friends exit.)*

Scene Eight

Narrator: But Rio soon found out that wasn't true at all.

Mrs. Bradbury: *(enters)* Rio, I'd like for you to take this letter home tonight.

Rio: Letter? What kind of letter?

Mrs. Bradbury: An *important* letter. I really need a quick response from your parents.

Rio: What kind of response? Maybe I could respond for them . . . if I knew the question.

Mrs. Bradbury: I don't think so. I need to know when they want to have our conference.

Rio: A conference? Now? The school year is almost over!

Mrs. Bradbury: That's why it's urgent that you get the letter home right away. The progress report asked your parents to set up a conference, but I haven't heard from them. So I set a time that I hope will work. The information is in the letter.

Rio: I don't know. … My parents are really busy these days. I don't think they can come in.

Mrs. Bradbury: I'm sure they'll make time for this meeting. I know how concerned they are about your future. *(starts to exit)*

Rio: Mrs. Bradbury!

Mrs. Bradbury: Yes, Rio.

Rio: I … uh … just wanted to say … your hair looks lovely today.

Mrs. Bradbury: Thank you, Rio.

From Diana R. Jenkins, *All Year Long! Funny Readers Theatre for Life's Special Times.* Westport, CT: Teacher Ideas Press. Copyright © 2007 by Diana R. Jenkins.

Rio: That style is so flattering!

Mrs. Bradbury: And so are you.

Rio: Huh?

Mrs. Bradbury: *(sighs)* I know you're worried about failing, dear. But flattery won't influence me. I have to do what's best for you without any consideration of our personal relationship.

Rio: You mean … I'm going to flunk?

Mrs. Bradbury: I can't tell you that right now. Please take the letter home tonight. *(exits)*

Rio: Man! Why does she always do this top-secret sealed envelope thing when she sends a note home from school? If this letter mentions that progress report, my parents will wonder why they never saw it. They'll probably blame me! And even if there's nothing about that, they'll go to the conference and find out I'm in danger of flunking. I bet I'll get the blame for that, too!

Narrator: Unbelievable!

Rio: I know. Man! Why does this stuff always happen to me?

Scene Nine

Narrator: Rio didn't know what to do. All her big plans had failed, and now she was in a worse mess than ever. She hated to tell her friends about how she had intercepted the progress report in the mail. *(as friends enter)* But she decided she had to do it because she needed their help.

Caitlin: You stole the progress report out of the mail?

Darius: That's a crime, you know. Punishable by law!

Rio: Oh, come on. Like the police care that I looked at my own progress report!

Malone: It was addressed to your parents. It was their mail.

Darius: Yeah, what you did was illegal.

Selah: *(kindly)* And just not right, Rio. You know that.

Rio: But I only looked because I didn't want to be grounded again for bad grades. I didn't know it was going to say I was totally flunking! And now I have to worry about this stupid letter about some stupid conference. What should I do, you guys? Should I lose it accidentally on purpose? Should I write a fake reply? Come on! You have to help me figure a way out of this!

Malone: Like how?

Caitlin: What can we do?

Darius: I don't have any ideas.

Rio: So you're just going to sit by while Mrs. Bradbury ruins my life? What kind of friends are you?

Selah: *(finally mad)* How can you say that? We've been very good friends to you! Don't we always try to help when you get yourself into these situations?

Rio: What do you mean … when I get myself into situations? You act like all this is my fault!

From Diana R. Jenkins, *All Year Long! Funny Readers Theatre for Life's Special Times.* Westport, CT: Teacher Ideas Press. Copyright © 2007 by Diana R. Jenkins.

Selah: Because it is, Rio! Instead of blaming somebody else for your problems, why don't you take responsibility for yourself for once?

Rio: Well, why don't you just … just … get out of my life!

Selah: Okay! Gladly! *(exits)*

Rio: I cannot believe her. *(snorts)* "Take responsibility." Sheesh! She sounds like my parents. They're always harping on *(mocks)* responsibility. *(back to normal)* Like I can somehow keep bad stuff from happening to me! Brother! So … any ideas, you guys?

Darius: Yeah. I have one. Straighten out your mess yourself. *(exits)*

Caitlin: Yeah. *(exits)*

Malone: Selah's right about you. *(exits)*

Rio: Great. Now what am I supposed to do about this stupid letter?

Scene Ten

Narrator: Rio's friends didn't speak to her for the rest of the day, but Rio couldn't think about that. She had a much bigger problem to worry about.

Rio: If only I knew how things were going to come out in the end! Is Mrs. Bradbury passing me or not? Should I give my parents this letter? Or not? Maybe I'd better keep them away from that conference until I convince Mrs. Bradbury to pass me. But what if it's too late for that? Aaargh!

Narrator: By the time Rio got home that afternoon, she had decided she had to read the note before she could make any other schemes … uh … plans.

Rio: If my parents wonder why it's not in a sealed envelope like usual, I'll just tell them Mrs. Bradbury ran out of envelopes because it's close to the end and her supplies are getting low.

Narrator: She read the note …

Rio: "Dear *(mumble)* end is near *(mumble)* Rio's future *(mumble)* possible retention! *(mumble)* Please meet *(mumble)* Hey, she said "possible retention"! That means I can still change her mind. But I have to keep my parents out of this until I do.

Narrator: So Rio destroyed the letter, then sat down and did her homework.

Rio: I think I'll do the extra math problems in the back of the book, too. That'll show Mrs. Bradbury how hard I'm trying. Maybe she'll even give me some extra credit.

Narrator: When her parents got home, Rio was writing an essay about her favorite teacher even though that teacher already said she wouldn't be swayed by flattery.

Rio: Hey, she's only human.

Mom: *(entering with Dad)* I'm impressed. You've really been putting forth a good effort lately.

Dad: You are making us so proud, Rio.

Mom: *(getting emotional)* I've been really worried about you and your schoolwork. I'm so glad to see you pulling it together like this.

Dad: *(getting emotional)* You're the best daughter a father could ask for.

Mom: Or a mother!

Dad: *(overly emotional)* Why, you're what gives my life meaning.

Mom: Mine, too. Mine, too. *(sniffling)* Excuse me. I need a tissue. *(exits)*

Dad: Me, too! *(exits)*

Narrator: It usually feels great to make your parents proud, but for some reason Rio felt like …

Rio: *(glumly)* Scum. Now I wish I had never kept the truth from them. But … well … I had to do it.

Narrator: What?

Rio: I had to do it! I had to do it! I mean … Mrs. Bradbury forced my hand with that stupid progress report. I had to do it!

Narrator: Uh-huh.

Rio: *(muttering)* I had to do it.

Scene Eleven

Narrator: Rio had a hard time sleeping that night. A guilty conscience will do that to a person.

Rio: Right. How can I be guilty when I just did what I had to do? I mean … none of this is my fault! I just feel bad for my parents, that's all. They're going to be so disappointed if I fail. And if they find out … everything. Man! How did my life get to be such a mess?

Narrator: Her friends still didn't talk to her at school the next day. Rio tried to tell herself she didn't care, but she felt terrible about that, too.

Rio: Hey, if they don't want to be friends, that's their problem. It's not my fault! Okay, I could have treated them a little better. I guess I do kind of dump my problems on them too much. And I could have been a better friend back to them. Rats! Why doesn't anything ever go right for me?

Narrator: But something did go right for Rio that day.

Mrs. Bradbury: *(enters)* I've been checking your averages. Your grades are improving!

Rio: They are?

Mrs. Bradbury: I wish you had worked as hard the rest of the year as you have here at the end.

Rio: Does this mean I'm going to pass?

Mrs. Bradbury: I can't tell you that right now. Your parents and I need to discuss some things first. I will be hearing from them soon, won't I?

Rio: Yes, ma'am.

Mrs. Bradbury: Good. I'm very proud of you, Rio. *(exits)*

Rio: I should have done my work and studied and all that a lot earlier. Yeah. I should have gotten busy months ago. Like at the beginning of the year. My parents wouldn't have hassled me … and … and worried about me. Mrs. Bradbury wouldn't have sent any of those progress reports. And I wouldn't have gotten into this whole stupid mess! Hey … .

From Diana R. Jenkins, *All Year Long! Funny Readers Theatre for Life's Special Times.* Westport, CT: Teacher Ideas Press. Copyright © 2007 by Diana R. Jenkins.

Narrator: Finally … finally … Rio had to admit the truth.

Rio: I started everything! I didn't do what I should have in the first place and then I kept not doing it except for when I was grounded and so I ended up in real danger but I did all the wrong things to save myself from the problem I caused in the first place! It's my fault. It's all my fault.

Narrator: So … you're saying it's your fault?

Rio: Not funny, okay? My life is in ruins! And I ruined it! And there's no way to unruin it.

Narrator: *Un*ruin?

Rio: Wait. Maybe there is a way to make things … well, not right … but at least less ruined.

Narrator: Okay.

Scene Twelve

Narrator: *(as friends enter)* First, Rio apologized to her friends.

Rio: So, anyway, I'm sorry I acted like that and I'm sorry I didn't appreciate you guys and I'm sorry about … you know … everything.

Malone: So … you're saying you're—

Rio: Sorry! Yeah. Really, you guys.

Malone: Okay.

Caitlin: It's all right.

Darius: We're cool.

Rio: *(to Selah)* Can you forgive me for the stuff I said?

Selah: *(smiling)* Sure.

Narrator: *(as friends exit, Mrs. Bradbury enters)* Next, Rio confessed to Mrs. Bradbury …

Mrs. Bradbury: Oh, my! I'm really disappointed in you, Rio.

Narrator: *(as Mom and Dad enter)* And her parents …

Mom: Rio!

Dad: What were you thinking, young lady?

Narrator: Of course, she got in huge trouble—grounded from everything but detention with Mrs. Bradbury every day. And she still didn't know if she was passing the grade or not.

Mrs. Bradbury: *(to Mom and Dad)* Thank you for coming in. I think we have a lot to discuss.

Mom: *(as adults exit)* We certainly do!

Rio: I wish I had thought about the end of this year all the way back at the beginning. Now I'm doomed.

Narrator: But Rio got a big surprise when that conference was over.

Mrs. Bradbury: *(entering with Mom and Dad)* Summer school!

Rio: I'm going to summer school?

Mom: Yes. And if you do well, you'll pass to the next grade.

Dad: You'll have to work hard.

Rio: Oh, I will! I will!

Mrs. Bradbury: *(teasing)* I understand you'll have plenty of time to study since you're grounded for life.

Rio: *(laughing)* Yeah. *(serious)* Thanks for giving me a chance.

Mrs. Bradbury: You're welcome, dear. *(exits with Mom and Dad)*

Rio: Wow. Things worked out better than I thought they would.

Narrator: So Rio learned an important lesson. The end.

Rio: No, it's not! I'm straightening my life out and making a fresh start.

Narrator: Okay then. *(to audience)* The beginning.

From Diana R. Jenkins, *All Year Long! Funny Readers Theatre for Life's Special Times.* Westport, CT: Teacher Ideas Press. Copyright © 2007 by Diana R. Jenkins.

Index

About the Author

DIANA R. JENKINS is the author of more than three hundred stories, comic strips, and articles for children and teens and a number of essays and education-related articles. She earned a bachelor's degree in special education from Ball State University and a reading specialist master's degree from the University of Arkansas at Little Rock. After twenty-plus years as a special education teacher, she became a freelance writer. She lives in Montgomery, Ohio, with her husband, a medical physicist.